you have it made

Ellie Krieger

you have it made

Delicious, Healthy, Do-Ahead Meals

Ellie Krieger

with photography by QUENTIN BACON

HOUGHTON MIFFLIN HARCOURT
Boston New York
2016

For Thom and Isabella

For information about permission to reproduce selections from
this book, write to trade.permissions@hmhco.com or to Permissions,
Houghton Mifflin Harcourt Publishing Company,
3 Park Avenue, 19th Floor, New York, New York 10016.

www.hmhco.com

Library of Congress Cataloging-in-Publication Data
Krieger, Ellie, author.
    You have it made! : delicious, healthy do-ahead meals / Ellie Krieger ;
    photography by Quentin Bacon.
        pages cm
    ISBN 978-0-544-57930-9 (paper over board)
    ISBN 978-0-544-57932-3 (ebook)
    1. Make-ahead cooking. I. Title.
    TX714.K763 2016

    641.5′55—dc23   2015028798

Book design by Rachel Newborn

Printed in China
TOP 10 9 8 7 6 5 4 3 2 1

CONTENTS

ACKNOWLEDGMENTS

I AM TREMENDOUSLY GRATEFUL for THE talented, creative, and hardworking people who put so much of themselves into bringing this book to life.

Adeena Sussman and Anat Abramov, thank you for your culinary talent and hard work, and for making even the most demanding schedule a joyful experience. Mostly, though, thank you for your enduring friendship. Thanks, Lori Powell, for your inspired and delicious contributions, and for having every last detail done right; and thank you, also, chefs Natalia Hancock, RD, and Jackie Ourman.

Thank you Melissa O'Shea MS RD, for your hard work, precision and expertise with the nutrition data. And thanks Quentin Bacon, Suzanne Lenzer, Kate Schmidt, and Maeve Sheridan, not only for creating such stunning, mouthwatering images, but also for making the photo shoot such a pleasure; and Suzanne Katz and Ivonne Frowein for making me look and feel good.

Thank you to my A-team management, Robert Flutie and Danielle Iturbe, agents Jane Dystel and Miriam Goderich, and publicists Janell Vantrease, Crystal Wang, and Marcus Braham. It is an honor and a joy to be able to work with each of you.

Thanks to everyone at HMH, especially my editor Justin Schwartz, and Natalie Chapman for all of your support, as well as Rebecca Liss, Brad Parsons, and Jessica Gilo. It amazes me how the HMH team turns a manuscript into a real work of art that people can hold, pore over, and get so much pleasure and use out of. Thanks for working your magic on mine.

INTRODUCTION

THIS BOOK IS MUCH MORE than a collection of recipes. It is a step-by-step guide to turning your refrigerator and freezer into a treasure chest of meals to make your life deliciously easier and healthier.

Imagine, on the busiest weekday morning, being able to get a sumptuously flavorful, energizing breakfast ready in less time than it takes to brew a cup of coffee. Or, later that evening, when the inevitable question "what's for dinner?" comes up, breezily choosing from a menu of craveable, healthful options, right at your fingertips. Think about entertaining—for a holiday meal, Sunday brunch, or just having some friends over to watch the game—and how nice it would be to relax and enjoy your guests while treating them to a feast of memorable, crowd-pleasing dishes.

In your hands right now is a remarkable tool to make that happen: 150 luscious make-ahead recipes that hit what I call the "sweet spot," where delicious and healthy meet. And for each, I give you complete directions to successfully refrigerate and/or freeze it, as well as serve it when you are ready.

As a passionate food lover, taste is number one for me, and each of these dishes is full-out delicious. But they are good-for-you too, something that is important to me as a nutritionist and mom. They emphasize fresh, seasonal, minimally processed ingredients, and follow my tried-and-true Usually-Sometimes-Rarely food philosophy, which I introduced in my first book *Small Changes Big Results*, and has guided all my work and every recipe I have created since. My golden rule: no food is ever off-limits. Rather, I categorize food as Usually, Sometimes, or Rarely. Usually foods are those I use most plentifully and are the backbone of healthy eating: vegetables, whole fruit, beans, nuts and seeds, lean protein, seafood, lower-fat dairy, whole grains, and healthy oils. I sprinkle in Sometimes foods here and there for flavor and variety. They may be a bit more processed, like all-purpose flour, less nutrient rich, like honey, or a little higher in saturated fat, like chicken thighs. Rarely foods—like refined sugar, cream, bacon, and butter—are foods that many nutritionists forbid and many cooks use with a heavy hand. I have found the ideal midpoint by using these foods strategically, in small amounts for maximum impact.

The idea is that there is no need to deprive yourself or go to extremes to be healthy. In fact, extremes are usually unhealthy and trap us into a diet mentality. Rather, balance is key. If you are eating mostly nutrient-rich, whole foods, there is room for some butter in your mashed potatoes, some brown sugar in your oatmeal, or even a slice of rich chocolate cake once in a while.

I also believe in focusing on pure, minimally processed ingredients and steering clear of artificial and keep it in the freezer, ready to be poured into a ready-made crust; aromatic meals in foil pouches that go straight from oven to freezer; flavorful freezable simmer-sauces to quickly thaw and pour over just-browned meat; and freezer-marinades where chops, roasts or chicken breasts are frozen in a tasty mix of seasonings before cooking, so all you need to do is thaw, then grill, or pop the dish in the oven. There are meals made in adorable, convenient jars,

> If you are eating mostly nutrient-rich, whole foods, there is room for some butter in your mashed potatoes, some brown sugar in your oatmeal, or even a slice of rich chocolate cake once in a while.

additives. I will use reduced-fat foods only if they work taste-wise and are not laden with chemical additives. So I use low-fat milk and yogurt for example, but you won't get me within a yard of fat-free whipped topping. (Have you ever read the ingredient list on that stuff?) I'll take a little good old-fashioned whipped cream any day. And when it comes to cheeses like Parmesan, blue cheeses, and sharp cheddar, there is just no substitute. Besides, they are so flavorful that just a bit goes a long way.

There are many familiar favorites in this book that likely come to mind when you think "make-ahead": richly satisfying stews and chilis, heartwarming soups, homey casseroles, cheesy pasta bakes, slaws, and breakfast baked goods. But far from being the same-old, same-old, each one here has an inspiring twist that gives it an easy-to-achieve "wow" factor, healthfully, of course, and without taking you too far out of your comfort zone.

On top of that, there are dozens of fun, do-ahead ideas here that might surprise you. There's a sumptuous quiche where you make the filling ahead,

like overnight oats with fruit, and layered vegetable and grain salads; and there are mini meatloaves, two-bite frittatas, and individual mac-n-cheese cups made in muffin tins.

For each I give you storage and reheating instructions to maximize the convenience for you and help you make the most of the space in your freezer. Many of the meals can be stored in individual portions, which I find incredibly practical these days when everyone seems to be running in different directions. It makes it easy to pull out one, two, or a few portions of a meal as needed. And since I give you detailed reheating instructions it is a no-brainer for older children, spouses, or a caregiver to reheat a meal if you can't be there for dinner that night or someone has to eat on a different schedule than the rest of the group. There are also many instances where there's the option of splitting a larger casserole or bake into two batches so you can literally cook it once and eat twice. What's more, most of the meals here can go directly from freezer to oven or stove top, so you don't even need to worry about remembering to thaw.

As soon as you start cooking from this book you will realize how helpful it is to have a bounty of wonderful meals tucked away, but it is even more valuable than you might realize. One of the best things you can do for your health is to cook at home. When you do, you are more likely to eat smarter portions with fewer calories, much less saturated fat and sodium, and more nutrients than if you went the restaurant or prepared food route. Plus, you save money. But life's crazy pace can get in the way of putting food on the table that you really feel good about.

That's why cooking ahead is such an important strategy to help you regain control of the way you eat and your well being. It can be a lifesaver, literally and figuratively. Besides, it's more fun to cook when you are relaxed, so carve out a little time on the weekend or later in the evenings when things have settled down a bit, and make a meal to pack away. Or, make one of the dishes here; eat some, and save some for later. Ultimately, cooking ahead takes the stress out of meal time and helps you and your loved ones have a happier, healthier life—one where you really do have it made.

ABOUT THE NUTRITION FACTS

I DON'T COOK WITH A calculator at hand to get a certain nutrient profile from a recipe. Rather, I set out to make a delicious dish, using the principles laid out in my "Usually-Sometimes-Rarely" food philosophy. Incredibly, when I do so, the numbers tend to work out on their own. But while I prefer to focus on the balance and quality of the food, because numbers can be a helpful guide I have included the nutrition facts for each recipe, with the amount of calories, fat, protein, carbohydrate, fiber, cholesterol, and sodium in each serving. Since some fats are beneficial and others detrimental I further break down fat into saturated (bad fat), and monounsaturated and polyunsaturated (good fats).

I have also listed good and excellent sources of essential nutrients in each recipe. To qualify as a good source a serving must contain at least 10% of the Daily Value (the standard daily recommended intake) and to be called an excellent source it needs to provide at least 20% of the Daily Value. I encourage you not to get hung up on these values, but factor them in when planning your meals and let them serve as a reminder that vitamins and minerals are not just found in powders and pills as so many marketers would have us believe. They are bountifully present in delicious, wholesome foods.

Keep in mind that the nutrition information excludes optional ingredients or anything added to taste, and if there is a choice of ingredients, like "nonfat or low-fat yogurt," I always use the first option listed for the analysis. Also, the type of salt I use throughout is finely ground. If you use course ground or flaked salt you may need to add a bit more.

Regarding portion size, since everyone has different appetites and different calorie needs, there will always be a range of how many people a given recipe serves. But in order to do the nutrition analysis I had to pick one number. So I chose to base the serving sizes on amounts that would satisfy most moderately active women. If you are serving a group of high school football players, you are training for a marathon, or you are not as active as you'd like to be, adjust the portions accordingly.

THE 411 ON STORING, THAWING, AND REHEATING

FOR EACH RECIPE IN THIS book I provide the specific directions for how best to store, thaw, and reheat each dish. But here is a quick primer on the essential tools you need, tricks and strategies for making the most of your refrigerator and freezer, and reheating food to get the best tasting results.

MUST-HAVES AND NICE-TO-HAVES

THERE ARE A FEW INEXPENSIVE food storage tools that are essential, and a few items that are not totally necessary, but certainly good to have. Assuming you already have basic cooking gear—pots, pans, baking trays and pie plates, a large casserole dish, etc.—you will need the following to be able to refrigerate or freeze and reheat optimally:

Must-haves

* Heavy-duty aluminum foil

    For wrapping foods that will go in the oven and an extra layer of freezer protection

* Plastic wrap

    For an extra layer of freezer protection

* Sealable plastic freezer bags in quart, 1-gallon, and 2-gallon sizes

    Quart-sized bags are ideal for single servings of stews, soups, and sauces, 1-gallon bags are perfect for wrapped individual foods, and 2-gallon bags will hold a roast or medium-sized casserole dish.

* A permanent marker

    There is a designated space on most freezer bags for marking the contents of the bag and the date. You could also write directly on a foil wrapper.

Nice-to-Haves:

* A set of sealable, microwave-safe food containers in various sizes

    For refrigerating leftovers

* Six to eight individual serving size (2 to 4 cup capacity) airtight containers that are oven, freezer, and microwave safe

For freezing or refrigerating individual servings of casseroles and bakes. Helpful hint: square is more space-efficient than round.

* **Two 8-inch square casserole dishes that are oven and freezer safe**
  For making a larger casserole in two batches so you can eat one and freeze one

* **Six to eight 1½-cup capacity jars (12 ounce or 500 ml) with lids**
  For attractive storage of layered salads and breakfast parfaits

* **Food Labels**
  Unlike tape and office labels, which do not adhere well to cold surfaces, food labels are designed to stick to food containers in the refrigerator and freezer.

* **Refrigerator and freezer thermometer**
  So you really know if your food is being stored at a safe and optimal temperature. Keep your refrigerator between 32°F and 40°F and your freezer at 0°F or below.

* **A microwave splatter guard**
  This lid maintains the right moisture level and prevents messes with microwave reheating.

* **A vacuum packing system**
  This appliance removes all the air from, and then heat-seals, the heavy-duty plastic bags that the food is placed in. Although they can be expensive, they are excellent for protecting flavor and avoiding freezer burn.

THE FREEZER FOUR-STEP: CHILL. PACK. LABEL. STACK.

1) Chill

CHILLING FOOD BEFORE FREEZING IT helps prevent ice crystals from forming on the surface. Place cooked food in the refrigerator as soon as possible so it cools

quickly. (You do not have to let it cool at room temperature and should definitely not let food sit at room temperature for more than 2 hours.) Once the food is chilled, freeze it quickly by packing it in small quantities, and making sure your freezer is at 0°F or colder. If your freezer has a "quick-freeze" setting, use it.

2) Pack

TO PREVENT FREEZER-BURN AND OFF tastes from developing, be sure your food is as well-sealed and airtight as possible. If you are using containers with lids, "burp" them to remove excess air. Double wrap individual food items, first in plastic or foil, then in sealable plastic bags with the air squeezed out of them. Place soups and stews in doubled plastic freezer bags, pressing the air out before sealing.

To leave both of your hands free for scooping when transferring food into plastic bags, place the bag into a tall glass or pitcher, fitting the opening of the bag over the mouth of the vessel to hold the bag open in place.

Although sometimes you have to tear a bag to remove the frozen food, most times a bag will be reusable, so wash, dry, and reuse whenever possible.

3) Label

LABEL EACH BAG OR DISH with exactly what is inside and the date. While frozen foods remain safe indefinitely, their taste and texture become compromised over time. The freezer storage times suggested in this book are for optimal quality.

4) Stack

LAYING BAGS OF LIQUIDY FOODS flat to freeze allows you to stack them like books once frozen, which optimizes the space you have. Freeze them unstacked so they freeze quickly, then stack them later.

SAFE THAWING

MANY OF THE FREEZER-FRIENDLY DISHES in this book do not need to be thawed at all. Rather, they go directly from freezer to oven or, once released from their container by running them under hot water for 30 seconds, they can be thawed directly on the stove, which makes them extra-convenient.

When you do need to thaw a dish, it is critical to do it safely, and the golden rule is never to thaw at room temperature where harmful bacteria thrive. Instead you may thaw safely in the refrigerator, in the microwave, or in a cold water bath. When thawing in the refrigerator, place the food on a rimmed plate or in a bowl to catch any leaks or drips. Once a food is thawed you should cook it as soon as possible. Also keep in mind that most foods take longer to thaw in the refrigerator than you might think. Some will thaw overnight, but most take 24 to 48 hours.

A WORD ABOUT REHEATING

FOR JUST ABOUT EVERY RECIPE served hot, I provide two ways to reheat it; in the oven/on the stove, or in the microwave, and I include the approximate time required. Keep in mind that regardless of what method you choose there are many variables that affect thawing and reheating time, such as the dish you are using, the temperature of your refrigerator, etc. The times provided here are intended as a general guide.

TIPS FOR USING THE MICROWAVE

IF YOU ARE MICROWAVING, HERE are a few tips and tricks to make the most of it:

* Cover the food as I indicate in the recipe directions. Sometimes a food is best reheated wrapped in a paper towel, other times it is best to use a splatter guard. If you do not have a splatter guard you can use a microwave-safe bowl or container, upside down, to tent over the food.

* Only microwave food in a microwave-safe plate or container. Do not use take-out containers or plastic food tubs.

* At the midpoint of the cooking/defrosting time, give the food a stir, or flip it over.

* After heating, allow the food to rest, covered, for a minute or so before eating, to allow the heat to distribute evenly throughout the food.

* Food thawed in the microwave should be cooked and eaten immediately afterward.

* The cooking times I provide here were determined using my 1000-watt microwave oven, where "high" is 100 percent power and "defrost" is 30 percent power. You will need to adjust cooking times if your microwave wattage is different. This online calculator easily converts the numbers for you: www.microwavewatt.com.

* The cooking time required for a microwave also depends on the amount of food being heated. Throughout this book I have provided microwave instructions for a single portion of a given dish. To thaw and/or warm twice that amount you need to multiply the cooking time by 1.5. To heat more than that, it would not be accurate to simply multiply, so it is best to increase the cooking time minute by minute, checking frequently for doneness.

Breakfast & Brunch

Mango-Chai Breakfast Rice Pudding

• MAKES 6 SERVINGS •

RICE PUDDING FOR BREAKFAST? SURE, why not? Especially when it is made with brown rice, low-fat milk, whole fruit, and just a touch of honey. The mango and warm chai spices give it a tropical essence and enticing aroma, and a finishing dollop of yogurt is like icing on the, um, pudding. Go ahead and treat yourself!

- 1 CUP SHORT-GRAIN BROWN RICE, SUCH AS ARBORIO
- 3 CUPS 1% MILK
- 3 TABLESPOONS HONEY
- ½ TEASPOON PURE VANILLA EXTRACT
- ½ TEASPOON GROUND CINNAMON
- ½ TEASPOON GROUND GINGER
- ¼ TEASPOON GROUND CARDAMOM
- ¼ TEASPOON GROUND NUTMEG
- ¼ TEASPOON SALT
- ⅛ TEASPOON FRESHLY GROUND BLACK PEPPER
- 2 CUPS DICED MANGO, THAWED IF FROZEN, DIVIDED

FOR SERVING:
- ¾ CUP NONFAT OR LOW-FAT PLAIN GREEK YOGURT
- 1 TABLESPOON HONEY
- ¼ TEASPOON GROUND CINNAMON

1 Bring 2 cups of water to a boil in a heavy, ovenproof pot, such as a Dutch oven. Add the rice, cover, and simmer over low heat until the rice is nearly cooked, 40 to 45 minutes.

2 Preheat the oven to 375°F. Add the milk, honey, vanilla, cinnamon, ginger, cardamom, nutmeg, salt, and pepper to the pot with the rice and stir to combine well. Cover, place in the oven, and cook for 30 minutes, stirring once or twice. Then add 1 cup of the mango and cook for 15 minutes more.

3 Remove the pot from the oven and allow to cool, uncovered, for 15 minutes, then stir in the remaining 1 cup mango. The pudding will be slightly soupy at this stage but the liquid will continue to absorb into the rice and thicken as the pudding cools.

4 Distribute the pudding among six 12-ounce cups or jars, cover, and refrigerate for at least 4 hours. To serve, dollop with the yogurt, drizzle with the honey, and sprinkle with the cinnamon.

---

* **Serving size:** Scant 1 cup pudding, and 2 tablespoons yogurt; **Per serving:** Calories 260; Total Fat 2g (Mono Fat 0.4g, Poly Fat 0.1g, Sat Fat 1g); Protein 10g; Carb 52g; Fiber 2g; Cholesterol 10mg; Sodium 160mg; **Excellent source of:** Riboflavin, Vitamin C; **Good source of:** Calcium, Phosphorus, Potassium, Protein, Vitamin A

TO REFRIGERATE
Cover tightly and refrigerate for up to 4 days.

Herbed Ham and Cheese Bread Pudding

• MAKES 8 SERVINGS •

THE SUMPTUOUS, SAVORY STRATA IS fragrant with nutty gruyère cheese, smoky ham, and fresh thyme. It is moist and rich tasting, a real treat for a celebratory Sunday brunch. But it is so much better for you than most, thanks to the use of whole-grain bread, low-fat milk, and a balanced amount of cheese.

It's also easy and convenient to make—you pull the simple ingredients together the day before and let it sit in the refrigerator overnight. The next day you just pop it in the oven and sip your morning coffee while it cooks and becomes puffed and golden. Leftovers reheat well, so don't wait for a special occasion to make it. Whip one up on any Saturday or Sunday and have breakfast on hand for the work week.

2 TABLESPOONS OLIVE OIL

1 LARGE ONION, THINLY SLICED INTO HALF-MOONS

12 LARGE EGGS

2 CUPS 1% PERCENT MILK

1 TABLESPOON DIJON MUSTARD

½ TEASPOON SALT

½ TEASPOON FRESHLY GROUND BLACK PEPPER

1 CUP GRATED GRUYÈRE CHEESE (4 OUNCES)

4 OUNCES THINLY SLICED SMOKED HAM, SUCH AS BLACK FOREST HAM, CUT INTO THIN STRIPS

¼ CUP CHOPPED FRESH ITALIAN PARSLEY LEAVES

1 TABLESPOON FINELY CHOPPED FRESH THYME

COOKING SPRAY

1 POUND WHOLE-GRAIN CRUSTY BREAD, CUT INTO 1-INCH CUBES

1 Heat the oil in a large skillet over medium-high heat. Add the onion and cook, stirring, until translucent and slightly golden, 8 to 9 minutes. Remove from the heat and allow to cool.

2 In a large bowl, whisk together the eggs, milk, mustard, salt, and pepper until well combined. Stir in the cheese, ham, parsley, and thyme and stir gently. Spray a 9 × 13-inch glass baking dish with cooking spray and arrange the bread evenly in the dish. Pour the ham-egg mixture over the bread, moving some of the bread around to ensure the liquid is evenly distributed. Cover and refrigerate for at least 8 hours and up to 24.

3 Preheat the oven to 350°F. Bake the bread pudding until the top is golden and eggs are cooked through, 60 to 65 minutes.

Recipe continues

* **Serving size:** One 4 × 3-inch piece; **Per serving:** Calories 400; Total Fat 18g (Mono Fat 7.2g, Poly Fat 3.1g, Sat Fat 6.4g); Protein 26g; Carb 31g; Fiber 5g; Cholesterol 305mg; Sodium 790mg; **Excellent source of:** Calcium, Iodine, Manganese, Phosphorus, Protein, Riboflavin, Selenium, Vitamin K; **Good source of:** Copper, Fiber, Folate, Iron, Magnesium, Molybdenum, Niacin, Pantothenic Acid, Potassium, Thiamin, Vitamin A, Vitamin B6, Vitamin B12, Vitamin D, Zinc

TO REFRIGERATE AND REHEAT

Once baked, chill uncovered in the refrigerator for 30 minutes, then cover tightly and refrigerate for up to 3 days. To reheat, allow to sit at room temperature while the oven preheats to 350°F. Uncover the casserole dish, or scoop the desired amount onto a sheet of foil and place in the oven for 20 to 30 minutes, depending on the amount. Alternatively, scoop onto a microwave-safe plate, cover with a splatter guard, and microwave on high for about 60 seconds for one portion.

Family Favorite Granola

I HAVE EXPERIMENTED WITH MANY variations of granola over the years, changing up the nuts and seeds, adding seasonings like vanilla and cinnamon, tossing in dried fruit, or using honey rather than maple syrup as a sweetener, but I come back to this one again and again at my family's request. It's extra-nutty, with three kinds of nuts and seeds, plus shredded coconut, and it's lightly sweetened with pure maple syrup and seasoned with just a bit of salt. Despite its simple ingredients, it has a deep flavor that develops from a good, long toasting in the oven. I like to leave it in for the full hour so it is extra well done. Play around with it and see what you like best. If you want to add dried fruit, toss it in after the granola has baked.

3 CUPS OLD-FASHIONED ROLLED OATS

1 CUP PECAN PIECES

1 CUP UNSWEETENED SHREDDED COCONUT

½ CUP SLICED ALMONDS

½ CUP HULLED SUNFLOWER SEEDS

½ CUP PURE MAPLE SYRUP

2 TABLESPOONS CANOLA OIL OR OTHER NEUTRAL TASTING OIL

¼ TEASPOON SALT

1 Preheat the oven to 300°F. Line a baking sheet with parchment paper.

2 In a large bowl, stir all the ingredients together until well combined. Spread the mixture onto the baking sheet and cook, stirring once or twice, for about 40 minutes for lightly toasted and golden brown, and up to 60 minutes for deeply toasted flavor and darker brown color.

3 Allow to cool at room temperature. Granola will crisp as it cools.

TO REFRIGERATE

Place in an airtight container in the refrigerator where it will keep for up to 2 weeks.

TO FREEZE

Place in a sealable freezer bag and freeze for up to 3 months. Thaw at room temperature for 1 to 2 hours before using.

＊ **Serving size:** ¼ cup; **Per serving:** Calories 150; Total Fat 10g (Mono Fat 3.3g, Poly Fat 1.7g, Sat Fat 2.8g); Protein 3g; Carb 14g; Fiber 2g; Cholesterol 0mg; Sodium 50mg; **Excellent source of:** Manganese

Blueberry-Chia Overnight Oats in Jars

WHEN YOU LET ROLLED OATS sit overnight in a mixture of milk and yogurt the oats soften and absorb the liquid, and you wake up to a treat that has the luxurious texture of a pudding. With that as the base you can run with all kinds of fruit, nut, and flavor combos. Here, fresh blueberries and blueberry jam add magnificent color and light sweetness, and chia seeds and almonds punch up the crunch factor while adding healthy fats, satisfying fiber, and protein. Using individual jars makes for an easy grab and go breakfast, or a fun way to serve for a brunch.

⅔ CUP WHOLE NATURAL ALMONDS, DIVIDED

1½ CUPS NONFAT OR 1% MILK

1 CUP NONFAT OR LOW-FAT PLAIN YOGURT (NOT GREEK-STYLE)

⅓ CUP ALL-FRUIT BLUEBERRY JAM

1 TEASPOON PURE VANILLA EXTRACT

1 CUP OLD-FASHIONED ROLLED OATS

2 TABLESPOONS CHIA SEEDS

2 CUPS BLUEBERRIES, DIVIDED

1 Toast the almonds in a dry skillet over medium-high heat, stirring frequently, until lightly browned and fragrant, 3 to 5 minutes. Allow to cool slightly, then chop them coarsely.

2 In a medium bowl, stir together the milk, yogurt, jam, and vanilla. Stir in the oats, chia seeds, and half of the almonds. Then stir in 1 cup of the blueberries.

3 Divide the mixture evenly among four 12-ounce (1½-cup) jars. Top each with the remaining blueberries and almonds. Cover tightly and refrigerate overnight or at least 8 hours. Serve chilled or at room temperature. (Note: the nuts on top will soften a bit in the refrigerator. If you want them extra-crunchy, sprinkle them on right before serving.)

＊**Serving size:** 1 jar containing about 1 cup oat mixture and ¼ cup topping; **Per serving:** Calories 410; Total Fat 15g (Mono Fat 8.2g, Poly Fat 4.8g, Sat Fat 1.5g); Protein 15g; Carb 57g; Fiber 9g; Cholesterol 5mg; Sodium 90mg; **Excellent source of:** Calcium, Fiber, Magnesium, Manganese, Phosphorus, Protein, Riboflavin, Vitamin E; **Good source of:** Copper, Iodine, Iron, Molybdenum, Potassium, Thiamin, Vitamin C, Vitamin D, Vitamin K, Zinc

TO REFRIGERATE
The jars will keep up to 4 days in the refrigerator.

Pumpkin Spice Overnight Oats in Jars

THIS VERSION OF THE PUDDING-LIKE, no-cook oatmeal celebrates autumn flavors with pumpkin puree, pure maple syrup, pumpkin seeds, dried cranberries, and fragrant pumpkin-pie spices.

½ CUP WALNUT PIECES, COARSELY CHOPPED, DIVIDED

⅓ CUP HULLED PUMPKIN SEEDS, DIVIDED

1 CUP NONFAT OR 1% MILK

1 CUP NONFAT OR LOW-FAT PLAIN YOGURT (NOT GREEK-STYLE)

1 CUP OLD-FASHIONED ROLLED OATS

½ CUP PUMPKIN PUREE

¼ CUP PURE MAPLE SYRUP

1 TEASPOON PURE VANILLA EXTRACT

¼ TEASPOON GROUND CINNAMON

⅛ TEASPOON GROUND NUTMEG

⅛ TEASPOON GROUND GINGER

½ CUP DRIED CRANBERRIES, DIVIDED

1 Toast the walnuts and pumpkin seeds in a dry skillet over medium-high heat, stirring frequently, until golden and fragrant, 3 to 5 minutes. Set aside to cool.

2 In a medium bowl, stir together the milk, yogurt, oats, pumpkin puree, maple syrup, vanilla, cinnamon, nutmeg, and ginger. Add half of the walnuts and pumpkin seeds and half of the dried cranberries and stir to combine.

3 Divide the mixture evenly among four 12-ounce (1½-cup) jars. Top each with the remaining walnuts, pumpkin seeds, and dried cranberries. Cover tightly and refrigerate overnight or at least 8 hours. Serve chilled or at room temperature. (Note: the nuts on top will soften a bit in the refrigerator. If you want them extra-crunchy, sprinkle them on right before serving.)

＊ **Serving size:** 1 jar containing about ¾ cup oat mixture and ¼ cup topping; **Per serving:** Calories 390; Total Fat 16g (Mono Fat 3.4g, Poly Fat 9.4g, Sat Fat 2.2g); Protein 13g; Carb 52g; Fiber 5g; Cholesterol 0mg; Sodium 80mg; **Excellent source of:** Calcium, Fiber, Magnesium, Manganese, Phosphorus, Protein, Riboflavin, Vitamin A; **Good source of:** Copper, Iodine, Iron, Vitamin C, Vitamin D, Zinc

TO REFRIGERATE
The jars will keep up to 4 days in the refrigerator.

Apple-Cinnamon Baked Oatmeal

• MAKES 6 SERVINGS •

THIS RECIPE IS LIKE GIVING your everyday bowl of oatmeal the fairy-godmother treatment, turning its basic ingredients, oats, fruit, nuts, and milk, almost magically, into an apple cake–like treat that is spiked with cinnamon, maple, and vanilla and studded with walnuts. Plus, you just have to prep it once for a week's worth of warm, satisfying breakfasts.

COOKING SPRAY

¾ CUP WALNUT PIECES, CHOPPED, DIVIDED

1 TABLESPOON LIGHT BROWN SUGAR

1 TEASPOON GROUND CINNAMON, DIVIDED

2 CUPS ROLLED OATS

1 TEASPOON BAKING POWDER

⅛ TEASPOON SALT

2 CUPS 1% MILK

⅓ CUP PURE MAPLE SYRUP

1 LARGE EGG

2 TABLESPOONS CANOLA OIL OR OTHER NEUTRAL TASTING OIL

1½ TEASPOONS PURE VANILLA EXTRACT

2 MEDIUM GOLDEN DELICIOUS APPLES, UNPEELED, CORED, AND CUT INTO ½-INCH PIECES (2 CUPS)

½ CUP RAISINS

1 Preheat the oven to 375°F. Coat an 8-inch square baking dish or 9-inch deep dish pie plate with cooking spray.

2 In a small bowl, mix together ½ cup of the walnuts, the brown sugar, and ¼ teaspoon of the cinnamon.

3 In a medium bowl, stir together the oats, the remaining ¼ cup of walnuts, baking powder, the remaining ¾ teaspoon of the cinnamon, and the salt. In another bowl, whisk together the milk, maple syrup, egg, oil, and vanilla. Pour the liquid ingredients over the oat mixture and stir to combine. Stir in the apple and raisins.

4 Pour into the prepared baking dish. Top with the walnut–brown sugar mixture. Bake for 40 to 45 minutes, until it is set and the top is golden.

Recipe continues

TO REFRIGERATE AND REHEAT

Chill uncovered for 30 minutes, then cover tightly with foil or plastic wrap and refrigerate for up to 4 days.

To reheat, allow to sit at room temperature as the oven preheats to 350°F. Bake, covered with foil for 20 to 40 minutes, depending on the amount. Alternatively, place on a microwave-safe plate, cover with a splatter guard, and microwave for about 60 seconds for a single portion.

TO FREEZE AND REHEAT

Allow to chill, uncovered, in the refrigerator for 1 hour. To freeze the whole dish, cover tightly with plastic wrap and then foil, or to freeze individual portions, slice, wrap each portion in foil, then place in a sealable freezer bag. Freeze for up to 3 months.

To reheat, there is no need to thaw. Remove the plastic wrap from the dish, and re-cover with the foil, or remove portions from the plastic bag, keeping them wrapped in foil. Place the frozen dish or foil packet(s) in a cold oven set to 350°F. Once the oven reaches temperature, cook for 20 minutes for a single portion to 40 minutes for the whole dish.

Alternatively, to microwave individual portions, remove from the foil and place on a microwave-safe dish. Cover with a splatter guard and microwave on high for 2 minutes for a single portion.

---

* **Serving size:** 1¼ cups; **Per serving:** Calories 420; Total Fat 18g (Mono Fat 5.5g, Poly Fat 9.1g, Sat Fat 2.4g); Protein 10g; Carb 58g; Fiber 6g; Cholesterol 35mg; Sodium 330mg; **Excellent source of:** Fiber, Calcium, Manganese, Protein, Riboflavin; **Good source of:** Copper, Iron, Magnesium, Phosphorus, Potassium

Sweet Ricotta and Berry Flatbread Breakfast Pizzas

• MAKES 4 SERVINGS •

SPREADING CREAMY, PROTEIN-RICH RICOTTA CHEESE on whole-grain flatbread and topping it with plump berries and a drizzle of lemon and honey is fast and easy to do, but even that can seem like too much on a hectic weekday morning. Luckily, you can make these ahead and keep them in the freezer for completely effortless, tasty nourishment, even when you think you have no time for breakfast.

- 4 WHOLE-GRAIN FLATBREADS, SUCH AS PITA OR NAAN (2 OUNCES EACH)
- 2 TEASPOONS OLIVE OIL
- 2 TABLESPOONS HONEY, DIVIDED
- ¾ CUP PART-SKIM RICOTTA CHEESE
- 1 CUP FRESH BLUEBERRIES, OR FROZEN UNTHAWED
- 1 CUP FRESH RASPBERRIES, OR FROZEN UNTHAWED
- 2 TEASPOONS FRESH LEMON JUICE

1 Brush the top of each piece of bread lightly with the oil and then brush each with about 1 teaspoon of the honey.

2 Spread 3 tablespoons of the ricotta cheese on top of each flatbread, then scatter each with ¼ cup of the blueberries and ¼ cup of the raspberries.

3 Mix the remaining honey with the lemon juice until combined and drizzle some over each pizza. The pizzas may be frozen at this stage.

4 To serve, place a foil-lined baking sheet in the oven and preheat it along with the oven to 450°F. Place the pizza on the tray and cook until the berries are warmed through and nearly bursting and the bread is crisped, 8 to 10 minutes.

---

* **Serving size:** 1 pizza; **Per serving:** Calories 300; Total Fat 8g (Mono Fat 2.9g, Poly Fat 1.1g, Sat Fat 2.9g); Protein 12g; Carb 51g; Fiber 7g; Cholesterol 15mg; Sodium 300mg; **Excellent source of:** Fiber, Manganese, Phosphorus, Protein, Selenium, Vitamin C; **Good source of:** Calcium, Copper, Iron, Magnesium, Thiamin, Vitamin K, Zinc

Refrigerating not recommended.

TO FREEZE AND HEAT
Place each pizza onto a large piece of foil. Fold the foil around the pizzas to form a packet. Place the packets into one or two large sealable freezer bags and freeze for up to 3 months. Do not thaw. When ready to serve, open the packets completely and cook in a 450°F oven for about 12 minutes.

English Muffin Breakfast Pizzas · MAKES 4 SERVINGS ·

PIZZA LEFTOVER FROM THE PREVIOUS night's dinner suits me just fine for breakfast, especially if I have made it myself with really good ingredients. Whether, like me, you already love a slice as your first meal of the day, or you need to ease in to the pizza-for-breakfast concept, this is the perfect recipe. In it, familiar breakfast favorites—English muffins and Canadian bacon—meet classic pizza ingredients, tomato sauce and mozzarella cheese, for a freezer-friendly melt that will make everyone happy.

4 WHOLE-WHEAT ENGLISH MUFFINS (NOT HONEY-WHEAT)

2 TABLESPOONS OLIVE OIL, DIVIDED

4 SLICES (3 OUNCES) CANADIAN BACON, THINLY SLICED INTO STRIPS

3 CUPS LIGHTLY PACKED FRESH BABY SPINACH LEAVES, COARSELY CHOPPED

½ CUP SIMPLE MARINARA SAUCE (PAGE 214) OR STORE-BOUGHT MARINARA

1 CUP SHREDDED PART-SKIM MOZZARELLA CHEESE (4 OUNCES)

1 Split the English muffins and brush the cut side of each with oil, using a total of 1 tablespoon of the oil.

2 Heat the remaining 1 tablespoon of oil in a medium skillet over medium-high heat. Add the Canadian bacon and cook, stirring once or twice, until browned, 2 minutes. Add the spinach and cook, stirring, until wilted, 1 minute. If planning to freeze the pizzas, allow the spinach mixture to cool completely.

3 Top each English muffin half with 1 tablespoon of the marinara sauce, then 1 heaping tablespoon of the spinach mixture, then 2 tablespoons of the cheese. If freezing, do so at this stage.

4 To serve now, place a baking sheet in the oven and preheat it along with the oven to 450°F. Place the pizza on the baking sheet and bake for 8 to 10 minutes until the English muffin is toasted and the cheese is melted and beginning to brown. Allow to cool slightly before eating.

✻ **Serving size:** 2 rounds; **Per serving:** Calories 300; Total Fat 14g (Mono Fat 6.9g, Poly Fat 1.0g, Sat Fat 4.1g); Protein 18g; Carb 27g; Fiber 4g; Cholesterol 30mg; Sodium 660mg; **Excellent source of:** Calcium, Protein, Vitamin A, Vitamin K; **Good source of:** Chloride, Fiber, Folate, Iron, Manganese, Phosphorus, Selenium, Vitamin C

Refrigerating not recommended.

TO FREEZE AND HEAT
Place 2 pizza rounds onto a large piece of foil. Fold the foil around the pizzas to form a packet. Place the packets into one or two large sealable freezer bags and freeze for up to 3 months. Do not thaw. When ready to serve, open the packets completely and cook in a 450°F oven for about 12 minutes.

Broccoli Cheddar "Quiche in a Bag" with Melt-in-Your-Mouth No-Roll Olive Oil Pie Crust

• MAKES 6 SERVINGS •

YOU'D BE WISE TO RULE out keeping a finished quiche in the freezer, because cooked eggs tend to get rubbery and watery if frozen. But a little known secret is that raw egg freezes beautifully, so you can store a prepared quiche filling in a bag in your freezer, ready to be thawed and baked whenever you need it. Once cooked, it will keep in the refrigerator for several days. This quiche is lightened up calorie-wise from your typical recipe, but its creamy egg custard is full of cheesy, rich flavor and is undeniably delicious.

1 TABLESPOON OLIVE OIL

1 SMALL ONION, DICED

2 CUPS BROCCOLI FLORETS, COARSELY CHOPPED

1 TEASPOON MUSTARD POWDER

¼ TEASPOON SALT

¼ TEASPOON FRESHLY GROUND BLACK PEPPER

1 CUP 1% MILK

3 TABLESPOONS ALL-PURPOSE FLOUR

4 LARGE EGGS

¾ CUP SHREDDED SHARP CHEDDAR CHEESE (3 OUNCES)

FOR SERVING:

1 MELT-IN-YOUR-MOUTH NO-ROLL OLIVE OIL PIE CRUST (PAGE 35) OR A STORE BOUGHT, PRE-BAKED DEEP-DISH WHOLE-GRAIN PIE CRUST

1 Heat the oil in a medium skillet over medium heat. Add the onion and cook, stirring, until translucent, 3 minutes. Add the broccoli and cook, stirring frequently, until the broccoli begins to soften, 3 minutes. Stir in the mustard powder, salt, and pepper. Allow to cool completely.

2 In a large bowl, whisk together the milk and flour until the flour is dissolved. Add the eggs and whisk to incorporate.

3 Pour the egg mixture into a gallon sized sealable plastic freezer bag. (Helpful hint: fit the bag over a small deep pot or large measuring pitcher to make it easier to fill). Add the vegetable mixture and the cheese to the bag and squish it around to distribute the ingredients evenly. The quiche mixture may be refrigerated or frozen at this stage.

4 To continue, preheat the oven to 350°F. Pour the (thawed, if frozen) filling into the pie crust and bake until a knife inserted into the middle comes out clean, 50 to 65 minutes. Allow to cool for 5 minutes before slicing.

Recipe continues

For the uncooked filling:

TO REFRIGERATE

Uncooked mixture may be refrigerated for 1 day. Pour into a bowl and stir to redistribute the ingredients, then follow the "to continue" instructions in the recipe.

TO FREEZE

Freeze the uncooked mixture for up to 2 months. To thaw, place on a plate or in a container to prevent any leaks and thaw completely in the refrigerator for 36 to 48 hours. Once thawed, transfer to a bowl and stir to redistribute ingredients, then follow the "to continue" instructions in the recipe.

For the cooked quiche:

TO REFRIGERATE AND REHEAT

Chill uncovered in the refrigerator for 30 minutes, then cover tightly with foil or plastic wrap and refrigerate for up to 4 days.

To reheat, allow to sit at room temperature as the oven preheats to 350°F. Heat in the pie dish, uncovered, or place a single serving on a sheet of foil on a baking tray for 10 to 30 minutes, depending on the amount. Alternatively, uncover, place on a microwave-safe plate, top with a splatter guard, and microwave on high for about 30 seconds for a single portion.

✳ **Serving Size:** ⅙ of quiche; **Per serving:** Calories 370; Total Fat 23g (Mono Fat 12.2g, Poly Fat 2.3g, Sat Fat 6.4g); Protein 13g; Carb 28g; Fiber 3g; Cholesterol 140mg; Sodium 360mg; **Excellent source of:** Protein, Riboflavin, Selenium, Vitamin C, Vitamin K; **Good source of:** Calcium, Fiber, Folate, Iodine, Iron, Molybdenum, Phosphorus, Thiamin, Vitamin E

MELT-IN-YOUR-MOUTH NO-ROLL OLIVE OIL PIE CRUST
• MAKES 1 DEEP-DISH PIE CRUST OR TART CRUST; SERVES 6 •

I THINK YOU WILL FIND this recipe a revelation. It has everything you want in a pie crust (rich but delicate flavor, tender melt-in-your-mouth texture, and easy prep) without the things you don't want (all the saturated fat, refined flour, and skill required to make it turn out right). As a bonus, you get the health benefits of olive oil and whole-grain flour. Bake up a couple and keep them in your freezer so they are on hand for the next time you feel a quiche or pie coming on.

⅔ CUP WHOLE-GRAIN PASTRY FLOUR

½ CUP ALL-PURPOSE FLOUR

¼ TEASPOON SALT

2 TABLESPOONS COLD 1% MILK

⅓ CUP OLIVE OIL, PLUS 1 TEASPOON FOR BRUSHING

TO REFRIGERATE
Wrap the ball of raw dough in plastic wrap or wrap the baked pie or tart shell, in its dish, in foil, and then tightly in plastic wrap and refrigerate for up to 4 days. Allow the ball of dough to come to room temperature for 1 hour before using. The pre-baked shell may be used right out of the refrigerator.

TO FREEZE
Wrap the ball of raw dough in plastic wrap, then place in a sealable plastic freezer bag, or wrap the baked pie or tart shell in its dish in foil then place in a 2 gallon sealable plastic freezer bag and freeze for up to 3 months. When ready to use thaw in the refrigerator for 8 to 12 hours.

1 Preheat the oven to 400°F.

2 In a medium bowl, whisk together the whole-grain pastry flour, all-purpose flour, and salt. In a small bowl or spouted pitcher, whisk the milk into ⅓ cup of the olive oil until it is well integrated. Make a well in the flour mixture, pour in the oil mixture, then combine with a fork until crumbly. Gather the dough up into a ball and refrigerate or freeze, or continue to prebake.

3 Brush a 9-inch deep-dish pie plate or tart pan and one side of a 10-inch square piece of foil with the remaining teaspoon of oil. Pat the mixture into the prepared pie plate or tart pan as you would a graham cracker crust.

4 Prick the pie crust in a few spots with a fork. Line the crust with foil (oiled side touching the crust) and top with pie weights or raw rice and bake for 10 minutes. Remove the weights or rice and the foil and bake for another 5 minutes, until golden. Allow to cool completely.

∗ **Serving size:** ⅙ pie crust; **Per serving:** Calories 210; Total Fat 13g (Mono Fat 9.2g, Poly Fat 1.4g, Sat Fat 1.8g); Protein 3g; Carb 19g; Fiber 2g; Cholesterol 0mg; Sodium 100mg

Pumpkin Waffles

THE VERY ANTICIPATION OF THE pumpkin-spice aroma of these waffles will make you want to get out of bed in the morning. They are crisp outside, tender inside, and filled with loads of energizing power ingredients to help fuel your day: 100 percent whole-grain flour, pure pumpkin puree, flax seed, milk, yogurt, and eggs. And just like the store-bought kind, you can pop these into the toaster, or toaster oven, straight from the freezer.

1¾ CUPS WHOLE-WHEAT FLOUR

¼ CUP GROUND FLAX SEED

1½ TEASPOON BAKING POWDER

½ TEASPOON BAKING SODA

½ TEASPOON GROUND CINNAMON

¼ TEASPOON GROUND GINGER

¼ TEASPOON GROUND NUTMEG

¼ TEASPOON SALT

1½ CUPS LOW-FAT PLAIN YOGURT (NOT GREEK-STYLE)

1 CUP PUMPKIN PUREE

4 LARGE EGGS

½ CUP WHOLE MILK

3 TABLESPOONS MOLASSES

2 TABLESPOONS CANOLA OIL, OR OTHER NEUTRAL TASTING OIL

COOKING SPRAY

FOR SERVING:

1 CUP PURE MAPLE SYRUP

1 In a large bowl, whisk together the flour, flax seed, baking powder, baking soda, cinnamon, ginger, nutmeg, and salt. In a medium bowl, whisk together the yogurt, pumpkin puree, eggs, milk, molasses, and oil until well combined. Stir the wet ingredients into the dry ingredients, mixing just enough to combine them. The batter may be refrigerated at this stage.

2 Spray a waffle iron with cooking spray and preheat it. Ladle enough of the batter to cover three-fourths of the surface of the waffle iron, close it, and cook until golden brown, 3 to 5 minutes. Repeat with the remaining batter. The waffles may be frozen at this stage. To continue, keep warm on a baking sheet in a 350°F oven, if desired.

3 Serve the waffles drizzled with the maple syrup.

Recipe continues

TO REFRIGERATE AND SERVE

Uncooked batter may be refrigerated in an airtight container for up to 1 day. Stir before cooking as according to the recipe directions.

Refrigerating cooked waffles not recommended.

TO FREEZE AND REHEAT

Allow cooked waffles to cool at room temperature for 15 minutes, then wrap in foil or plastic wrap and place in a sealable plastic freezer bag for up to 2 months.

To reheat, place, uncovered, on a baking tray in a 350°F oven or toaster oven for 10 minutes, flipping once, or toast in a toaster set to medium darkness.

Microwave reheating not recommended.

---

* **Serving size:** 1 large or 2 small waffles; **Per serving:** Calories 350; Total Fat 9g (Mono Fat 3.8g, Poly Fat 2.8g, Sat Fat 2.1g); Protein 11g; Carb 59g; Fiber 5g; Cholesterol 95mg; Sodium 330mg; **Excellent source of:** Calcium, Fiber, Iodine, Magnesium, Manganese, Phosphorus, Protein, Riboflavin, Selenium, Vitamin A; **Good source of:** Copper, Iron, Potassium, Thiamin, Vitamin B6, Zinc

Dutch Baby Pancake
with Fall Fruit Compote

• MAKES 4 SERVINGS •

A DUTCH BABY IS SO impressive looking it seems like it would take some special effort, but it is one of the easiest types of pancakes to make. All you do is pour a simple batter into a heated skillet and pop it in the oven. It comes out puffed, golden, and ready to be topped with compote.

⅔ CUP WHOLE-WHEAT PASTRY FLOUR OR REGULAR WHOLE-WHEAT FLOUR

¼ TEASPOON SALT

1 CUP 1% MILK

3 LARGE EGGS

1 TABLESPOON PURE MAPLE SYRUP

⅓ TEASPOON ALMOND EXTRACT

1 TABLESPOON UNSALTED BUTTER

1⅓ CUPS FALL FRUIT COMPOTE (RECIPE FOLLOWS)

1 In a medium bowl, whisk together the flour and salt. In another bowl, whisk the milk, eggs, maple syrup, and almond extract. Add the wet ingredients to the dry ingredients and mix until just combined. The batter may be refrigerated or frozen at this stage.

2 To continue, preheat the oven to 450°F. In a heavy 10-inch cast-iron or ovenproof nonstick skillet, heat the butter until it is very hot but not smoking. Pour the batter into the skillet and quickly transfer it to the oven. Bake until golden brown and puffed, 15 to 20 minutes; do not open oven during baking. Spread the warm compote on top of the pancake, then cut the pancake into 4 wedges. Serve immediately.

For the uncooked batter:

TO REFRIGERATE

Place the batter in an airtight container and refrigerate for up to 1 day. Stir to blend evenly, then follow the "to continue" directions above.

TO FREEZE

Transfer the batter to a gallon-sized sealable freezer bag and freeze for up to 2 months. Allow to thaw in the refrigerator completely, 24 to 36 hours, transfer to a bowl and stir to blend evenly, then follow the "to continue" directions above.

For the cooked pancake:

TO REFRIGERATE AND REHEAT

Wrap leftover pancake in an airtight container and refrigerate for up to 2 days. To reheat, wrap in foil and heat in a 350°F oven for 15 minutes, or place on a microwave-safe plate, cover with a splatter guard, and microwave on high for about 40 seconds for a single portion.

∗ **Serving size:** ¼ Dutch Baby and ⅓ cup compote; **Per serving:** Calories 320; Total Fat 9g (Mono Fat 2.7g, Poly Fat 1.2g, Sat Fat 4.4g); Protein 10g; Carb 51g; Fiber 6g; Cholesterol 155mg; Sodium 270mg; **Excellent source of:** Fiber, Manganese, Phosphorus, Riboflavin, Selenium; **Good source of:** Calcium, Copper, Iodine, Magnesium, Pantothenic Acid, Protein, Potassium, Thiamin, Vitamin B6, Vitamin B12, Vitamin C, Zinc

FALL FRUIT COMPOTE

• MAKES 8 SERVINGS •

COOKING SLICED APPLES AND PEARS in a touch of butter, until they are softened and caramelized, brings out their inherent sweetness and releases their autumnal aroma. The rest of the ingredients elevate them further for a sumptuous treat that is perfect for piling onto pancakes or waffles, serving with yogurt as a breakfast or snack, or even topping with a scoop of vanilla ice cream for dessert.

- 1 TABLESPOON UNSALTED BUTTER
- 2 GOLDEN DELICIOUS APPLES, UNPEELED, SLICED INTO ¼-INCH-THICK SLICES (4 CUPS)
- 3 FIRM-RIPE BOSC PEARS, UNPEELED, SLICED INTO ¼-INCH-THICK SLICES (4 CUPS)
- ¼ CUP DRIED UNSWEETENED CRANBERRIES, SOAKED IN HOT WATER FOR 10 MINUTES, DRAINED
- ⅓ CUP PURE MAPLE SYRUP
- 2 TABLESPOONS FRESH ORANGE JUICE
- 1 TEASPOON GROUND CINNAMON
- ¼ TEASPOON FINELY GRATED ORANGE ZEST
- ⅛ TEASPOON SALT

1 Heat the butter in a large nonstick skillet over medium-high heat. Add the apples and pears and cook, stirring a few times, until they are softened and browned but still retain their shape, about 10 minutes. Stir in the cranberries, maple syrup, orange juice, cinnamon, orange zest, and salt and cook, stirring, until the liquid has thickened, 1 minute. Serve warm or chilled.

TO REFRIGERATE AND REHEAT

Place in an airtight container in the refrigerator where compote will keep for up to 1 week. Reheat in a covered pot on the stove over low heat, stirring occasionally, until warmed through, 2 to 10 minutes, depending on the amount. Or place in a microwave-safe dish, cover with a splatter guard, and microwave on high for 15 seconds for one portion to 1 minute for the entire batch.

TO FREEZE AND REHEAT

Allow to chill in the refrigerator for 30 minutes, then place in an airtight container or sealable plastic freezer bag and freeze for up to 3 months. Thaw in the refrigerator for 10 to 12 hours. Alternatively, run the bag under hot water for 30 seconds to release the compote, place in a microwave-safe bowl, and microwave on the defrost setting for 3 minutes for one portion to 10 minutes for the entire batch.

＊ **Serving size:** About ⅓ cup; **Per serving:** Calories 130; Total Fat 1.5g (Mono Fat 0.4g, Poly Fat 0.1g, Sat Fat 0.9g); Protein 0g; Carb 30g; Fiber 3g; Cholesterol 5mg; Sodium 40mg; **Excellent source of:** Manganese; **Good source of:** Fiber, Riboflavin, Vitamin C

DIY Whole-Grain Buttermilk Pancake Mix

• MAKES 16 SERVINGS (4 BATCHES) •

PANCAKES ARE, HANDS DOWN, MY daughter's favorite breakfast. We often make them together on weekends, but she would beg for them on weekdays too. I mostly had to say "no" since it was too much to pull together on a busy morning, and I couldn't bring myself to buy a pancake mix, knowing it's not much more than a few simple dry ingredients whisked together. So, I came up with this DIY pancake mix so I could say "yes" to her on school days too. I amp up the protein and nutrition further by using milk in the final batter, but you could also use water if need be, like if you are on a camping trip.

FOR THE MIX

3½ CUPS WHOLE-WHEAT PASTRY FLOUR

1 CUP LOW-FAT DRY BUTTERMILK

½ CUP CORNMEAL

¼ CUP TOASTED WHEAT GERM

1 TABLESPOON PLUS 1 TEASPOON BAKING POWER

1 TABLESPOON GRANULATED SUGAR, OPTIONAL

2 TEASPOONS BAKING SODA

¼ TEASPOON SALT

FOR THE PANCAKES • MAKES 4 SERVINGS •

1⅓ CUPS DIY WHOLE-GRAIN BUTTERMILK PANCAKE MIX

1 CUP 1% MILK

1 LARGE EGG

¼ CUP PURE MAPLE SYRUP, FOR SERVING

1 **To make the mix,** whisk all the mix ingredients together in a large bowl until combined. Store in the refrigerator in an airtight container for up to 3 months. Makes about 5⅓ cups of mix.

2 **To make the pancakes,** place 1⅓ cup of the mix into a medium bowl. Whisk the milk and egg together in a medium bowl or spouted pitcher. Add to the pancake mix and stir until there are no dry spots or large lumps. It is OK if there are some small lumps.

3 Heat a large nonstick griddle over medium heat. Ladle about ¼ cup of the batter per pancake. Flip when the pancake tops are covered with bubbles and the underside is browned, about 2 minutes. Cook until the pancakes are golden brown on both sides and cooked through, about 1 to 2 minutes more. Serve immediately with the maple syrup.

＊ **Serving size:** Two 5-inch pancakes and 1 tablespoon maple syrup; **Per serving (prepared pancakes):** Calories 210; Total Fat 3g (Mono Fat 0.8g, Poly Fat 0.4g, Sat Fat 1g); Protein 9g; Carb 38g; Fiber 3g; Cholesterol 55mg; Sodium 510mg; **Excellent source of:** Calcium, Manganese, Riboflavin; **Good source of:** Fiber, Iodine, Phosphorus, Protein, Selenium, Vitamin B12

TO REFRIGERATE

The dry mix will keep in an airtight container in the refrigerator for up to 3 months. The prepared batter will keep in the refrigerator in an airtight container for 1 day. Stir well and add a bit more milk or water if it seems too thick.

Mini Frittatas with Leeks and Asparagus

• MAKES 6 SERVINGS •

THESE THREE-BITE VEGETABLE FRITTATAS ARE tasty, beautiful, and fun to serve as part of a brunch spread, but they are equally welcomed at an evening cocktail party, and great to have on hand for an easy, satisfying weekday breakfast with some whole-grain toast, or even as an energizing afternoon snack. Made in a muffin pan, they will help you see that familiar kitchen basic in a new, exciting way.

COOKING SPRAY

1 TABLESPOON OLIVE OIL

2 CUPS CHOPPED LEEKS, WHITE AND LIGHT GREEN PARTS ONLY

1 BUNCH ASPARAGUS (1 POUND), SLICED ON THE BIAS INTO ½-INCH PIECES (2 CUPS)

6 MEDIUM WHITE BUTTON MUSHROOMS, SLICED (4 OUNCES)

7 LARGE EGGS

¼ CUP 1% MILK

¼ CUP GRATED PARMESAN CHEESE

½ TEASPOON SALT

⅛ TEASPOON FRESHLY GROUND BLACK PEPPER

1 Preheat the oven to 375°F. Spray a muffin pan with cooking spray.

2 Heat the oil in a medium skillet over medium heat. Add the leek, asparagus, and mushrooms and cook, stirring occasionally, until the vegetables have softened, about 6 minutes. Allow to cool slightly.

3 Meanwhile, in a medium bowl, whisk the eggs and milk together. Stir in the cooked vegetables, cheese, salt, and pepper.

4 Distribute the mixture evenly into the muffin pan. Bake until set in the center, 18 to 20 minutes. Serve warm or at room temperature.

＊ **Serving size:** 2 mini frittatas; **Per serving:** Calories 150; Total Fat 9g (Mono Fat 4.8g, Poly Fat 1.5g, Sat Fat 2.8g); Protein 11g; Carb 8g; Fiber 2g; Cholesterol 220mg; Sodium 340mg; **Excellent source of:** Iodine, Protein, Selenium, Thiamin, Vitamin A, Vitamin K; **Good source of:** Calcium, Copper, Folate, Iron, Manganese, Molybdenum, Pantothenic Acid, Phosphorus, Vitamin B6, Vitamin C, Vitamin D

TO REFRIGERATE AND REHEAT

Allow to cool in the refrigerator, uncovered, for 30 minutes. Then transfer the frittatas to an airtight container and refrigerate for up to 3 days. Frittatas may be served at room temperature, or reheated. To reheat, place on a foil-lined baking tray and warm in a 350°F oven, uncovered, for 5 to 8 minutes, or place on a microwave-safe plate, cover with a splatter guard, and microwave for 30 seconds for a single portion.

Freezing is not recommended.

Harvest Breakfast Cookies · MAKES 8 SERVINGS ·

MY FRIEND CINDY GIFTED ME with a batch of big, soft, whole-grain, treats that were like a cross between a muffin and a cookie, positively brimming with apples, cranberries, and pecans. It was a recipe she came up with after years of tinkering with one she had found on a package somewhere. I couldn't stop thinking about how delicious they were, and how much I wanted a stash in my freezer at all times, so I decided to come up with my own version. Thanks, Cindy, for the inspiration. These have become a staple in my home as an on-the-go breakfast or afternoon snack.

1 CUP PECAN PIECES

1 CUP WHOLE-WHEAT FLOUR

1 TEASPOON BAKING POWDER

1 TEASPOON GROUND CINNAMON

¼ TEASPOON SALT

½ CUP PURE MAPLE SYRUP

⅓ CUP CANOLA OIL, OR OTHER NEUTRAL TASTING OIL

1 LARGE EGG

1 TEASPOON PURE VANILLA EXTRACT

1 CUP ROLLED OATS

1 MEDIUM GOLDEN DELICIOUS APPLE, UNPEELED, DICED INTO ¼-INCH PIECES

1 CUP FRESH CRANBERRIES, OR FROZEN UNTHAWED, HALVED

¼ CUP DRIED CRANBERRIES

1 Preheat the oven to 350°F.

2 Place the pecans on a baking sheet and toast until fragrant, 8 minutes. Set aside to cool.

3 Meanwhile, in a medium bowl, whisk together the flour, baking powder, cinnamon, and salt. In a large bowl, beat together the maple syrup, canola oil, egg, and vanilla, until well incorporated.

4 Pour the dry ingredients into the wet ingredients and mix to combine. Add the oats, apple, fresh and dried cranberries, and pecans and stir to distribute evenly.

5 Line a baking sheet with parchment paper. Using a ½-cup measure or large ice cream scoop, scoop the batter into 8 large balls (a scant ½ cup each) and drop onto the parchment-lined baking sheet. Bake until set and lightly browned on the bottom, 20 to 25 minutes. Transfer to a cooling rack to cool.

Recipe continues

TO REFRIGERATE AND REHEAT
Allow the cookies to cool completely at room temperature, then place in an airtight container and refrigerate for up to 1 week. Allow to come to room temperature before eating, or warm in a 325°F oven, uncovered, on a baking tray, for 8 minutes. Or warm in the microwave on high, uncovered, for 15 seconds for one cookie.

TO FREEZE AND REHEAT
Allow the cookies to cool completely at room temperature, then wrap individually in foil or plastic wrap and place in a sealable plastic freezer bag for up to 3 months. There is no need to thaw before reheating; just place frozen cookie(s) uncovered on a baking tray in a cold oven and set to 325°F. Once the oven comes to temperature, continue to heat for 12 to 15 minutes. Alternatively, place frozen cookie(s) on a microwave-safe plate, uncovered, and microwave on high for 25 to 30 seconds for one serving. Also, the cookies will thaw at room temperature in 2 hours and may be eaten at room temperature.

---

* **Serving size:** 1 cookie; **Per serving:** Calories 350; Total Fat 20g (Mono Fat 11.4g, Poly Fat 5.8g, Sat Fat 1.9g); Protein 5g; Carb 40g; Fiber 5g; Cholesterol 25mg; Sodium 150mg; **Excellent source of:** Fiber, Manganese; **Good source of:** Copper, Magnesium, Phosphorus, Protein, Riboflavin, Selenium, Thiamin, Vitamin E, Vitamin K

PB and J Breakfast Bake · MAKES 8 SERVINGS ·

HEY, YOU GOT YOUR PEANUT butter and jelly in my breakfast bake! Just like in the famous Reese's commercial, this mash-up of tastes is an aha! flavor combination. It has all the elements of a sweet bread-pudding-like bake where cubed bread soaks overnight in a vanilla-cinnamon infused egg mixture. But here, the bread is cut up peanut butter and grape jelly sandwiches, and there are fresh grapes and crunchy peanuts scattered on top to echo those flavors. As the dish bakes, the peanut butter and jelly melt in and infuse the soufflé-like center with richness and a nutty aroma. The top crisps to golden brown as the grapes roast, becoming softer and more deeply flavored. The result is a decadent dish that turns a lunchbox staple into an extraordinary breakfast.

COOKING SPRAY

10 SLICES WHOLE-GRAIN BREAD

⅓ CUP NATURAL PEANUT BUTTER

¼ CUP GRAPE JELLY

12 LARGE EGGS

2 CUPS 1% MILK

2 TABLESPOONS PURE MAPLE SYRUP, PLUS MORE FOR SERVING, OPTIONAL

1 TEASPOON PURE VANILLA EXTRACT

½ TEASPOON GROUND CINNAMON

2 CUPS HALVED BLACK OR RED GRAPES

¼ CUP UNSALTED PEANUTS, COARSELY CHOPPED

1 Spray a 9 × 13-inch baking dish with cooking spray.

2 Make 5 peanut butter and jelly sandwiches by spreading five of the slices of bread with about 1 tablespoon each of the peanut butter and the other five slices with about 2 teaspoons each of the jelly, and then putting the peanut butter and jelly halves together. Slice each sandwich into 8 pieces, then scatter the sandwich pieces, unevenly, into the prepared baking dish.

3 In a large bowl, whisk together the eggs, milk, 2 tablespoons maple syrup, vanilla, and cinnamon until well combined. Pour the egg mixture over the sandwiches in the pan. Press the sandwiches down a bit so they are all moistened, but after moistening it is OK if some edges are sticking up out of the liquid.

4 Sprinkle the top with the grapes and peanuts, then cover tightly and place in the refrigerator at least 8 hours or overnight.

5 Preheat the oven to 350°F. Uncover and bake until puffed and browned and the egg mixture is set, 55 to 65 minutes.

Recipe continues

＊ **Serving size:** One 4 × 3-inch piece; **Per serving:** Calories 380; Total Fat 17g (Mono Fat 4.3g, Poly Fat 2.8g, Sat Fat 4.2g); Protein 20g; Carb 38g; Fiber 4g; Cholesterol 280mg; Sodium 260mg; **Excellent source of:** Iodine, Manganese, Phosphorus, Protein, Riboflavin, Selenium; **Good source of:** Calcium, Copper, Fiber, Folate, Iron, Magnesium, Molybdenum, Niacin, Pantothenic Acid, Potassium, Thiamin, Vitamin B6, Vitamin B12, Vitamin D, Zinc

TO REFRIGERATE AND REHEAT

Once baked, allow to chill, uncovered, in the refrigerator for 30 minutes, then cover tightly and refrigerate for up to 3 days.

Allow to sit at room temperature while the oven preheats to 350°F. Uncover the casserole dish, or scoop desired amount onto a sheet of foil and place in the oven for 20 to 30 minutes, depending on the amount. Alternatively, scoop the desired amount onto a microwave-safe plate, cover with a splatter guard, and microwave on high for about 60 seconds for one portion.

Freezing is not recommended.

Savory French Toast Sandwiches
with Tomato Jam with Honey • MAKES 6 SERVINGS •

THESE BREAKFAST SANDWICHES HAVE THAT irresistible savory-sweet-smoky balance that lights up all your taste buds. It starts with French toast made savory with a Parmesan and mustard seasoned egg batter. That is spread with a luscious tomato jam that's been simmered with a hint of honey, and then sandwiched with a generous slice of smoky ham. It's a super-satisfying dish that is impressive enough to serve company for brunch, but that's also convenient to eat on the go.

- 4 LARGE EGGS
- ½ CUP NONFAT MILK
- ½ TEASPOON DRY MUSTARD POWDER
- ¼ TEASPOON FRESHLY GROUND BLACK PEPPER
- ½ CUP GRATED PARMESAN CHEESE (1½ OUNCES)
- OLIVE OIL COOKING SPRAY
- 12 SLICES WHOLE-GRAIN ITALIAN BREAD (EACH ABOUT ½-INCH THICK, 3 INCHES HIGH × 4½ INCHES WIDE)
- 6 TABLESPOONS TOMATO JAM (RECIPE FOLLOWS)
- 6 OUNCES SLICED SMOKED HAM, SUCH AS BLACK FOREST

1 In a large bowl, whisk together the eggs, milk, mustard powder, and pepper. Stir in the cheese.

2 Spray a large nonstick skillet with cooking spray and preheat over medium heat. Dip 4 of the pieces of bread, one at a time, into the egg mixture until completely moistened and coated with cheese. Then place them in the skillet and cook until the outside is golden brown and the center is warm, about 2 minutes per side. Transfer to a plate. Repeat with two more batches of the bread slices, wiping the pan out with a paper towel and respraying with oil between each batch.

3 Spread ½ tablespoon of the tomato jam onto one side of each piece of the French toast, then fold a slice of the ham onto each of 6 of the pieces and top with the remaining French toast to form a ham sandwich.

TO REFRIGERATE AND REHEAT
Allow sandwiches to chill, uncovered, in the refrigerator for 30 minutes, then wrap in plastic wrap or foil and refrigerate for up to 4 days.

To reheat, preheat the oven to 350°F, wrap the sandwich in foil, and bake until warmed through, about 20 minutes. Alternatively, unwrap the sandwich, rewrap in a paper towel, and microwave on high for about 1 minute per sandwich.

TO FREEZE AND REHEAT
Allow sandwiches to chill, uncovered, in the refrigerator for 30 minutes, then wrap in plastic wrap or foil and place in a sealable freezer bag in the freezer for up to 3 months.

To reheat, there is no need to thaw. Place, wrapped in foil, in a cold oven as it preheats to 350°F. Once the oven reaches temperature, continue to cook for 25 to 30 minutes until warmed through. Or, remove any foil or plastic, rewrap in a paper towel, and microwave for 2 minutes on high for one serving.

❊ **Serving size:** 1 sandwich; **Per serving:** Calories 290; Total Fat 9g (Mono Fat 3g, Poly Fat 2g, Sat Fat 3.3g); Protein 21g; Carb 31g; Fiber 5g; Cholesterol 145mg; Sodium 690mg; **Excellent source of:** Manganese, Phosphorus, Protein, Riboflavin, Selenium, Thiamin; **Good source of:** Calcium, Copper, Fiber, Folate, Iodine, Iron, Magnesium, Molybdenum, Niacin, Potassium, Vitamin A, Vitamin B6, Vitamin B12, Vitamin C, Vitamin D, Zinc

TOMATO JAM WITH HONEY   • MAKES 24 SERVINGS •

WHEN YOU COOK FRESH TOMATOES low and slow with a little vinegar, some sweetener, and salt, you wind up with a tomato jam that tastes like a fresher, chunkier, upgraded cousin of ketchup. This version is lightly sweetened compared to most recipes (and I think more flavor balanced) and it's done with honey, so there is no refined sugar involved. This tomato jam is essential for the Savory French Toast Sandwiches, but it will also elevate a simple grilled cheese, turkey, or grilled vegetable sandwich and is delicious on a turkey burger, or spread on crostini with some soft goat cheese.

4½ POUNDS RIPE PLUM TOMATOES, SEEDED AND COARSELY CHOPPED (ABOUT 10 CUPS)

½ CUP HONEY

¼ CUP CIDER VINEGAR

¾ TEASPOON SALT

❊ **Serving size:** 2 tablespoons; **Per serving:** Calories 35; Total Fat 0g (Mono Fat 0g, Poly Fat 0g, Sat Fat 0g); Protein 1g; Carb 9g; Fiber 1g; Cholesterol 0mg; Sodium 75mg; **Good source of:** Vitamin A, Vitamin C

Combine the tomatoes, honey, vinegar, and salt in a large, heavy pot. Bring to a boil over medium-high heat, then lower the heat to medium-low and cook, adjusting the heat as needed to keep the mixture at a simmer, stirring occasionally, until the tomatoes have broken down and the mixture has thickened to a jam-like consistency, 1 to 2 hours. (Once the mixture has begun to thicken, you will need to stir more frequently to prevent burning.)

TO REFRIGERATE
Transfer to an airtight container and store in the refrigerator for about 2 weeks.

TO FREEZE AND THAW
Chill in the refrigerator for 30 minutes, then place into a sealable plastic freezer bag or pour into ice cube trays and freeze. Once frozen, transfer the cubes of sauce to a sealable plastic freezer bag where it will keep for up to 3 months.

Thaw in the refrigerator for 18 to 24 hours. Allow to come to room temperature before serving. Alternatively, place in a microwave-safe dish, cover, and microwave on high for about 20 seconds for one portion to 1 minute for the entire batch.

Cheese Blintzes
with Strawberry Rhubarb Compote   • MAKES 8 SERVINGS •

WHEN I WAS A KID we always had boxes of frozen blintzes in the house that I remember reheating myself when I was old enough to do so. As an adult I learned how to make and freeze them myself, which seriously upped the ante on their tastiness and healthfulness.

In case you have never had them, cheese blintzes are tender, golden crepes filled with a lightly sweetened cheese mixture, and then rolled up and browned in a skillet until they are crisp outside and soft and melty inside. I enjoy them with a warm fruit compote, along with some Greek yogurt.

FOR THE FILLING:

10 OUNCES (1½ CUPS PACKED) FARMER'S CHEESE

1 CUP REDUCED-FAT COTTAGE CHEESE

1½ TABLESPOONS HONEY

PINCH OF GROUND NUTMEG

FOR THE CREPES:

4 LARGE EGGS

⅔ CUP 1% MILK

⅔ CUP WHOLE-WHEAT PASTRY FLOUR, (OR ⅓ CUP ALL-PURPOSE FLOUR AND ⅓ CUP REGULAR WHOLE-WHEAT FLOUR)

4 TEASPOONS CANOLA OIL, OR OTHER NEUTRAL TASTING OIL

⅛ TEASPOON SALT

COOKING SPRAY

FOR SERVING:

COOKING SPRAY

1 RECIPE STRAWBERRY RHUBARB COMPOTE (RECIPE FOLLOWS)

LOW-FAT PLAIN GREEK YOGURT, OPTIONAL

1 For the filling, stir together the farmer's cheese, cottage cheese, honey, and nutmeg in a medium bowl, until well combined.

2 To make the crepes, place the eggs, milk, flour, oil, and salt in a blender and blend until smooth. Heat an 8-inch nonstick skillet over medium heat. Coat it lightly with cooking spray, then ladle 2 tablespoons of the batter into the center of the skillet, swirling to coat the bottom of the pan evenly with the batter. Cook for 20 to 25 seconds, then flip, and cook for 5 to 10 seconds more. Turn out onto a plate and repeat with the remaining batter, separating them with a paper towel or wax paper to prevent sticking.

3 Place a crepe on a clean work surface and dollop 3 tablespoons of the filling just below the center of the crepe. Fold over the sides, then pull edges over filling, rolling up burrito-style, into a blintz. Repeat with the remaining crepes and filling. The blintzes may be refrigerated or frozen at this stage.

4 To continue, spray a nonstick skillet, large enough to hold the quantity you are browning, with cooking spray, heat over medium heat, and cook the blintzes until browned and warmed through, about 1 to 2 minutes per side. Serve with the Strawberry Rhubarb Compote and a dollop of yogurt.

TO REFRIGERATE AND SERVE

Place unbrowned blintzes in an airtight container in the refrigerator where they will keep for up to 2 days. To serve, follow the "to continue" directions in the recipe, adding about 1 minute to the cooking time.

TO FREEZE AND SERVE

Wrap unbrowned blintzes individually in plastic wrap, then place them in a sealable plastic freezer bag and freeze for up to 3 months. There is no need to thaw. To serve, spray a nonstick skillet large enough to hold the amount you are browning with cooking spray. Heat over medium-low heat and cook the blintzes 3 minutes on one side, then flip and cook for 2 minutes on the other side. Reduce the heat to low, cover, and cook for 2 minutes more until browned and warmed through.

✳ **Serving size:** 2 blintzes and ¼ cup compote; **Per serving:** Calories 200; Total Fat 7g (Mono Fat 2.6g, Poly Fat 1.2g, Sat Fat 2.3g); Protein 12g; Carb 24g; Fiber 1g; Cholesterol 100mg; Sodium 300mg; **Excellent source of:** Protein, Manganese, Riboflavin, Selenium, Vitamin C; **Good source of:** Calcium, Phosphorus, Vitamin B12

STRAWBERRY RHUBARB COMPOTE • MAKES 2 CUPS; 8 SERVINGS •

THIS GLORIOUS SAUCE IS WONDERFUL on the blintzes, but also heavenly on the Dutch Baby Pancake, page 39, and the pancakes made with the DIY Whole-Grain Buttermilk Pancake Mix, page 41. It is also delicious simply spooned over yogurt.

1 CUP FRESH RHUBARB PIECES (½-INCH WIDE)

⅓ CUP PURE MAPLE SYRUP

2 TABLESPOONS ORANGE JUICE

3 CUPS QUARTERED STRAWBERRIES (ABOUT 12 MEDIUM)

✳ **Serving size:** ¼ cup; **Per serving:** Calories 45; Total Fat 0g (Mono Fat 0g, Poly Fat 0g, Sat Fat 0g); Protein 0g; Carb 11g; Fiber 1g; Cholesterol 0mg; Sodium 0mg; **Excellent source of:** Manganese, Vitamin C; **Good source of:** Riboflavin

Place the rhubarb, maple syrup, and orange juice in a small saucepan. Bring to a boil, lower the heat to medium, and simmer for 5 minutes until the rhubarb has softened and is beginning to break down. Add the strawberries. Return to a boil, and then lower the heat slightly and cook, stirring occasionally, until the strawberries have softened and the liquid is thickened, about 5 minutes. Remove from the heat.

TO REFRIGERATE AND REHEAT

Place in an airtight container in the refrigerator where compote will keep for up to 1 week. Reheat in a covered pot on the stove over low heat, stirring occasionally, until warmed through, 2 to 10 minutes, depending on the amount. Or place in a microwave-safe dish, cover with a splatter guard, and microwave on high for 15 seconds for one portion to 1 minute for the entire batch.

TO FREEZE AND REHEAT

Allow to chill in the refrigerator for 30 minutes, then place in an airtight container or sealable plastic freezer bag and freeze for up to 3 months. Thaw in the refrigerator for 10 to 12 hours. Alternatively, run the bag under hot water for 30 seconds to release the compote, place in a microwave-safe bowl, and microwave on the defrost setting for 3 minutes for one portion to 10 minutes for the entire batch.

Peach-Cherry Breakfast Cobbler

• MAKES 6 SERVINGS •

I HAVE BEEN KNOWN TO indulge in leftover fruit crisp or cobbler with a scoop of Greek yogurt the morning after a dinner party, so, I figured, why not come up with one that is specifically designed as a healthy way to start the day? This breakfast cobbler is packed with fresh summer fruit, ever so lightly sweetened with honey, and topped with a tender whole-grain biscuit made with a touch of healthy oil to reduce the amount of butter needed. Served with a dollop of yogurt, it has all the nutrition you want in a breakfast, and you get to eat cobbler!

4 LARGE RIPE PEACHES OR 4 CUPS UNSWEETENED FROZEN SLICED PEACHES, THAWED

1 CUP HALVED PITTED SWEET CHERRIES, OR FROZEN, THAWED, AND HALVED

4 TABLESPOONS HONEY, DIVIDED

1 TABLESPOON FRESH LEMON JUICE

1 TABLESPOON CORNSTARCH

¾ CUP WHOLE-WHEAT PASTRY OR WHITE WHOLE-WHEAT FLOUR

¾ TEASPOON BAKING POWDER

¼ TEASPOON BAKING SODA

¼ TEASPOON SALT

3 TABLESPOONS VERY COLD UNSALTED BUTTER, CUT INTO SMALL PIECES

½ CUP LOW-FAT PLAIN GREEK YOGURT

2 TABLESPOONS NONFAT OR 1% LOW-FAT MILK

2 TABLESPOONS CANOLA OIL, OR OTHER NEUTRAL TASTING OIL

FOR SERVING:

2 CUPS LOW-FAT PLAIN GREEK YOGURT

1 Preheat oven to 375°F.

2 If using fresh peaches, bring a 4-quart pot of water to a boil and fill a large bowl with ice water. With a paring knife, slice through each peach skin from end to end, but leave the peach intact. Place the peaches in the boiling water for 30 seconds. Then, using a slotted spoon, transfer the peaches to the ice water for 30 seconds. Remove the skin from the peaches. Then split the peaches in half, remove the pits, and slice each half into 4 slices.

3 In an 8-inch square baking dish, toss together the sliced peaches, cherries, 3 tablespoons of the honey, the lemon juice, and cornstarch.

4 To make the crust, place the flour, baking powder, baking soda, and salt into a food processor and pulse a few times to combine. Add the butter and pulse about 10 times, or until pebble-size pieces form.

Recipe continues

5 In a small bowl or pitcher, whisk together the yogurt, milk, oil, and the remaining 1 tablespoon honey. Add to the food processor and pulse until the mixture is just moistened. Drop the batter in 6 mounds on top of the fruit, spreading each mound out slightly.

6 Bake for 30 to 40 minutes, until the fruit is bubbling and the biscuits are cooked through and deep golden brown on top. Let rest 5 minutes before serving.

7 Serve warm with a dollop of the Greek yogurt alongside.

TO REFRIGERATE AND REHEAT
Allow to chill uncovered in the refrigerator for 30 minutes, then cover tightly with foil and refrigerate for up to 4 days. To reheat, allow to sit at room temperature while the oven preheats to 350°F. Cook, covered, for 10 minutes, then uncover and cook for 10 minutes more, until warmed through. Alternatively, scoop onto a microwave-safe plate, cover with a splatter guard, and microwave on high for about 60 seconds for one portion.

NOTE: *Biscuit will not re-crisp with microwave reheating.*

TO FREEZE AND REHEAT
Allow to cool at room temperature for 30 minutes, then cover with plastic wrap and then foil and refrigerate for 30 minutes. Transfer to the freezer for up to 3 months. To reheat, remove the plastic wrap and re-cover with the foil. Place in a cold oven and set the oven to preheat to 350°F. Once the oven reaches temperature, cook, covered, for 20 minutes, then uncover and cook until bubbling and the topping is warmed through, 10 minutes more.

✳ **Serving Size:** ¾ cup; **Per serving:** Calories 310; Total Fat 13g (Mono Fat 4.6g, Poly Fat 1.8g, Sat Fat 5.3g); Protein 11g; Carb 42g; Fiber 4g; Cholesterol 20mg; Sodium 250mg; **Excellent source of:** Manganese, Protein; **Good source of:** Calcium, Fiber, Selenium, Vitamin A, Vitamin C

Eggs in a Skillet with Spiced Tomato Sauce, Chard, and Goat Cheese (Shakshuka) • MAKES 6 SERVINGS •

MY ISRAELI FRIENDS TURNED ME on to shakshuka, a dish of eggs poached in a skillet of aromatically spiced tomato sauce, often topped with cheese. Eaten with warm pita, it is a big comfort food for them and it quickly became one for me too. But I find it even more comforting to know I can make the tomato base ahead and have it in my refrigerator or freezer so it is there when I want it. When you are ready to eat you just need to heat it, then add the eggs and cheese. And don't pigeonhole this dish into the A.M. time slot; it also works well for lunch or dinner.

1 LARGE BUNCH SWISS CHARD (12 OUNCES)

2 TABLESPOONS OLIVE OIL

1 LARGE ONION, CHOPPED

3 CLOVES GARLIC, MINCED

1 TEASPOON GROUND CUMIN

1 TEASPOON PAPRIKA

½ TEASPOON CRUSHED RED PEPPER FLAKES

½ TEASPOON SALT

ONE 28-OUNCE CAN NO-SALT-ADDED CRUSHED TOMATOES

ONE 14-OUNCE CAN NO-SALT-ADDED DICED TOMATOES

FOR SERVING:

6 LARGE EGGS

4 OUNCES SOFT GOAT CHEESE

1 Remove the chard leaves from the stalks. Thinly slice the stems. Stack the leaves, roll them into a log, and slice them into thin shreds.

2 In a large skillet, heat the oil over medium heat. Add the onion and cook, stirring, until softened, 6 to 7 minutes. Add the chard stems and garlic and cook, stirring, 1 minute more. Add the cumin, paprika, red pepper flakes, and salt and cook, stirring, 1 additional minute.

3 Add the crushed and diced tomatoes with their juices, bring to a boil, then lower the heat to medium-low and simmer until the mixture thickens, 10 minutes. Add the shredded chard leaves and cook, stirring, until wilted, 5 minutes. The sauce may be refrigerated or frozen at this stage.

4 To continue, form a well in the sauce in the skillet and crack one egg into it. Repeat with the remaining eggs. Scatter the goat cheese around the surface. Cover and cook until the egg whites become opaque and the yolks are still slightly runny, 4 to 5 minutes.

Recipe continues

TO REFRIGERATE AND REHEAT

Place the sauce in an airtight container in the refrigerator for up to 4 days. To reheat, place in a large skillet, cover, and warm over medium-low heat for 8 to 12 minutes, until bubbling. Then continue cooking from the "to continue" instructions in the recipe.

TO FREEZE AND REHEAT

Allow the sauce to cool in the refrigerator for 30 minutes, then place in a sealable freezer bag and freeze for up to 3 months.

Thaw in the refrigerator for 24 to 36 hours, then reheat following the "to refrigerate" directions. Or, to thaw quickly, run the bag under hot water for 30 seconds to release the sauce, then transfer it to a large deep skillet, cover, and cook over medium heat for 25 minutes, turning the frozen mass over once or twice, and breaking it up with a spoon occasionally as it thaws, until hot and bubbling. Then reduce the heat to medium-low and follow the "to continue" directions in the recipe.

✳ **Serving size:** 1 cup sauce and 1 egg; **Per serving:** Calories 250; Total Fat 15g (Mono Fat 6.4g, Poly Fat 1.6g, Sat Fat 6g); Protein 13g; Carb 14g; Fiber 3g; Cholesterol 200 mg; Sodium 490mg; **Excellent source of:** Phosphorus, Protein, Riboflavin, Selenium, Vitamin A, Vitamin C, Vitamin K; **Good source of:** Calcium, Copper, Fiber, Iodine, Iron, Magnesium, Manganese, Molybdenum, Potassium, Vitamin B6, Vitamin D

Honey-Nut Energy Bars • MAKES 15 SERVINGS •

THESE BARS HAVE A FRESH-MADE taste that reflects the pure ingredients they are made with: hearty whole grains; a generous helping of nuts, seeds, and dried fruit; a hint of cinnamon; and just the right amount of honey. They have a tender and cookie-like texture, striking the perfect balance between crunchy and chewy. They are extra easy to make if you pulse the nuts, seeds and dried cherries all together in the food processor until just chopped.

- 1 CUP ROLLED OATS
- ¾ CUP WHOLE-WHEAT FLOUR
- 1 TEASPOON GROUND CINNAMON
- ¼ TEASPOON SALT
- ½ CUP HONEY
- ⅓ CUP UNSWEETENED APPLESAUCE
- ¼ CUP OLIVE OIL
- 1 LARGE EGG, LIGHTLY BEATEN
- ½ CUP DRIED TART CHERRIES, CHOPPED
- ½ CUP WALNUT PIECES, CHOPPED
- ½ CUP WHOLE NATURAL ALMONDS, CHOPPED
- ½ CUP PISTACHIOS, CHOPPED
- ½ CUP HULLED PUMPKIN SEEDS, CHOPPED
- COOKING SPRAY

1 Preheat the oven to 325°F.

2 In a medium bowl, whisk together the oats, flour, cinnamon, and salt.

3 In a large bowl, whisk together the honey, applesauce, oil, and egg until well combined. Stir in the oat mixture until combined. Stir in the dried cherries, walnuts, almonds, pistachios, and pumpkin seeds.

4 Coat an 8-inch square baking pan with cooking spray. Spread the mixture into the prepared pan and bake until a toothpick inserted in the center comes out clean, 25 to 30 minutes. Allow to cool completely, then cut into 15 bars, about 2½ inches by 1½ inches each.

TO KEEP AT ROOM TEMPERATURE
Place in an airtight container at room temperature for up to 3 days.

TO REFRIGERATE
Place in an airtight container in the refrigerator for up to 2 weeks.

TO FREEZE
Wrap individually in plastic wrap and store in a sealable plastic freezer bag in the freezer where they will keep for up to 3 months. Thaw at room temperature for 2 hours, in a 350°F oven on a baking tray for 10 to 12 minutes, or wrap in a paper towel and microwave on high for 20 to 30 seconds for one bar.

✳ **Serving size:** 1 bar; **Per serving:** Calories 220; Total Fat 12g (Mono Fat 5.8g, Poly Fat 4.2g, Sat Fat 1.6g); Protein 5g; Carb 24g; Fiber 4g; Cholesterol 10mg; Sodium 45mg; **Excellent source of:** Manganese; **Good source of:** Fiber, Protein

Salads

Four Bean Salad

THIS SALAD UPS THE ANTE on the well-loved three-bean classic in more ways than one. First, it adds another bean into the mix for even more color and hearty bean protein, and second, it gives you that mouthwatering, sweet-tart dressing without any added sugar by taking advantage of naturally sweet dried figs, which are simply pureed with the rest of the dressing ingredients.

- ¾ POUND GREEN BEANS, TRIMMED
- ½ CUP CHOPPED SHALLOT
- 6 TABLESPOONS CIDER VINEGAR
- 6 DRIED MISSION FIGS (ABOUT 2¼ OUNCES), STEMS TRIMMED, QUARTERED
- 3 TABLESPOONS EXTRA-VIRGIN OLIVE OIL
- 2 TEASPOONS DIJON MUSTARD
- ¾ TEASPOON SALT
- ¼ TEASPOON FRESHLY GROUND BLACK PEPPER
- ONE 15-OUNCE CAN LOW-SODIUM DARK RED KIDNEY BEANS, DRAINED AND RINSED
- ONE 15-OUNCE CAN LOW-SODIUM CANNELLINI BEANS, DRAINED AND RINSED
- ONE 15-OUNCE CAN LOW-SODIUM BLACK BEANS, DRAINED AND RINSED

1 Place the green beans in a steamer basket set over a pot of boiling water. Cover and steam for 4 minutes, then transfer them to a bowl and place in the refrigerator to cool for at least 15 minutes. Alternatively you can "steam" the beans in a microwave-safe bowl with 1 tablespoon water, tightly covered, for 4 minutes on high, then drain and chill. Cut into ¼ to ½-inch pieces.

2 Meanwhile, place the shallot, vinegar, figs, oil, mustard, salt, and pepper in a food processor and pulse until almost smooth.

3 In a large bowl, combine the green beans with the kidney, cannellini, and black beans. Add the dressing and toss to coat.

∗ **Serving size:** 1 cup; **Per serving:** Calories 290; Total Fat 7g (Mono Fat 5g, Poly Fat 0.9g, Sat Fat 1.1g); Protein 14g; Carb 46g; Fiber 13g; Cholesterol 0mg; Sodium 529mg; **Excellent source of:** Fiber, Folate, Manganese, Potassium, Protein; **Good source of:** Calcium, Copper, Magnesium, Iron, Phosphorus, Thiamin, Vitamin C, Vitamin K

TO REFRIGERATE

The salad will keep in the refrigerator in an airtight container for up to 4 days. Allow to come to room temperature and toss well before serving.

Grilled Corn and Poblano Salad

• MAKES 6 SERVINGS •

THIS MEXICAN STYLE SALAD HAS the unmistakable smoky flavor of char-grilled sweet corn and peppers, the brightness of lime, and a dressing made lightly creamy with a mix of yogurt and mayo. It's a few ingredients that come together in an extraordinary way—perfect for serving at a summer barbecue.

6 EARS CORN, HUSKED

1 TABLESPOON OLIVE OIL

½ TEASPOON SALT, DIVIDED

½ TEASPOON PEPPER, DIVIDED

1 MEDIUM POBLANO PEPPER

2 TABLESPOONS PLAIN LOW-FAT YOGURT

1 TABLESPOON FRESH LIME JUICE

1 TABLESPOON MAYONNAISE

1 Preheat a lightly oiled grill, or grill pan, over medium heat. Rub the corn with the oil and ¼ teaspoon each of the salt and pepper and grill, in batches if necessary, along with the whole poblano pepper, turning them each a few times, until the corn is softened and charred in spots and the pepper is blistered, 8 to 10 minutes.

2 Transfer the pepper to a bowl and cover with plastic wrap until cooled. Once cool enough to handle, remove the skin from the pepper, seed it, and chop it.

3 Cut the kernels from corn cobs and transfer the kernels to a large bowl along with the chopped pepper. Add the yogurt, lime juice, mayonnaise, and remaining ¼ teaspoon each salt and pepper and toss. Serve warm or chilled.

---

* **Serving size:** ¾ cup; **Per serving:** Calories 130; Total Fat 6g (Mono Fat 2.5g, Poly Fat 1.9g, Sat Fat 1g); Protein 4g; Carb 20g; Fiber 3g; Cholesterol 0mg; Sodium 230mg; **Good source of:** Fiber, Folate, Thiamin, Vitamin A, Vitamin C

TO REFRIGERATE

The salad will keep in the refrigerator in an airtight container for up to 4 days. Toss well and add additional lime juice to taste if needed before serving.

Asian Slaw

THIS COLORFUL, CRISP SLAW IS packed with punchy flavor thanks to its dressing's irresistible balance of tangy lime and sweet honey, with just the right kick of chili sauce. It is perfect with just about any kind of grilled meat or fish, or even stuffed into a wrap sandwich, but it was born to be served with the East Meets West Brisket on page 135.

⅓ CUP RICE WINE VINEGAR

4 TABLESPOONS CANOLA OIL, OR OTHER NEUTRAL TASTING OIL

3 TABLESPOONS FRESH LIME JUICE

1½ TEASPOONS HONEY

1 TEASPOON CHILI-GARLIC SAUCE, SUCH AS SRIRACHA

¾ TEASPOON SALT

½ RED CABBAGE (1 POUND), SHREDDED (4 CUPS)

½ LARGE DAIKON RADISH, SHREDDED (2 CUPS)

2 LARGE CARROTS, PEELED AND SHREDDED (2 CUPS)

½ SMALL RED ONION, VERY THINLY SLICED

1 In a medium bowl, whisk together the vinegar, oil, lime juice, honey, chili garlic sauce, and salt. In a large bowl, toss together the cabbage, radish, carrots, and onion. The salad and dressing may be made ahead to this stage.

2 To serve, drizzle the dressing over the salad and toss to coat.

✳ **Serving size:** 1 cup; **Per serving:** Calories 100; Total Fat 7g (Mono Fat 4.5g, Poly Fat 2.1g, Sat Fat 0.6g); Protein 1g; Carb 9g; Fiber 2g; Cholesterol 0mg; Sodium 270mg; **Excellent source of:** Vitamin A, Vitamin C, Vitamin K

TO REFRIGERATE

Store the salad and dressing in separate airtight containers in the refrigerator. The salad will keep for up to 4 days. The dressing will keep for up to 1 week. Dress up to 2 hours before serving. Add a splash of lime juice if needed, as the acidity tends to fade with storage.

Spring Pea Salad   • MAKES 8 SERVINGS •

THIS SALAD IS A VERDANT celebration of spring, with a gorgeous green triple-play of peas—shelled, snap, and snow—splashed with crisp red and white radishes and fresh mint in a light lemon Dijon vinaigrette. It's a lovely, easy, everyday salad that would also be a treat on an Easter, Passover, or Mother's Day holiday table.

- 2 TABLESPOONS EXTRA-VIRGIN OLIVE OIL
- 2 TABLESPOONS FRESH LEMON JUICE
- 1 TEASPOON FINELY GRATED FRESH LEMON ZEST
- 1 TEASPOON DIJON MUSTARD
- ¾ TEASPOON SALT
- ½ TEASPOON FRESHLY GROUND BLACK PEPPER
- 3 TABLESPOONS CHOPPED FRESH MINT
- 2 TABLESPOONS FINELY CHOPPED SHALLOT
- 2 CUPS SHELLED FRESH PEAS, OR FROZEN, THAWED (10 OUNCES)
- 1 POUND SUGAR SNAP PEAS (5 CUPS), TRIMMED AND HALVED ON THE DIAGONAL
- ¼ POUND SNOW PEAS (1½ CUPS), TRIMMED AND HALVED ON THE DIAGONAL
- 1 CUP THINLY SLICED RADISHES (ABOUT A SMALL BUNCH)

1 In a small bowl, whisk together the oil, lemon juice, zest, mustard, salt, and pepper. Stir in the mint and shallot.

2 Bring a large pot of water to a boil and have ready a large bowl of ice water. If using fresh peas, add them to the boiling water and cook until tender, about 3 minutes, then transfer them with a slotted spoon to the bowl of ice water to cool. Drain from the ice water and transfer to a large bowl. If using frozen, thawed peas, place them in the large bowl.

3 Add the sugar snap peas and snow peas to the boiling water and cook until just tender, about 1 minute. Drain and add to the bowl of ice water until cooled. Then drain well and transfer to the large bowl with the other peas. Add the radish and toss to combine.

4 Just before serving, toss with the vinaigrette until well combined.

✳ **Serving size:** About ¾ cup; **Per serving:** Calories 100; Total Fat 3.5g (Mono Fat 2.5g, Poly Fat 0.4g, Sat Fat 0.5g); Protein 4g; Carb 12g; Fiber 4g; Cholesterol 0mg; Sodium 270mg; **Excellent source of:** Vitamin C; **Good source of:** Fiber, Iron, Vitamin A, Vitamin K

TO REFRIGERATE
Store the salad and dressing in separate airtight containers in the refrigerator. The salad will keep for up to 4 days. The dressing will keep for up to 1 week. Dress just before serving, adding a splash of lemon juice if needed, as the acidity tends to fade with storage.

Cauliflower Tabbouleh

• MAKES 6 SERVINGS •

WHEN YOU GRATE RAW CAULIFLOWER florets in a food processor or on a box grater, it takes on the texture of a grain, and it is fun to experiment with ways to use it like one. Here it subs for bulgur in a tantalizing version of a classic Middle Eastern tabbouleh salad, which is packed with aromatic herbs in a lemony cumin dressing. Serve it alongside hummus and pita, with grilled chicken or fish, or as a starter with a stew such as Fragrant Chicken and Eggplant Stew, page 179 or Savory Lamb and Chickpea Stew, page 155. (I also use grated cauliflower as "rice" in a pilaf on page 308).

½ HEAD CAULIFLOWER

1 PINT GRAPE TOMATOES, QUARTERED

½ LARGE ENGLISH CUCUMBER, SEEDED AND DICED (ABOUT 2 CUPS)

2 CUPS CHOPPED FRESH ITALIAN PARSLEY LEAVES

½ CUP DICED RED ONION

⅓ CUP CHOPPED FRESH MINT LEAVES

¼ CUP OLIVE OIL

¼ CUP LEMON JUICE

1 TEASPOON GROUND CUMIN

¾ TEASPOON FINELY GRATED LEMON ZEST

¼ TEASPOON SALT

¼ TEASPOON FRESHLY GROUND BLACK PEPPER

1 Cut the cauliflower into two or three large pieces, each with some stem attached. Holding each piece by the stem, grate the top part of the cauliflower on the large holes of a box grater to form rice-like pieces, until you have about 3 cups. Alternatively, you can cut the cauliflower into florets, removing as much of the stem as possible, and grate the florets in the food processor using the grater attachment. Save the stems and any remaining cauliflower for another use.

2 In a large bowl, toss together the grated cauliflower, tomatoes, cucumber, parsley, onion, and mint leaves.

3 In a small bowl, whisk together the oil, lemon juice, cumin, lemon zest, salt, and pepper. Pour the dressing over the cauliflower mixture and toss well to combine. Cover tightly and place in the refrigerator for at least 1 hour and up to 3 days.

∗ **Serving size:** 1¼ cups; **Per serving:** Calories 120; Total Fat 10g (Mono Fat 6.7g, Poly Fat 1g, Sat Fat 1.3g); Protein 3g; Carb 9g; Fiber 3g; Cholesterol 0mg; Sodium 125mg; **Excellent source of:** Vitamin A, Vitamin C, Vitamin K; **Good source of:** Fiber, Folate, Iron, Potassium, Manganese

TO REFRIGERATE
The salad will keep in the refrigerator in an airtight container for up to 3 days. Toss well and add additional lemon juice to taste if needed before serving.

Spinach Salad with Roasted Squash, Pumpkin Seeds, and Pomegranate

• MAKES 4 SERVINGS •

THIS SALAD IS A TRUE celebration of the tastes and colors of the fall-winter season, with chunks of sweet, orange squash contrasting the juicy, tart crunch of pomegranate and nutty, toasted pumpkin seeds, all atop fresh leafy greens dressed in a maple-sweetened vinaigrette. It is a stunning way to start a holiday meal or to make an everyday dinner feel special. Add some roasted chicken, pork, or beans to make it a main course.

4 CUPS (½-INCH CUBES) BUTTERNUT SQUASH (ABOUT 1 POUND)

¼ CUP EXTRA-VIRGIN OLIVE OIL, DIVIDED

1 TABLESPOON PLUS 2 TEASPOONS PURE MAPLE SYRUP, DIVIDED

½ TEASPOON SALT, DIVIDED

⅓ CUP HULLED PUMPKIN SEEDS

2 TABLESPOONS CIDER VINEGAR

1½ TEASPOONS DIJON MUSTARD

⅛ TEASPOON FRESHLY GROUND BLACK PEPPER

5 CUPS LIGHTLY PACKED BABY SPINACH, OR BABY KALE

½ CUP POMEGRANATE ARILS

1 Preheat the oven to 400°F.

2 Toss the squash with 1 tablespoon of the oil, 2 teaspoons of the maple syrup, and ¼ teaspoon of the salt and place in a single layer on a baking tray. Roast, stirring once, until tender and browned, 35 to 40 minutes. Set aside to cool.

3 Spread the pumpkin seeds out on another baking tray and place in the oven until fragrant and toasted, 6 minutes. Set aside to cool.

4 In a small bowl, whisk together the remaining 3 tablespoons olive oil, the cider vinegar, the remaining 1 tablespoon maple syrup, the mustard, the remaining ¼ teaspoon of salt, and the pepper. The salad may be made ahead up to this point.

5 To serve, toss the spinach with the dressing, put about 1¼ cups on each serving plate, then top each with about ⅓ cup roasted squash, a heaping tablespoon of the pumpkin seeds, and 2 tablespoons of the pomegranate arils.

Recipe continues

* **Serving size:** 1¼ cups greens, ⅓ cup squash, 1 heaping tablespoon pumpkin seeds, and 2 tablespoons pomegranate arils; **Per serving:** Calories 310; Total Fat 20g (Mono Fat 11.7g, Poly Fat 4g, Sat Fat 2.9g); Protein 8g; Carb 32g; Fiber 7g; Cholesterol 0mg; Sodium 380mg; **Excellent source of:** Copper, Fiber, Folate, Magnesium, Manganese, Phosphorus, Potassium, Vitamin A, Vitamin B6, Vitamin C, Vitamin E, Vitamin K; **Good source of:** Calcium, Iron, Molybdenum, Niacin, Protein, Riboflavin, Thiamin, Zinc

TO REFRIGERATE

Store the roasted squash, toasted nuts, dressing, and washed and dried spinach separately in the refrigerator for up to 4 days. Allow the dressing to come to room temperature before serving.

To make an individual serving, toss 1 tablespoon of the dressing with 1¼ cups spinach, then proceed with the remaining "to serve" directions.

"Pickled" Cucumber Salad

• MAKES 6 SERVINGS •

MARINATING CUCUMBERS FOR 20 MINUTES in a lightly sweetened vinegar and dill mixture gives it the taste of a "new" pickle with the fresh appeal of a salad. It's great to serve at a picnic or BBQ.

- 1 CUP UNSEASONED RICE VINEGAR
- 2 TABLESPOONS HONEY
- ¼ TEASPOON SALT
- 2 ENGLISH CUCUMBERS, THINLY SLICED (ABOUT 4 CUPS)
- 1 SMALL RED ONION, SLICED
- 2 TABLESPOONS CHOPPED FRESH DILL

1 Whisk together the vinegar, honey, and salt in a large bowl until the honey is dissolved. Stir in the cucumbers, onion, and dill. Let stand at least 20 minutes and up to 1 hour at room temperature. Drain and discard liquid, (or reserve to whisk with some oil for future use as salad dressing) and then serve or refrigerate.

---

* **Serving size:** ¾ cup; **Per serving:** Calories 60; Total Fat 0g (Mono Fat 0g, Poly Fat 0g, Sat Fat 0g); Protein 1g; Carb 14g; Fiber 1g; Cholesterol 0mg; Sodium 100mg; **Good source of:** Vitamin C

TO REFRIGERATE
The salad will keep in the refrigerator in an airtight container for up to 2 days.

Roasted Beet, Fennel, and Citrus Salad

• MAKES 8 SERVINGS •

SWEET, EARTHY BEETS AND TANGY, bright citrus are a heavenly pair, but when you toss some cool, crisp fennel into the mix you have a truly memorable trio. A honey-touched citrus vinaigrette ties them all together, and the stunning crimson mixture sits royally on a bed of fresh greens. For extra convenience you can skip roasting the beets and purchase the vacuum-packed, precooked beets (unseasoned), found in the refrigerator section at the grocery store. Try this salad as a starter before the Chicken Braised in Red Wine, page 207, or with the Creamy Zucchini Soup, page 111.

6 MEDIUM BEETS

2 MEDIUM ORANGES

2 MEDIUM RUBY RED GRAPEFRUITS

3 TABLESPOONS EXTRA-VIRGIN OLIVE OIL

3 TABLESPOONS WHITE WINE VINEGAR

1 TABLESPOON FINELY CHOPPED SHALLOT

2 TEASPOONS HONEY

½ TEASPOON SALT

¼ TEASPOON FRESHLY GROUND BLACK PEPPER

2 MEDIUM BULBS FENNEL, TRIMMED, CORED, AND THINLY SLICED

FOR SERVING:
4 CUPS LIGHTLY PACKED MIXED GREENS

1 Preheat the oven to 400°F.

2 Slice any stems and leaves off of the beets, leaving just about a half inch of stem on the beet. Scrub the beets well, then wrap each beet in foil and place on a baking sheet. Bake until easily pierced with a fork or metal skewer, about 1 hour. Allow to cool until you can handle them comfortably, then peel the beets using your fingers and paring knife as needed. Cut the stems off and discard, then slice the beets thinly into half-moons.

3 Cut the oranges and grapefruits into segments by slicing off the top and bottom of the fruit, then, standing it on one end, cut downward, following the line of the fruit, to remove the peel and white pith. Then with a paring knife, working over a bowl, remove the fruit segments from their membranes. Separate the juice and the segments, reserving both.

Recipe continues

4   In a small bowl, whisk together the oil, vinegar, shallot, honey, salt, pepper, and 3 tablespoons of the reserved citrus juice. (Reserve any remaining juice to drink or use in a future recipe.)

5   In a large bowl, gently toss the beets, citrus segments, and fennel with the dressing. To make ahead, refrigerate at this stage. Serve over the mixed greens.

＊ Serving size: ¾ cup beet salad and ½ cup greens; **Per serving:** Calories 130; Total Fat 5g (Mono Fat 3.8g, Poly Fat 0.6g, Sat Fat 0.8g); Protein 2g; Carb 22g; Fiber 7g; Cholesterol 0mg; Sodium 220mg; **Excellent source of:** Fiber, Vitamin A, Vitamin C, Vitamin K; **Good source of:** Folate, Manganese, Potassium

TO REFRIGERATE

Place the dressed beet, fennel, and citrus mixture in an airtight container where it will keep for up to 3 days. Stir well and drain some of the accumulated liquid off before spooning over the greens, if desired, or serve in bowls and savor the juices.

Potato and Chickpea Salad
with Mango Lime Dressing • MAKES 6 SERVINGS •

THIS SALAD IS INSPIRED BY an Indian street-food favorite, *aloo chana chat*, which translates to "Potato and Chickpea Snack." Here, the nibble becomes a salad with the fresh addition of tomatoes and cucumber, and a dressing of sweet mango and tangy lime juice. A generous handful of cool mint and cilantro leaves seal the deal for a salad that is lusciously exotic, but totally accessible. Try it with the Green "Tandoori" Grilled Chicken, page 209.

2 LARGE RED POTATOES (10 OUNCES), CUT INTO ½-INCH CUBES (4 CUPS)

ONE 15-OUNCE CAN NO-SALT-ADDED CHICKPEAS, DRAINED AND RINSED

1 PINT GRAPE TOMATOES, HALVED

½ ENGLISH CUCUMBER, CHOPPED (1 CUP)

½ SMALL RED ONION, DICED (⅓ CUP)

1 JALAPEÑO PEPPER (¾ OUNCE), SEEDED AND FINELY DICED

FOR THE DRESSING:

1 CUP DICED RIPE MANGO CHUNKS (6 OUNCES), THAWED IF FROZEN

½ CUP FRESH LIME JUICE

2 TABLESPOONS CANOLA OIL

1½ TABLESPOONS LIGHT BROWN SUGAR

1 SMALL CLOVE GARLIC

1 TEASPOON CHILI POWDER

1 TEASPOON GROUND CORIANDER

1 TEASPOON GROUND CUMIN

1 TEASPOON GROUND GINGER

1 TEASPOON SALT

¼ TEASPOON GROUND BLACK PEPPER

FOR SERVING:

⅓ CUP PACKED FRESH MINT LEAVES

¼ CUP PACKED FRESH CILANTRO LEAVES

1 Place the potatoes in a steamer basket set over a pot of boiling water. Cover and steam until they are just tender, 8 to 10 minutes. Transfer to the refrigerator to cool completely. In a large bowl, toss together the potatoes, chickpeas, tomatoes, cucumber, onion, and jalapeño.

2 Combine all of the dressing ingredients in the small bowl of a food processor or in a mini-chopper and process until smooth. If planning to serve later, store the dressing and salad separately at this stage.

3 To serve, add the mint, cilantro, and dressing to the salad and toss to combine.

TO REFRIGERATE
Store the salad, dressing, and herbs in separate airtight containers for up to 4 days. Once dressed, the salad will keep in the refrigerator for up to 1 day.

※ **Serving size:** 1⅓ cups; **Per serving:** Calories 200; Total Fat 6g (Mono Fat 3.2g, Poly Fat 1.4g, Sat Fat 0.4g); Protein 6g; Carb 33g; Fiber 5g; Cholesterol 0mg; Sodium 410mg; **Excellent source of:** Fiber, Copper, Vitamin C; **Good source of:** Magnesium, Phosphorus, Potassium, Protein, Vitamin A, Vitamin K

Southwestern Layered Salad • MAKES 6 SERVINGS •

THE BRIGHT RAINBOW OF COLORS in this salad impresses immediately, but only when you dig in do you realize it also boasts a full spectrum of tastes and textures—cool, crunchy jícama and carrots; creamy avocado; sweet, juicy corn; and hearty black beans—seasoned with fresh lime, cilantro, and Southwestern spices. It is a sure winner at a tailgate or barbecue as an accompaniment for grilled meats, or packed into individual jars as a fun picnic dish. It also makes for a complete vegetarian main course.

TWO 15-OUNCE CANS LOW-SODIUM BLACK BEANS, DRAINED AND RINSED

¼ CUP CHOPPED SCALLION GREENS

8 TABLESPOONS FRESH LIME JUICE, DIVIDED

6 TABLESPOONS CHOPPED FRESH CILANTRO, DIVIDED

1 TABLESPOON PLUS 1 TEASPOON EXTRA-VIRGIN OLIVE OIL

1 TEASPOON CHILI POWDER

1 TEASPOON GROUND CUMIN

1¼ TEASPOONS SALT, DIVIDED

2 CUPS FRESH CORN KERNELS (FROM ABOUT 3½ EARS), OR FROZEN, THAWED

2 MEDIUM RIPE AVOCADOS

1 SMALL CLOVE GARLIC, MINCED

6 MEDIUM CARROTS, SHREDDED (4 CUPS)

1 LARGE JÍCAMA (1 POUND), PEELED AND CUT INTO ¼-INCH DICE

1 In a medium bowl, toss the beans with the scallion, 2 tablespoons of the lime juice, 2 tablespoons of the cilantro, 1 tablespoon of the oil, the chili powder, ½ teaspoon of the cumin, and ¼ teaspoon of the salt. Place the beans in the bottom of one large serving bowl, ideally a clear one that will display the layers of the final salad, or divide among six 2-cup capacity jars.

2 Wipe out the bowl and use it to toss the corn with 1 tablespoon of the lime juice and ¼ teaspoon of the salt. Add the corn layer on top of the black beans in the serving bowl or jars.

3 Halve, pit, and scoop the flesh from the avocado into the same mixing bowl. Mash the avocado with 3 tablespoons of the lime juice, 2 tablespoons of the cilantro, the garlic, and ¼ teaspoon of the salt. Add the avocado to the serving dish(es), creating another layer on top of the corn. Place a piece of plastic wrap directly on top of the avocado layer and refrigerate until you have the next layers ready.

4 In another medium bowl, toss the jícama with 1 tablespoon of the lime juice and ¼ teaspoon of the salt. Then, in another small bowl, toss the carrot with the remaining 1 tablespoon lime juice, 2 tablespoons cilantro, 1 teaspoon oil, ½ teaspoon cumin, and ¼ teaspoon salt.

5 Remove the plastic wrap from the avocado layer, and make two more layers, first with the jícama, then finally with the carrot. Cover tightly and chill until you are ready to serve.

TO REFRIGERATE

The salad will keep in the refrigerator, covered tightly, for up to 2 days.

✱ **Serving size:** About 1⅔ cups; **Per serving:** Calories 310; Total Fat 14g (Mono Fat 8.8g, Poly Fat 1.7g, Sat Fat 1.9g); Protein 10g; Carb 48g; Fiber 18g; Cholesterol 0mg; Sodium 624mg; **Excellent source of:** Fiber, Folate, Potassium, Vitamin A, Vitamin C, Vitamin K; **Good source of:** Copper, Iron, Manganese, Pantothenic Acid, Protein, Vitamin B6, Vitamin E

Tuscan Lentil and Macaroni Salad

• MAKES 6 MAIN COURSE SERVINGS •

THIS IS THE KIND OF pasta salad you can imagine yourself eating on the patio of a trattoria overlooking the Italian countryside. It is a hearty and elegant mix of lentils and whole-grain elbow pasta, tossed with artichokes, tomatoes, carrots, and fresh herbs in an olive oil vinaigrette. It is a satisfying meal in itself, but it also works well as a side dish.

- 2 CUPS LOW-SODIUM CHICKEN BROTH
- 1 CUP GREEN LENTILS
- 2 MEDIUM CARROTS, DICED
- 8 OUNCES WHOLE-GRAIN ELBOW MACARONI
- ¼ CUP EXTRA-VIRGIN OLIVE OIL, DIVIDED
- 2 TABLESPOONS CHAMPAGNE VINEGAR OR WHITE WINE VINEGAR
- 1 TABLESPOON CHOPPED FRESH OREGANO OR 1 TEASPOON DRIED OREGANO
- 1 TABLESPOON DIJON MUSTARD
- ¾ TEASPOON SALT
- ¼ TEASPOON FRESHLY GROUND BLACK PEPPER
- ONE 10-OUNCE PACKAGE FROZEN ARTICHOKES, THAWED, DRAINED, AND CHOPPED
- 1½ CUPS GRAPE TOMATOES, QUARTERED
- ¼ CUP CHOPPED FRESH ITALIAN PARSLEY LEAVES

1 Combine the broth and lentils in a small saucepan and bring to a boil. Lower the heat to medium-low, cover, and simmer for 25 minutes. Add the carrots and cook until the lentils are tender but still retain their shape, 5 to 10 minutes more. Drain any remaining liquid and allow to cool to room temperature.

2 Meanwhile, bring a large pot of water to a boil. Add the macaroni and cook for 1 minute fewer than it says on the package directions. Drain, toss with 1 tablespoon of the oil, and allow to cool.

3 In a large bowl, whisk together the remaining 3 tablespoons oil, the vinegar, oregano, mustard, salt, and pepper. Add the pasta, lentils and carrots, artichoke hearts, tomatoes, and parsley and toss to combine.

∗ **Serving size:** 1⅓ cups; **Per serving:** Calories 360; Total Fat 11g (Mono Fat 6.7g, Poly Fat 1.2g, Sat Fat 1.5g); Protein 15g; Carb 55g; Fiber 12g; Cholesterol 0mg; Sodium 440mg; **Excellent source of:** Fiber, Iron, Manganese, Protein, Vitamin A, Vitamin K; **Good source of:** Copper, Magnesium, Niacin, Phosphorus, Potassium, Thiamin, Vitamin C

TO REFRIGERATE
The salad will keep in an airtight container in the refrigerator for up to 4 days. Stir well and add a splash of vinegar before serving if desired, as the acidity tends to fade over time.

Herbed Salmon Salad · MAKES 6 SERVINGS ·

BORED OF YOUR USUAL TUNA salad? This recipe is the perfect solution. It makes the most of another canned fish, salmon, by tossing it with crunchy chopped vegetables and fresh herbs in an olive oil, lemon, and Dijon vinaigrette. Just a touch of mayo adds a sumptuous creaminess. It's a delicious way to switch things up, healthfully, without going out of your comfort zone.

TWO 14.75-OUNCE CANS OF SALMON, DRAINED, SKIN AND BONES REMOVED, OR THREE 5-OUNCE POUCHES SKINLESS, BONELESS SALMON

2 STALKS CELERY, FINELY DICED

3 MEDIUM RADISHES, FINELY DICED

⅓ CUP CHOPPED FRESH ITALIAN PARSLEY LEAVES

¼ CUP CHOPPED FRESH CHIVES

2 TABLESPOONS CAPERS, DRAINED AND RINSED

3 TABLESPOONS EXTRA-VIRGIN OLIVE OIL

3 TABLESPOONS FRESH LEMON JUICE

2 TEASPOONS DIJON MUSTARD

¼ TEASPOON FRESHLY GROUND BLACK PEPPER

3 TABLESPOONS MAYONNAISE

1 Place the salmon in a large bowl and flake it into small pieces with a fork. Add the celery, radishes, parsley, chives, and capers and toss to combine.

2 In a small bowl, whisk together the oil, lemon juice, mustard, and pepper. Pour the dressing over the salmon, add the mayonnaise, and stir until evenly combined.

✳ **Serving size:** ⅔ cup; **Per serving:** Calories 300; Total Fat 18g (Mono Fat 7.5g, Poly Fat 5.6g, Sat Fat 2.8g); Protein 35g; Carb 2g; Fiber 1g; Cholesterol 120mg; Sodium 678mg; **Excellent source of:** Niacin, Phosphorus, Protein, Selenium, Vitamin B12, Vitamin K; **Good source of:** Potassium, Riboflavin, Vitamin A, Vitamin C, Vitamin D, Vitamin E

TO REFRIGERATE
Place in an airtight container in the refrigerator for up to 3 days.

Red Cabbage and Kale Salad
with Sunflower Seeds and Chickpeas • MAKES 6 SERVINGS •

ONE OF MY GO-TO LUNCH spots in New York is City Bakery on West 18th Street. They have an enticing self-serve spread that changes based on whatever is in season at the Union Square farmer's market nearby. The only trick is making it past their mesmerizing display of baked goods without getting something each time! This satisfying, jewel-toned salad with meaty chickpeas and a crunch of sunflower seeds is inspired by one I get there often, usually with some sliced chicken alongside, and, once in a while, with a cookie or tart for later.

⅓ CUP UNSALTED, HULLED SUNFLOWER SEEDS

¼ CUP WALNUT OIL OR EXTRA-VIRGIN OLIVE OIL

1 TABLESPOON HONEY

3 TEASPOONS CIDER VINEGAR

½ TEASPOON SALT

¼ TEASPOON FRESHLY GROUND BLACK PEPPER

5 CUPS CHOPPED RED CABBAGE

2 CUPS CHOPPED KALE LEAVES

1 LARGE CARROT, SHREDDED

ONE 15-OUNCE CAN LOW-SODIUM CHICKPEAS, DRAINED AND RINSED

1 Toast the sunflower seeds in a dry skillet over medium-high heat, stirring frequently, until fragrant and lightly browned, about 3 minutes. Set aside to cool.

2 In a small bowl, whisk together the oil, honey, vinegar, salt, and pepper until combined.

3 In a large bowl, toss together the cabbage, kale, carrot, chickpeas, and sunflower seeds. Add the dressing and toss to coat.

✴ **Serving size:** 1 cup; **Per serving:** Calories 230; Total Fat 14g (Mono Fat 6.9g, Poly Fat 1.7g, Sat Fat 1.8g); Protein 7g; Carb 22g; Fiber 7g; Cholesterol 0mg; Sodium 292mg; **Excellent source of:** Copper, Fiber, Manganese, Vitamin A, Vitamin B6, Vitamin C, Vitamin K; **Good source of:** Calcium, Folate, Iron, Magnesium, Phosphorus, Potassium, Protein

TO REFRIGERATE
The salad will keep well in the refrigerator in an airtight container for up to 4 days. The taste of the vinegar fades with time, so taste it before serving and add a teaspoon or so more if needed.

Cranberry Chicken Salad

• MAKES 6 SERVINGS •

THIS SALAD IS CHOCK-FULL OF Thanksgiving-inspired flavors and colors—fresh and dried cranberries, fennel, walnuts, red onion, and parsley—all in a creamy Dijon dressing made with a blend of Greek yogurt and just a touch of mayo. It is a favorite all autumn long, but ideal for using up ingredients from a holiday meal; you can even swap the chicken out for turkey if you have some left over.

½ CUP WALNUT PIECES

¾ CUP FRESH OR FROZEN CRANBERRIES

⅓ CUP PLAIN NONFAT OR LOW-FAT GREEK YOGURT

3 TABLESPOONS MAYONNAISE

1 TABLESPOON DIJON MUSTARD

⅛ TEASPOON SALT

⅛ TEASPOON FRESHLY GROUND BLACK PEPPER

1 RECIPE CHILLED OVEN-POACHED CHICKEN (RECIPE FOLLOWS), CHOPPED, OR 4 CUPS CHOPPED, COOKED CHICKEN OR TURKEY BREAST

1 CUP CHOPPED FENNEL BULB OR CELERY

⅓ CUP CHOPPED FRESH ITALIAN PARSLEY LEAVES

⅓ CUP DRIED CRANBERRIES

¼ CUP FINELY CHOPPED RED ONION

1 Toast the walnuts in a dry skillet over medium-high heat, stirring frequently, until fragrant, about 3 minutes, or place them on a baking tray and toast them in a 350°F oven for 8 minutes. Set aside to cool and then roughly chop.

2 Place the cranberries in a small saucepan with 2 tablespoons of water. Cover and heat over medium heat until the cranberries burst, about 3 minutes. Allow to cool.

3 In a large bowl, whisk together the yogurt, mayonnaise, mustard, salt, and pepper. Stir in the cooked cranberries. Add the chicken, fennel, toasted walnuts, parsley, dried cranberries, and onion and toss to combine.

✻ **Serving size:** 1 cup; **Per serving:** Calories 340; Total Fat 17g (Mono Fat 6g, Poly Fat 7.1g, Sat Fat 1.8g); Protein 37g; Carb 10g; Fiber 2g; Cholesterol 115mg; Sodium 290mg; **Excellent source of:** Manganese, Niacin, Pantothenic Acid, Phosphorus, Protein, Selenium, Vitamin B6, Vitamin K; **Good source of:** Copper, Magnesium, Potassium, Riboflavin, Thiamin, Vitamin C

TO REFRIGERATE

The salad will keep in an airtight container in the refrigerator for up to 4 days. Stir well before serving.

Chilled Oven-Poached Chicken

• MAKES 6 SERVINGS; ABOUT 4 CUPS CHOPPED CHICKEN •

POACHED CHICKEN IS PERFECT FOR salads because it cooks up juicy and tender throughout, and has a mild, neutral flavor that is a blank canvas for just about any flavor profile. It technically involves cooking on the stovetop in liquid, and is not especially difficult; but if you are not careful it is easy to overcook the meat, making it tough and rubbery. This oven method achieves a similar result, but it is much more foolproof. Use it for any dish that calls for cooked chicken, or add it to a vegetable salad to turn it into a complete meal.

2 POUNDS SKINLESS, BONELESS CHICKEN BREASTS, POUNDED TO ½-INCH THICKNESS

1 TEASPOON OLIVE OIL

⅛ TEASPOON SALT

PINCH FRESHLY GROUND BLACK PEPPER

1 Preheat the oven to 350°F.

2 Place the chicken breasts in a baking dish, drizzle both sides with the oil, and season with the salt and pepper. Cover with foil and bake until cooked through, 20 minutes. Chill for at least 30 minutes at room temperature, then chill for at least 30 minutes and up to 4 days in the refrigerator. The chicken may also be frozen at this stage. Slice or chop right before using.

TO REFRIGERATE
Place in an airtight container and refrigerate for up to 4 days.

TO FREEZE
Wrap each piece of chicken individually in plastic wrap, then place in a sealable freezer bag and freeze for up to 3 months. Thaw in the refrigerator for 24 hours. To thaw quickly, place on a microwave-safe plate, cover with a splatter guard, and microwave on the defrost setting for 4 minutes for one serving.

* **Serving size:** About ½ chicken breast, ⅔ cup chopped; **Per serving:** Calories 190; Total Fat 4.5g (Mono Fat 1.6g, Poly Fat 0.7g, Sat Fat 0.9g); Protein 34g; Carb 0g; Fiber 0g; Cholesterol 110mg; Sodium 115mg; **Excellent source of:** Niacin, Pantothenic Acid, Phosphorus, Protein, Selenium, Vitamin B6; **Good source of:** Magnesium, Potassium, Riboflavin

Buffalo Chicken Salad   • MAKES 6 SERVINGS •

HERE, TENDER CHICKEN BREAST IS tossed in a creamy dressing spiked with cayenne pepper sauce, which gives it that distinctive Buffalo wings flavor. I don't often recommend brand-name sauces, but in this case, it's worth picking up a bottle of Frank's Red Hot for the most authentic taste. Lots of crisp, cool celery and a sprinkle of blue cheese complete the picture for a healthier way to get your favorite bar-food flavor fix.

⅓ CUP PLAIN NONFAT OR LOW-FAT GREEK YOGURT

3 TABLESPOONS CAYENNE PEPPER SAUCE, PREFERABLY FRANK'S RED HOT

2½ TABLESPOONS MAYONNAISE

1 RECIPE CHILLED OVEN-POACHED CHICKEN, CHOPPED (PAGE 85), OR 4 CUPS CHOPPED, COOKED CHICKEN BREAST

6 CELERY STALKS FROM THE MORE TENDER, INNER PART OF THE BUNCH, CUT THINLY ON THE BIAS, WITH LEAVES (4 CUPS)

2 LARGE SCALLIONS, THINLY SLICED

FOR SERVING:

1 HEAD OF ROMAINE LETTUCE

⅓ CUP CRUMBLED BLUE CHEESE

ADDITIONAL CAYENNE PEPPER SAUCE, TO TASTE

1 Place the yogurt, hot sauce, and mayonnaise in a large bowl and stir to combine. Stir in the chicken, celery, and scallions and toss to combine. The salad may be refrigerated at this stage.

2 Serve over a bed of whole romaine lettuce leaves, garnished with the blue cheese and additional hot sauce if desired.

＊ **Serving size:** 1⅓ cups salad and 3 to 4 lettuce leaves; **Per serving:** Calories 300; Total Fat 13g (Mono Fat 5.1g, Poly Fat 2.4g, Sat Fat 2.6g); Protein 38g; Carb 7g; Fiber 3g; Cholesterol 120mg; Sodium 550mg; **Excellent source of:** Folate, Niacin, Pantothenic Acid, Phosphorus, Potassium, Protein, Riboflavin, Selenium, Vitamin A, Vitamin B6, Vitamin C, Vitamin K; **Good source of:** Fiber, Iron, Calcium, Magnesium, Thiamin, Zinc

TO REFRIGERATE

The salad will keep in an airtight container in the refrigerator for up to 4 days. Stir well before serving.

Marinated Chicken and Antipasto Salad

• MAKES 6 SERVINGS •

THIS SALAD TAKES ITS INSPIRATION from the delicious bites you might find on an antipasto platter. Crisp-tender cauliflower florets and a colorful array of bell peppers are married as they absorb the tastes of a sumptuous marinade made with fruity olive oil, a bright kick of vinegar, fresh garlic, and thyme. Tossed with green olives and grilled chicken, and finished with a sprinkle of fragrant basil leaves, it is as beautiful as it is boldly flavorful.

½ LARGE HEAD CAULIFLOWER, CUT INTO 1-INCH FLORETS (ABOUT 5 CUPS)

½ CUP EXTRA-VIRGIN OLIVE OIL

½ CUP WHITE WINE VINEGAR

2 CLOVES GARLIC, MINCED

2 TEASPOONS CHOPPED FRESH THYME LEAVES OR 1 TEASPOON DRIED THYME

1 TEASPOON FINELY GRATED LEMON ZEST

1 TEASPOON SALT

¼ TEASPOON FRESHLY GROUND BLACK PEPPER

1½ POUNDS THIN-CUT SKINLESS, BONELESS CHICKEN BREAST

2 MEDIUM BELL PEPPERS (RED, ORANGE, OR YELLOW) CUT INTO 1-INCH PIECES

1 CUP PITTED GREEN OLIVES, HALVED

FOR SERVING:

1 CUP LIGHTLY PACKED FRESH BASIL LEAVES (¾ OUNCE), TORN

1 Place the cauliflower into a steamer basket set over a pot of boiling water. Cover and steam until somewhat softened but still quite firm, about 4 minutes. Remove the basket from the boiling water and set aside to cool.

2 In a large bowl, whisk together the oil, vinegar, ¼ cup of water, the garlic, thyme, lemon zest, salt, and pepper. Transfer ⅓ cup of the marinade to a sealable plastic bag. Add the chicken to the bag and place in the refrigerator for 1 hour.

3 Add the cooled cauliflower, bell peppers, and olives to the remaining marinade in the bowl, and toss to coat. Cover and marinate at room temperature for 1 hour, stirring two or three times.

4 Using a slotted spoon, transfer the vegetables to another bowl. Transfer the remaining vegetable marinade to an airtight container in the refrigerator to use as a salad dressing or marinade for a future dish.

Recipe continues

5 Remove the chicken from the plastic bag and discard its marinade. Spray a grill or grill pan with cooking spray and heat over medium-high heat. Cook the chicken, in two batches if necessary, until cooked through, and grill marks are formed, about 2 minutes per side. Allow to cool and then cut into bite-sized pieces and toss with the vegetables in the bowl.

6 Right before serving, toss with the fresh basil leaves.

* **Serving size:** About 1¾ cups; **Per serving:** Calories 280; Total Fat 16g (Mono Fat 7.4g, Poly Fat 1.5g, Sat Fat 1.9g); Protein 28g; Carb 8g; Fiber 3g; Cholesterol 85mg; Sodium 440mg; **Excellent source of:** Folate, Niacin, Pantothenic Acid, Phosphorus, Potassium, Protein, Selenium, Vitamin A, Vitamin B6, Vitamin C, Vitamin K; **Good source of:** Fiber, Magnesium, Manganese, Riboflavin, Thiamin, Vitamin E

TO REFRIGERATE
The salad will keep in an airtight container in the refrigerator for up to 4 days. Stir well before serving. Remaining vegetable marinade will keep for up to 1 week.

Layered Farro Salad with Kale, Feta, and Grapes

• MAKES 8 SERVINGS •

FARRO IS ONE OF THE ancient grains that's made a big comeback, and with good reason, as it brings flair, flavor, and whole-grain nutrition to the table in an easy, accessible way. It is a type of wheat that resembles grains of barley, but with a nuttier flavor and delightful chewiness. It's also simple to make—the semipearled variety, which is the kind typically sold in the United States, is basically boiled just like rice—and is ready in about 30 minutes, no soaking necessary. And, like rice, you can serve it hot, or chill it for salads.

Here, farro is the base of a layered, main course salad with hearty kale, sweet juicy grapes, crunchy walnuts, and bold feta cheese. Each of the ingredients add a flavor element that plays off the other and they all come together for a truly singular dish. You can layer it in one large dish, or in individual jars to take to work, or to a picnic.

1 CUP FARRO

1¼ CUPS WALNUT PIECES

¼ CUP EXTRA-VIRGIN OLIVE OIL

3 TABLESPOONS FRESH LEMON JUICE

¼ TEASPOON SALT

¼ TEASPOON FRESHLY GROUND BLACK PEPPER

3 CUPS SHREDDED KALE LEAVES

½ CUP FINELY DICED RED ONION

¼ CUP FINELY CHOPPED FRESH ITALIAN PARSLEY LEAVES

1¼ CUPS CRUMBLED FETA CHEESE (6 OUNCES)

2 CUPS QUARTERED RED OR BLACK GRAPES

1 Cook the farro according to the directions on the package. Drain well, then place in the refrigerator to cool completely.

2 Toast the walnuts in a dry skillet over medium-high heat, stirring frequently, until fragrant and lightly browned, 3 to 5 minutes. Set aside to cool, then chop.

3 In a small bowl, whisk together the oil, lemon juice, salt, and pepper. Place the kale in a medium bowl, add half of the dressing, and toss to combine. Add the onion, parsley, and remaining dressing to the farro and toss to combine.

4 To assemble the salad, place the farro in the bottom of a large glass bowl, patting down slightly. Add the kale on top. Sprinkle with the feta cheese. Then layer with the grapes and finally the walnuts. Alternatively, make individual salads by layering the ingredients in wide-mouthed 12-ounce (500 ml) jars.

Recipe continues

∗ **Serving size:** 1¼ cups; **Per serving:** Calories 370;
Total Fat 24g (Mono Fat 7.7g, Poly Fat 9.6g, Sat Fat
5.6g); Protein 11g; Carb 30g; Fiber 5g; Cholesterol
20mg; Sodium 300mg; **Excellent source of:** Fiber,
Copper, Manganese, Protein, Vitamin A, Vitamin C,
Vitamin K; **Good source of:** Calcium, Chloride, Folate,
Iron, Magnesium, Molybdenum, Phosphorus, Riboflavin,
Thiamin, Vitamin B6

TO REFRIGERATE
The salad will keep in the refrigerator, covered tightly, for up
to 3 days.

Corn and Edamame "Succotash" Salad with Ginger Lime Dressing • MAKES 6 SERVINGS •

SUCCOTASH IS A CENTURIES-OLD NATIVE American dish made with corn and beans that remains a comfort-food staple to this day. Swapping in edamame for the typical lima beans and using a lime-ginger dressing, laced with aromatic sesame oil, gives it a refreshing and flavorful Asian twist. Red bell peppers add color and crunch, and watercress provides a pleasantly peppery contrast to the sweet corn. Try serving it with Grilled Chicken with Cherry Bourbon BBQ Sauce, page 185.

4 LARGE EARS FRESH CORN, HUSKED, OR 3½ CUPS FROZEN, THAWED, CORN KERNELS

1 CUP FROZEN, SHELLED EDAMAME

2 CUPS LIGHTLY PACKED WATERCRESS, COARSELY CHOPPED

1 SMALL RED BELL PEPPER, FINELY DICED

2 SCALLIONS, THINLY SLICED

¼ CUP MAYONNAISE

¼ CUP FRESH LIME JUICE

1 TEASPOON TOASTED SESAME OIL

1 TEASPOON HONEY

1 TEASPOON FINELY GRATED FRESH GINGER

¾ TEASPOON SALT

½ TEASPOON FRESHLY GROUND BLACK PEPPER

1 If using fresh corn, fill a large stock pot ⅔ full with water and bring to a boil. Otherwise bring a medium pot of water to a boil.

2 Add the fresh ears of corn, if using, to the stock pot and cook until it is firm-tender, about 3 minutes. With tongs, transfer the corn to an ice water bath to cool quickly. (Keep the pot of water boiling for the edamame.) Remove the corn from the ice water once cool, about 3 minutes. Cut the kernels off of the cob and place them, or the thawed corn kernels, in a large bowl.

3 Add the edamame to the boiling water, allow to return to a boil, then cook until tender, 3 to 5 minutes. Drain and then transfer to an ice water bath to cool quickly. Remove from the ice water once cool, 1 to 2 minutes. Pat the edamame dry and add it to the bowl with the corn.

4 Add the watercress, bell pepper, and scallions to the bowl and toss to combine.

5 In a medium bowl, whisk together the mayonnaise, lime juice, sesame oil, honey, ginger, salt, and pepper. Add the dressing to the salad and toss to coat.

Recipe continues

* **Serving size:** 1 cup; **Per serving:** Calories 210;
Total Fat 11g (Mono Fat 4.8g, Poly Fat 2.8g, Sat Fat
1.1g); Protein 7g; Carb 24g; Fiber 4g; Cholesterol
5mg; Sodium 380mg; **Excellent source of:** Vitamin
C, Vitamin K; **Good source of:** Fiber, Magnesium,
Manganese, Phosphorus, Potassium, Protein, Thiamin

TO REFRIGERATE

The salad will keep in an airtight container in the refrigerator
for up to 3 days. Stir well before serving. As the salad sits, the
watercress wilts, but pleasantly so. If you prefer to keep it
unwilted, store it, already washed and dried, in a plastic bag
lined with a paper towel, and toss it into the salad right before
serving.

Shrimp and Snow Pea Salad   • MAKES 8 SERVINGS •

SLICING THE SNOW PEAS LENGTHWISE gives them a shredded effect, which, along with grated carrots and Napa cabbage and a mouthwatering soy-sesame dressing, makes for a brilliant Asian-style slaw studded with succulent shrimp.

- 2 POUNDS LARGE CLEANED, PEELED SHRIMP
- ½ TEASPOON SALT
- ½ TEASPOON FRESHLY GROUND BLACK PEPPER
- ¼ CUP PLUS 1 TABLESPOON CANOLA OIL, OR OTHER NEUTRAL TASTING OIL, DIVIDED
- ½ CUP UNSEASONED RICE VINEGAR
- 2 TABLESPOONS HONEY
- 1 TABLESPOON TOASTED SESAME OIL
- 4 TEASPOONS REDUCED-SODIUM SOY SAUCE
- 2 TEASPOONS CHILI-GARLIC SAUCE, SUCH AS SRIRACHA, OR MORE TO TASTE
- 3 CLOVES GARLIC, MINCED
- 1 POUND SNOW PEAS, TRIMMED AND THINLY SLICED LENGTHWISE (4 CUPS SHREDDED)
- ½ SMALL HEAD NAPA CABBAGE, SHREDDED (4 CUPS)
- 2 LARGE CARROTS, PEELED AND SHREDDED (2 CUPS)
- 4 SCALLIONS, THINLY SLICED
- 2 TABLESPOONS SESAME SEEDS

1 Season the shrimp with the salt and pepper. Heat a large, heavy skillet over medium-high heat. Add 1 tablespoon of the canola oil to the skillet. Add half the shrimp, and cook until cooked through with slightly seared edges, turning once, 2 to 3 minutes total. Transfer the shrimp to a plate and repeat with the remaining shrimp. Place in the refrigerator and allow to cool completely.

2 In a medium bowl, whisk together the vinegar, the remaining ¼ cup canola oil, the honey, sesame oil, soy sauce, chili-garlic sauce, and garlic until combined. In a large bowl, toss together the shrimp, snow peas, cabbage, carrots, and scallions.

3 Toast the sesame seeds in a dry skillet over medium-high heat until they are fragrant and begin to pop, 1 to 2 minutes. Set aside to cool.

4 Just before serving, toss with the dressing and garnish with the sesame seeds.

* **Serving size:** 1½ cups; **Per serving:** Calories 280; Total Fat 12g (Mono Fat 6.4g, Poly Fat 3.4g, Sat Fat 1g); Protein 26g; Carb 17g; Fiber 4g; Cholesterol 185mg; Sodium 410mg; **Excellent source of:** Copper, Phosphorus, Protein, Vitamin A, Vitamin C, Vitamin K; **Good source of:** Fiber, Iron, Calcium, Magnesium, Manganese, Potassium, Zinc

TO REFRIGERATE

Store the salad, dressing, and sesame seeds in separate airtight containers in the refrigerator. The salad will keep for up to 3 days; the dressing will keep for up to 1 week; and the toasted sesame seeds up to 2 weeks.

If not stored previously, once dressed, the salad will keep in the refrigerator in an airtight container for 2 days.

Grilled Steak and Broccoli Salad
with Lemon-Tahini Dressing · MAKES 8 SERVINGS ·

HERE, SAVORY SLICES OF CUMIN-RUBBED grilled sirloin are matched with steamed broccoli that gets a turn on the grill as well. The smoky char they both develop ties the two together and readies them for a luxurious drizzle of lemony tahini dressing, for a satisfying main course salad that can be served warm or at room temperature. This recipe is easy to halve if you are not feeding a crowd.

2 HEADS OF BROCCOLI CUT INTO 2-INCH FLORETS (ABOUT 9 CUPS BROCCOLI FLORETS)

6 CLOVES GARLIC, FINELY MINCED

1 TABLESPOON OLIVE OIL

1 TEASPOON GROUND CUMIN

½ TEASPOON SALT, DIVIDED

¼ TEASPOON FRESHLY GROUND BLACK PEPPER

2 POUNDS TOP SIRLOIN STEAK

⅓ CUP PURE TAHINI PASTE

¼ CUP FRESH LEMON JUICE

2 TABLESPOONS FINELY CHOPPED FRESH ITALIAN PARSLEY LEAVES

PINCH CAYENNE PEPPER

COOKING SPRAY

1 Place the broccoli in a large microwave-safe bowl with 1 tablespoon of water or place it in a large steamer basket set over a pot of boiling water. Cover tightly and microwave on high, or steam, until it is bright green and just slightly tender, about 3 minutes. Drain and place in the refrigerator to chill.

2 Meanwhile, in a small bowl, combine the garlic, oil, cumin, ¼ teaspoon of the salt, and the pepper. Rub the spice mixture on the steak and let rest at room temperature while you make the dressing.

3 In a medium bowl, whisk together 5 tablespoons of water, the tahini, lemon juice, parsley, the remaining ¼ teaspoon of salt, and the cayenne. Add additional water by the tablespoonful as needed until the dressing is about the consistency of heavy cream.

4 Spray a grill or grill pan with cooking spray and heat it over medium-high heat. Grill the steak, 6 to 7 minutes per side for medium-rare. Remove to a cutting board to rest for 10 minutes, then slice thinly.

5 Place the broccoli onto the grill or grill pan, and cook, in batches if necessary, until lightly charred, 1 to 2 minutes per side.

6 Arrange the sliced steak and broccoli on serving plates. Drizzle with the dressing right before serving warm or at room temperature.

* **Serving size:** About 5 slices steak, 1 cup broccoli, and 2 tablespoons dressing; **Per serving:** Calories 320; Total Fat 21g (Mono Fat 10.4g, Poly Fat 2.8g, Sat Fat 6.2g); Protein 27g; Carb 10g; Fiber 3g; Cholesterol 75mg; Sodium 270mg; **Excellent source of:** Iron, Niacin, Phosphorus, Potassium, Protein, Riboflavin, Selenium, Thiamin, Vitamin B6, Vitamin B12, Vitamin C, Vitamin K, Zinc; **Good source of:** Copper, Fiber, Folate, Magnesium, Manganese, Vitamin A

TO REFRIGERATE
The steak, broccoli, and dressing may be made ahead and stored in separate airtight containers in the refrigerator. The steak and broccoli will keep for 4 days and the dressing will keep for 1 week. Allow all ingredients to come to room temperature for 30 minutes before serving.

Soups

Chicken and Wild Rice Soup • MAKES 8 SERVINGS •

THIS SOUP IS THE ULTIMATE comfort food, with a long-simmered, deeply flavorful chicken broth, tender carrots and celery, and the essence of fresh dill. It tastes just like one Grandma might have made, but it's even more healing and appealing thanks to the use of whole-grain wild rice instead of refined.

2 TABLESPOONS OLIVE OIL

1 LARGE ONION, CHOPPED

3 CLOVES GARLIC, MINCED

4 MEDIUM CARROTS, CUT INTO COINS

6 STALKS CELERY, CHOPPED

1 TEASPOON SALT

¼ TEASPOON FRESHLY GROUND PEPPER

8 CUPS LOW-SODIUM CHICKEN BROTH

2 LARGE BONE-IN CHICKEN BREAST HALVES (2 POUNDS), SKIN REMOVED

½ CUP WILD RICE

5 FRESH DILL SPRIGS

1 Heat the oil in a large soup pot over medium-high heat. Add the onion and cook, stirring, until translucent, about 7 minutes. Add the garlic and cook, stirring, 1 minute more. Add the carrots, celery, salt, and pepper and cook, stirring, until the carrots begin to soften, 5 minutes. Add the broth, chicken, 3 cups of water, the rice, and dill and bring to a boil over high heat. Skim and discard any solids that accumulate on top.

2 Lower the heat to medium-low and simmer, uncovered, for 1 hour. Remove the chicken to a plate and allow it to cool until it is easy to handle, about 15 minutes. Remove the chicken meat from the bone and chop it into bite-size pieces. Return the meat to the soup to warm through, 1 to 2 minutes. Remove the dill sprigs before serving.

TO REFRIGERATE AND REHEAT

Place in an airtight container in the refrigerator for up to 4 days. To reheat, ladle the amount to be warmed into a saucepan, cover, and heat over medium heat for 8 to 25 minutes, depending on the amount. Or place in a microwave-safe bowl, cover with a splatter guard, and microwave on high for 90 seconds to 2 minutes for one portion.

TO FREEZE AND REHEAT

Chill in the refrigerator for 30 minutes, then divide into sealable freezer bags in the portions desired.

When ready to heat, run the bag under hot water for 30 seconds to release the frozen soup from the bag. Then place it in a saucepan, cover, and heat over medium heat, breaking it up occasionally with a spoon, until thawed and warmed through, 15 to 45 minutes, depending on the amount.

Alternatively, after releasing the soup from the bag, transfer it to a microwave-safe bowl, cover with a splatter guard, and microwave on the defrost setting for about 10 minutes. Continue to microwave on high for about 90 seconds for one portion.

✳ **Serving size:** 2 cups; **Per serving:** Calories 220; Total Fat 6g (Mono Fat 3.1g, Poly Fat 0.9g, Sat Fat 1g); Protein 25g; Carb 15g; Fiber 2g; Cholesterol 65mg; Sodium 450mg; **Excellent source of:** Niacin, Phosphorus, Protein, Selenium, Vitamin A, Vitamin B6, Vitamin K; **Good source of:** Folate, Magnesium, Manganese, Pantothenic Acid, Potassium, Riboflavin

Chilled Beet and Yogurt Soup

• MAKES 6 SERVINGS •

IF YOU WANT SOMETHING FUN and refreshing yet satisfying on a hot summer's day, a dish you can whip up without breaking a sweat, this cool, brilliantly pink soup is just the answer. You simply whir some cooked beets and broth in the blender, then whisk in creamy yogurt and garden-fresh produce—cucumber, scallion, lemon, and dill—and chill until the flavors meld. To make it even more convenient, you can use a package of unseasoned, precooked vacuum-packed beets rather than boil your own. Serve it alongside a sandwich or with a salad, or a hardboiled egg on a slice of German-style black bread.

5 MEDIUM FRESH BEETS (1½ POUNDS)

2 CUPS LOW-SODIUM CHICKEN BROTH

2 CUPS PLAIN LOW-FAT GREEK YOGURT

½ MEDIUM ENGLISH CUCUMBER, SEEDED AND DICED

¼ CUP FRESH LEMON JUICE, PLUS MORE TO TASTE

¼ CUP CHOPPED FRESH DILL

1 SCALLION, WHITE AND GREEN PARTS ONLY, THINLY SLICED

1 TEASPOON SALT

FOR SERVING:

CHOPPED FRESH DILL

1 Place the beets in a large pot of water, bring to a boil, then lower the heat to medium-low and simmer until the beets are tender, about 40 minutes.

2 Transfer the beets to a bowl and place them in the refrigerator until they are cool enough to handle. Peel the cooled beets, using your fingers and paring knife as needed.

3 Place 3 of the beets in a blender along with the chicken broth, and puree until smooth. Dice the remaining beets. Transfer the puree to a large bowl or container and whisk in the yogurt until well combined. Stir in the diced beets, cucumber, lemon juice, dill, scallion, and salt. Chill for at least 4 hours before serving.

4 Serve garnished with dill.

---

* **Serving size:** 1¼ cups; **Per serving:** Calories 110; Total Fat 1.5g (Mono Fat 0g, Poly Fat 0.1g, Sat Fat 1g); Protein 9g; Carb 16g; Fiber 3g; Cholesterol 5mg; Sodium 520mg; **Excellent source of:** Folate; **Good source of:** Fiber, Manganese, Potassium, Protein, Vitamin C, Vitamin K

TO REFRIGERATE

The soup may be kept in an airtight container in the refrigerator for up to 4 days. Give it a stir before serving, and add additional lemon juice to taste, as the lemon tends to fade as the soup sits.

Freezing is not recommended.

Green-and-White Vegetable Soup with Basil Pesto

• MAKES 6 SERVINGS •

ALL GREEN AND WHITE INGREDIENTS—leeks, zucchini, green beans, celery root, parsnip, and white beans, with a bright splash of basil pesto as a garnish—make for a tasty soup that has an effortless elegance. It's important to add the pesto right before serving, so its color stays brilliant.

4 SPRIGS FRESH ITALIAN PARSLEY

2 SPRIGS FRESH THYME

1 SPRIG FRESH ROSEMARY

2 TABLESPOONS OLIVE OIL

2 LARGE LEEKS, WHITE AND LIGHT GREEN PARTS ONLY, THINLY SLICED

1 LARGE PARSNIP, PEELED AND DICED

½ MEDIUM CELERY ROOT, PEELED AND DICED (1 CUP)

2 LARGE CLOVES GARLIC, MINCED

1 TEASPOON SALT

½ TEASPOON FRESHLY GROUND BLACK PEPPER

8 CUPS LOW-SODIUM CHICKEN BROTH

ONE 15-OUNCE CAN LOW-SODIUM WHITE BEANS SUCH AS NAVY OR CANNELLINI, DRAINED AND RINSED

1 MEDIUM ZUCCHINI, TRIMMED AND DICED (1½ CUPS)

¼ POUND (ABOUT 40) THIN GREEN BEANS (HARICOTS VERTS), TRIMMED AND CUT INTO 1-INCH PIECES

FOR SERVING:

¼ CUP BASIL PESTO (RECIPE FOLLOWS), OR STORE-BOUGHT PESTO

1 Tie the parsley, thyme, and rosemary with a string into a bundle.

2 Heat the oil in a large soup pot over medium heat. Add the leeks and cook, stirring, until soft, 3 minutes. Add the parsnip, celery root, garlic, salt, and pepper and cook, stirring, until the vegetables begin to become tender, 3 to 5 minutes. Add the chicken broth, beans, and herb bundle and bring to a boil, then lower the heat to medium-low and simmer for 10 minutes. Add the zucchini and green beans and continue to simmer until the vegetables are tender, 10 minutes more. Remove the herb bundle. The soup may be refrigerated or frozen at this stage.

3 Right before serving, stir 2 teaspoons of the pesto into each bowl of soup.

Recipe continues

TO REFRIGERATE AND REHEAT

Place in an airtight container in the refrigerator for up to 4 days. To reheat, ladle the amount to be warmed into a saucepan, cover, and heat over medium heat for 8 to 25 minutes, depending on the amount. Or place in a microwave-safe bowl, cover with a splatter guard, and microwave on high for 90 seconds to 2 minutes for one portion.

TO FREEZE AND REHEAT

Chill in the refrigerator for 30 minutes, then divide into sealable freezer bags in the portions desired.

When ready to heat, run the bag under hot water for 30 seconds to release the frozen soup from the bag. Then place it in a saucepan, cover, and heat over medium heat, breaking it up occasionally with a spoon, until thawed and warmed through, 15 to 45 minutes, depending on the amount.

Alternatively, after releasing the soup from the bag, transfer it to a microwave-safe bowl, cover with a splatter guard, and microwave on the defrost setting for about 10 minutes. Continue to microwave on high for about 90 seconds for one portion.

---

* **Serving size:** About 2 cups; **Per serving:** Calories 220; Total Fat 11g (Mono Fat 6.9g, Poly Fat 1.6g, Sat Fat 1.6g); Protein 8g; Carb 22g; Fiber 5g; Cholesterol 0mg; Sodium 580mg ; **Excellent source of:** Thiamin, Vitamin C; **Good source of:** Fiber, Iron, Magnesium, Phosphorus, Potassium, Protein, Vitamin A

BASIL PESTO

THERE IS NO BETTER WAY to preserve a bounty of fresh summer basil, and having a batch of pesto in your refrigerator or freezer is a treasure any time of year. Its brilliant emerald color sure looks gem-like, and it will easily dress up a multitude of dishes with its rich, herbal flavor and hue. Simply drizzle it onto cooked chicken, fish, or scrambled eggs, toss it with grilled vegetables, spread it on a turkey sandwich, or stir it into pasta or soups.

¼ CUP PINE NUTS

2 CLOVES GARLIC, PEELED

3 CUPS LIGHTLY PACKED FRESH BASIL LEAVES

⅓ CUP FRESHLY GRATED PARMESAN CHEESE

1 TABLESPOON FRESH LEMON JUICE

½ CUP EXTRA-VIRGIN OLIVE OIL

¼ TEASPOON SALT

⅛ TEASPOON FRESHLY GROUND BLACK PEPPER

✱ **Serving size:** 2 tablespoons; **Per serving:** Calories 170; Total Fat 17g (Mono Fat 10.9g, Poly Fat 2.9g, Sat Fat 2.7g); Protein 2g; Carb 1g; Fiber 0g; Cholesterol 5mg; Sodium 125mg; **Excellent source of:** Manganese, Vitamin K; **Good source of:** Vitamin A, Vitamin E

1 Toast the pine nuts in a small, dry skillet over medium heat until fragrant and golden brown, shaking the pan frequently, about 3 minutes.

2 In a food processor, process the pine nuts and garlic together until minced. Add the basil, Parmesan, and lemon juice and process until finely minced. With the machine running, slowly pour the oil in a steady stream through the feed tube and process until well blended.

3 Season with the salt and pepper.

TO REFRIGERATE
Place in an airtight container in the refrigerator for up to 1 week.

TO FREEZE AND THAW
Place the sauce into a sealable plastic bag or pour into ice cube trays and freeze. Once frozen, transfer the cubes of sauce to a sealable plastic freezer bag where it will keep for up to 3 months.

Thaw in the refrigerator for 18 to 24 hours. Alternatively, place in a microwave-safe dish, cover, and microwave on high for about 20 seconds for one portion to 1 minute for the whole batch.

Russian Beef and Vegetable Soup (Borscht)

• MAKES: 6 SERVINGS •

THIS SOUP IS THE PERFECT antidote to a cold winter's night—it is warming and filling, plus chockfull of hearty, earthy vegetables and chunks of tender beef—and its vibrant red color, imparted by the beets in it, is sure to lift your spirits. A finishing dollop of cool sour cream provides luxurious taste and color contrast.

1 POUND LEAN BEEF STEW MEAT, CUT INTO ½-INCH CUBES

1 TEASPOON SALT, DIVIDED

½ TEASPOON FRESHLY GROUND BLACK PEPPER, DIVIDED

2 TABLESPOONS OLIVE OIL, DIVIDED

1 LARGE ONION, CHOPPED

3 CLOVES GARLIC, MINCED

½ SMALL HEAD GREEN CABBAGE, SHREDDED (4½ CUPS)

2 LARGE BEETS (1 POUND), PEELED AND CHOPPED

3 MEDIUM CARROTS, PEELED AND CUT INTO HALF COINS

4 CUPS LOW-SODIUM BEEF BROTH

ONE 28-OUNCE CAN NO-SALT-ADDED DICED TOMATOES

2 TABLESPOONS WHITE VINEGAR

FOR SERVING:

2 TABLESPOONS CHOPPED FRESH ITALIAN PARSLEY LEAVES OR DILL

⅔ CUP REDUCED-FAT SOUR CREAM OR LOW-FAT PLAIN GREEK YOGURT

1 Season the beef with ¼ teaspoon each of the salt and pepper. Heat 1 tablespoon of the oil in a large soup pot over high heat. Add the beef and cook, stirring occasionally, until browned, 5 minutes. Transfer the meat and any accumulated liquid to a plate.

2 Lower the heat to medium, heat the remaining 1 tablespoon oil, then add the onion and cook, stirring, until softened, 6 to 7 minutes. Add the garlic and cook 1 minute more. Add the cabbage, beets, carrots, the remaining ¾ teaspoon salt, the remaining ¼ teaspoon pepper, and the beef with its liquids. Add the broth, tomatoes with their juices, and 3½ cups of water and bring to a boil. Lower the heat to medium-low, and simmer, partially covered, until the meat and vegetables are tender, 1 hour. Stir in the vinegar. The soup may be refrigerated or frozen at this stage.

3 Serve garnished with the fresh herbs and a dollop of the sour cream.

Recipe continues

TO REFRIGERATE AND REHEAT

Place in an airtight container in the refrigerator for up to 4 days. To reheat, ladle the amount to be warmed into a saucepan, cover, and heat over medium heat for 8 to 25 minutes, depending on the amount. Or place in a microwave-safe bowl, cover with a splatter guard, and microwave on high for 90 seconds to 2 minutes for one portion.

TO FREEZE AND REHEAT

Chill in the refrigerator for 30 minutes, then divide into sealable freezer bags in the portions desired.

When ready to heat, run the bag under hot water for 30 seconds to release the frozen soup from the bag. Then place it in a saucepan, cover, and heat over medium heat, breaking it up occasionally with a spoon, until thawed and warmed through, 15 to 45 minutes, depending on the amount.

Alternatively, after releasing the soup from the bag, transfer it to a microwave-safe bowl, cover with a splatter guard, and microwave on the defrost setting for about 10 minutes. Continue to microwave on high for about 90 seconds for one portion.

✻ **Serving size:** 2 cups; **Per serving:** Calories 280; Total Fat 11g (Mono Fat 5.9g, Poly Fat 0.9g, Sat Fat 3.9g); Protein 22g; Carb 24g; Fiber 6g; Cholesterol 60mg; Sodium 660mg; **Excellent source of:** Fiber, Folate, Niacin, Phosphorus, Potassium, Protein, Selenium, Vitamin A, Vitamin B6, Vitamin B12, Vitamin C, Vitamin K, Zinc; **Good source of:** Calcium, Iron, Magnesium, Manganese, Riboflavin

Creamy Zucchini Soup · MAKES 6 SERVINGS ·

EVERY AUGUST ZUCCHINI IS SO plentiful no one seems to know what to do with it all. This recipe is a wonderful way to make the most of it, then and throughout the year. It is a smooth pureed soup made thick and protein-rich with the addition of white beans, which are blended up with it. A fragrant hint of fresh tarragon and a touch of lemon give it a lovely light flavor. It is delicious served chilled in the summer months, or hot when it is brisk outside.

2 TABLESPOONS OLIVE OIL

2 LARGE SHALLOTS, CHOPPED (ABOUT 1¼ CUPS)

3 CLOVES GARLIC, SLICED

1 TEASPOON SALT

½ TEASPOON FRESHLY GROUND BLACK PEPPER

3 POUNDS ZUCCHINI, HALVED LENGTHWISE AND SLICED CROSSWISE (ABOUT 10¼ CUPS)

4 CUPS LOW-SODIUM CHICKEN OR VEGETABLE BROTH

ONE 15-OUNCE CAN LOW-SODIUM GREAT NORTHERN OR CANNELLINI BEANS, RINSED AND DRAINED

2 TABLESPOONS FRESH TARRAGON LEAVES

1 TABLESPOON FRESH LEMON JUICE

½ TEASPOON FINELY GRATED FRESH LEMON ZEST

1 Heat the oil in a large pot over medium-low heat. Add the shallots, garlic, salt, and pepper and cook, stirring, until just tender, about 2 minutes. Add the zucchini and broth and bring to a boil over high heat.

2 Lower the heat to medium-low and simmer, covered, stirring occasionally, until very soft, about 10 minutes. Add the beans and tarragon, and return to a simmer. Stir in the lemon juice and zest.

3 Allow to cool for about 15 minutes, then puree in the blender in three batches until smooth, transferring the puree to a saucepan as blended. The soup may be refrigerated or frozen at this stage.

4 Return the soup to a simmer before serving, or refrigerate for at least 2 hours and serve chilled.

Recipe continues

TO REFRIGERATE AND REHEAT

Place in an airtight container and store in the refrigerator for up to 4 days. To reheat, ladle the amount to be warmed into a saucepan, cover, and heat over medium-low heat for 5 to 15 minutes, depending on the amount.

Microwave reheating not recommended.

TO FREEZE AND REHEAT

Chill in the refrigerator for 30 minutes, then divide into sealable freezer bags in the portions desired.

When ready to heat, run the bag under hot water for 30 seconds to release the frozen soup from the bag. Then place it in a saucepan, cover, and heat over medium-low heat, breaking it up occasionally with a spoon, until thawed and warmed through, 12 to 40 minutes, depending on the amount.

Microwave thawing not recommended.

✳ **Serving size:** About 1½ cups; **Per serving:** Calories 210; Total Fat 6g (Mono Fat 3.4g, Poly Fat 1g, Sat Fat 0.9g); Protein 14g; Carb 29g; Fiber 7g; Cholesterol 0mg; Sodium 520mg; **Excellent source of:** Fiber, Folate, Iron, Magnesium, Manganese, Phosphorus, Potassium, Protein, Vitamin A, Vitamin B6, Vitamin C, Zinc; **Good source of:** Copper, Calcium, Niacin, Pantothenic Acid, Thiamin

Butternut Squash and Apple Soup

• MAKES 6 SERVINGS •

THE SAYING GOES, "IF IT grows together, it goes together." It's a culinary rule of thumb that foods produced in the same region and season will pair perfectly flavor-wise. This autumnal soup is case in point, bringing together two highlights of the North American fall harvest: apples and squash. They are simmered, then pureed together to make a silken soup with a creamy sweetness and glorious color from the squash, and a bright fruitiness from the apple. A ping of fresh ginger and savory hint of sage tie them together and elevate them further.

1 TABLESPOON UNSALTED BUTTER

1 TABLESPOON OLIVE OIL

1 LARGE ONION, CHOPPED

2 POUNDS (¾- TO 1-INCH CUBES) BUTTERNUT SQUASH (ABOUT 7½ CUPS)

2 MEDIUM GRANNY SMITH APPLES, PEELED AND CHOPPED (ABOUT 3 CUPS)

1 TABLESPOON FINELY GRATED FRESH GINGER

2 CLOVES GARLIC, SLICED

1 TEASPOON DRIED RUBBED SAGE

1 TEASPOON SALT

½ TEASPOON FRESHLY GROUND BLACK PEPPER

5 CUPS LOW-SODIUM CHICKEN BROTH

¾ CUP APPLE CIDER

FOR SERVING:

½ CUP LOW-FAT PLAIN YOGURT

1 Heat the butter and oil in a soup pot over medium heat. Add the onion and cook, stirring, until softened, about 6 minutes. Stir in the squash, apples, ginger, garlic, sage, salt, and pepper. Add the broth and cider and bring to a boil. Lower the heat to medium-low, cover, and simmer, until the squash is very tender, about 25 minutes.

2 Uncover and allow to cool slightly, about 15 minutes, then puree in three batches in a blender until smooth, transferring the puree to a sauce pan as blended. The soup may be refrigerated or frozen at this stage.

3 To serve, bring the soup to a simmer. Serve garnished with the yogurt.

TO REFRIGERATE AND REHEAT

Place in an airtight container and store in the refrigerator for up to 4 days. To reheat, ladle the amount to be warmed into a saucepan, cover, and heat over medium heat for 5 to 25 minutes, depending on the amount. Or place a single portion in a microwave-safe bowl, cover with a splatter guard, and microwave on high for about 90 seconds.

TO FREEZE AND REHEAT

Chill in the refrigerator for 30 minutes, then divide into sealable freezer bags in the portions desired.

When ready to heat, run the bag under hot water for 30 seconds to release the frozen soup from the bag. Then place it in a saucepan, cover, and heat over medium heat, breaking it up occasionally with a spoon, until thawed and warmed through, 8 to 40 minutes, depending on the amount.

Alternatively, to microwave an individual portion, after releasing the soup from the bag, transfer it to a microwave-safe bowl, cover with a splatter guard, and microwave on the defrost setting for about 8 minutes, then continue to microwave on high for about 90 seconds.

＊**Serving size:** 1½ cups; **Per serving:** Calories 190; Total Fat 4.5g (Mono Fat 2.2g, Poly Fat 0.4g, Sat Fat 1.8g); Protein 5g; Carb 34g; Fiber 5g; Cholesterol 5mg; Sodium 470mg; **Excellent source of:** Fiber, Vitamin A, Vitamin C; **Good source of:** Calcium, Folate, Magnesium, Thiamin, Potassium, Vitamin B6, Vitamin E

Coconut Curried Lentil Soup

• MAKES 6 SERVINGS •

THE RED LENTILS USED TO make this Indian-inspired soup lose their shape completely with cooking, giving the dish a thick, hearty texture that puts it squarely in main course territory. They also change color to a soft yellow tone, which is punched up by the yellow curry powder, a spice mix which also provides a heady fragrance, big flavor, and remarkable health benefits. Don't forget the finishing squeeze of lemon and sprinkle of cilantro for a contrasting fresh brightness. Serve with a fresh green salad and some warm, whole-grain naan or other flatbread.

2 TABLESPOONS CANOLA OR VIRGIN COCONUT OIL

1 LARGE ONION, CHOPPED

4 CLOVES GARLIC, FINELY MINCED

1 TABLESPOON PLUS 2 TEASPOONS YELLOW CURRY POWDER

1½ CUPS DRIED RED LENTILS

1 LARGE TOMATO, DICED

1 BAY LEAF

7 CUPS LOW-SODIUM CHICKEN BROTH

1 CUP LIGHT COCONUT MILK

2 TABLESPOONS FRESH LEMON JUICE

1 TEASPOON SALT

FOR SERVING:

FRESH CILANTRO LEAVES

LEMON WEDGES

1 Heat the oil in a 4-quart stockpot over medium heat. Add the onion and cook, stirring, until tender and deep golden, 10 to 11 minutes. Add the garlic and curry powder and cook, stirring, 1 minute more. Stir in the lentils, tomato, and bay leaf, then add the chicken broth and bring to a boil. Lower the heat to medium-low and simmer, uncovered, until the lentils are tender and are breaking apart, 30 minutes. Remove and discard the bay leaf. Stir in the coconut milk, lemon juice, and salt and cook until incorporated and warmed through, 2 minutes more. The soup may be refrigerated or frozen at this stage.

2 To serve, garnish with cilantro leaves and serve with lemon wedges.

TO REFRIGERATE AND REHEAT

Place in an airtight container and store in the refrigerator for up to 4 days. To reheat, ladle the amount to be warmed into a saucepan, cover, and heat over medium heat for 5 to 25 minutes, depending on the amount. Or place a single portion in a microwave-safe bowl, cover with a splatter guard, and microwave on high for 90 seconds to 2 minutes.

TO FREEZE AND REHEAT

Chill in the refrigerator for 30 minutes, then divide into sealable freezer bags in the portions desired.

When ready to heat, run the bag under hot water for 30 seconds to release the frozen soup from the bag. Then place it in a saucepan, cover, and heat over medium heat, breaking it up occasionally with a spoon, until thawed and warmed through, 12 to 45 minutes, depending on the amount. Add 1 to 2 tablespoons of water if the pan appears dry.

Alternatively, after releasing the soup from the bag, transfer it to a microwave-safe bowl, cover with a splatter guard, and microwave on the defrost setting for about 12 minutes, then continue to microwave on high for 90 seconds to 2 minutes for one portion.

✳ **Serving size:** 1½ cups; **Per serving:** Calories 280, Total Fat 8g (Mono Fat 3.1g, Poly Fat 1.4g, Sat Fat 1.9g); Protein 16g; Carb 36g; Fiber 9g; Cholesterol 0mg; Sodium 490mg; **Excellent source of:** Fiber, Protein; **Good source of:** Iron, Manganese, Potassium

Go-To Gazpacho

AS SOON AS THE TOMATOES come into my local farmer's market my mind turns to one thing, like a mantra, gazpacho, gazpacho, gazpacho. I have made it dozens of different ways over the years, but this is my official, go-to recipe, the one I simply must have in my fridge all summer long. It is easy-breezy, basically akin to whirring a tomato, cucumber, and bell pepper salad in the blender. There is no need to fuss with peeling the tomatoes or straining the puree. I add a slice of bread (whole-grain) to give it extra body and creaminess and a finishing drizzle of good olive oil for a refreshing, sumptuous, elegant way to eat your vegetables that I bet you won't be able to stop thinking about.

1 MEDIUM CUCUMBER, PEELED AND SEEDED, DIVIDED

1 MEDIUM RED BELL PEPPER, CORED, DIVIDED

1½ POUNDS RIPE TOMATOES (4 TO 5 MEDIUM), CORED AND QUARTERED

1 SLICE WHOLE-WHEAT SANDWICH BREAD, CRUSTS REMOVED

3 TABLESPOONS EXTRA-VIRGIN OLIVE OIL

1 TABLESPOON SHERRY VINEGAR

1 SMALL CLOVE GARLIC, MINCED

¾ TEASPOON SALT

FOR SERVING:

4 TEASPOONS EXTRA-VIRGIN OLIVE OIL

1 Chop half of the cucumber and half of the pepper into large chunks and put them into a blender. Finely chop the remaining cucumber and pepper and set aside.

2 Add the tomatoes, ½ cup of water, the bread, oil, sherry vinegar, garlic, and salt to the blender and blend until smooth. Stir in the chopped peppers and cucumbers. Chill in the refrigerator in an airtight container for at least 2 hours.

3 Stir before serving and drizzle each bowl with 1 teaspoon of the oil.

∗ **Serving size:** About 1 cup; **Per serving:** Calories 190; Total Fat 15g (Mono Fat 10.8g, Poly Fat 1.8g, Sat Fat 2.1g); Protein 3g; Carb 13g; Fiber 3g; Cholesterol 0mg; Sodium 480mg; **Excellent source of:** Manganese, Vitamin C, Vitamin K; **Good source of:** Fiber, Molybdenum, Potassium, Vitamin B6

TO REFRIGERATE

The gazpacho will keep in the refrigerator in an airtight container for up to 4 days. Stir well before serving.

Freezing is not recommended.

Cuban Black Bean Soup

• MAKES 6 SERVINGS •

THIS CLASSIC CUBAN DISH IS the ultimate in slow food—you need to soak the beans the night before and simmer them for a couple of hours the next day—but there is not much actual effort involved, leaving you plenty of time to piddle around the house and relax as it cooks. You don't even have to do any chopping—that is done for you in the food processor. What you get is well worth the time: a deeply aromatic, hearty, creamy, belly-warming pot of pure comfort food. The final toppings are essential, as the soup itself becomes a rich, dark backdrop for their contrasting array of colors, flavors, and textures.

1 POUND DRIED BLACK BEANS

2 MEDIUM ONIONS, QUARTERED

1 MEDIUM RED BELL PEPPER, CORED, SEEDED, AND QUARTERED

1 MEDIUM GREEN BELL PEPPER, CORED, SEEDED, AND QUARTERED

4 CLOVES GARLIC, ROUGHLY CHOPPED

3 TABLESPOONS OLIVE OIL

2 TEASPOONS GROUND CUMIN

2 TEASPOONS DRIED OREGANO

1 TEASPOON SMOKED PAPRIKA

6 CUPS LOW-SODIUM CHICKEN BROTH AND/OR WATER

1¼ TEASPOONS SALT, PLUS MORE TO TASTE

½ TEASPOON FRESHLY GROUND BLACK PEPPER

2 BAY LEAVES

2 TABLESPOONS SHERRY VINEGAR

FOR SERVING:

½ CUP REDUCED-FAT SOUR CREAM OR LOW-FAT PLAIN GREEK YOGURT

1 TABLESPOON FRESH LIME JUICE

½ CUP FRESH CILANTRO LEAVES

½ SMALL RED ONION, FINELY CHOPPED

1 Place the beans in a colander and rinse under cold water, sorting through them to remove any pebbles. Transfer the beans to a pot or large bowl and add enough cold water to cover them by about an inch. Cover and place in the refrigerator to soak overnight, or at least 8 hours. Drain.

2 Place the onion, red and green bell peppers, and garlic in a food processor and process until finely minced. Add the oil and process until a puree is formed.

3 Transfer the puree to a large pot and cook over medium heat, stirring frequently, until most of the water has evaporated and the mixture begins to darken, about 15 minutes. Add the cumin, oregano, and paprika and cook for 1 minute more.

4 Add the soaked beans to the pot along with the broth or water. (You should have enough liquid to cover the beans by an inch. If needed, add more water.) Stir in the salt, pepper, and bay leaves.

5 Bring to a boil, then lower the heat to low and simmer, partially covered, for 2 hours, until the beans are tender and the soup has thickened. Transfer 3 cups of the bean soup to a blender and puree until smooth, then return the puree to the soup pot. Stir in the vinegar and 1 to 2 cups of water to reach the consistency you prefer. Pick out and discard the bay leaves and season with additional salt to taste. The soup may be refrigerated or frozen at this point.

6 To serve, stir the sour cream and lime juice together in a small bowl until combined. Serve each bowl of soup with a drizzle of the lime-sour cream mixture and a sprinkle each of the cilantro and onion.

TO REFRIGERATE AND REHEAT

Place in an airtight container and store in the refrigerator for up to 4 days. To reheat, ladle the amount to be warmed into a saucepan, cover, and heat over medium heat for 6 to 30 minutes, depending on the amount. Or place in a microwave-safe bowl, cover with a splatter guard, and microwave on high for 90 seconds to 2 minutes for one serving.

TO FREEZE AND REHEAT

Chill in the refrigerator for 30 minutes, then divide into sealable plastic freezer bags in the portions desired.

When ready to heat, run the bag under hot water for 30 seconds to release the frozen soup from the bag. Then place it in a saucepan, cover, and heat over medium heat, breaking it up occasionally with a spoon, until thawed and warmed through, 15 to 45 minutes. Add 1 to 2 tablespoons of water if the pan appears dry.

Alternatively, after releasing the soup from the bag, transfer it to a microwave-safe bowl, cover with a splatter guard, and microwave on the defrost setting for about 12 minutes, then continue to microwave on high for 90 seconds to 2 minutes for a single portion.

* **Serving size:** 1½ cups; **Per serving:** Calories 360; Total Fat 8g (Mono Fat 5g, Poly Fat 1.2g, Sat Fat 1.5g); Protein 21g; Carb 53g; Fiber 18g; Cholesterol 0mg; Sodium 570mg; **Excellent source of:** Copper, Folate, Fiber, Iron, Magnesium, Manganese, Molybdenum, Phosphorus, Potassium, Protein, Thiamin, Vitamin C; **Good source of:** Vitamin B6, Vitamin K, Zinc

Tuscan Seven Vegetable Soup

• MAKES 6 SERVINGS •

THIS ITALIAN TOMATO-BROTH BASED SOUP is fully loaded with seven kinds of vegetables, all cooked to tender perfection, and intoxicatingly aromatic thanks to plenty of garlic, onion, and herbs. It is an irresistible way to eat your vegetables when there is a chill in the air. If you have a rind of Parmesan cheese in your freezer (I recommend you store them there), pop it into the soup as it simmers for an extra flavor infusion.

2 TABLESPOONS OLIVE OIL

1 LARGE ONION, DICED

3 MEDIUM CARROTS, DICED

2 STALKS CELERY, DICED

1 MEDIUM RED BELL PEPPER, DICED

4 CLOVES GARLIC, MINCED

1 MEDIUM ZUCCHINI, DICED

1 TABLESPOON TOMATO PASTE

1¼ TEASPOONS SALT

1 TEASPOON DRIED THYME

1 TEASPOON DRIED BASIL

¼ TEASPOON FRESHLY GROUND BLACK PEPPER

6 CUPS LOW-SODIUM CHICKEN BROTH

ONE 14-OUNCE CAN NO-SALT-ADDED DICED TOMATOES

1½ CUPS COARSELY CHOPPED KALE LEAVES

FOR SERVING:

FRESHLY GRATED PARMESAN CHEESE, OPTIONAL

1 Heat the oil in a large stock pot over medium heat. Add the onion and cook, stirring, until it softens, about 5 minutes. Add the carrots, celery, and bell pepper and cook, stirring occasionally, until the vegetables are tender, about 10 minutes more. Add the garlic and cook, stirring, for 30 seconds more, then add the zucchini. Stir in the tomato paste, salt, thyme, basil, and black pepper. Add the chicken broth and tomatoes with their juices and bring to a boil. Lower the heat to medium-low and simmer, until the vegetables are tender and the flavors have melded, 15 minutes. Add the kale leaves and cook until they have wilted, 5 minutes.

2 Ladle into bowls and garnish each with a generous sprinkle of Parmesan.

TO REFRIGERATE AND REHEAT

Place in an airtight container in the refrigerator for up to 4 days. To reheat, ladle the amount to be warmed into a saucepan, cover, and heat over medium heat for 8 to 30 minutes, depending on the amount. Or place in a microwave-safe bowl, cover with a splatter guard, and microwave on high for about 2 minutes for one portion.

TO FREEZE AND REHEAT

Chill in the refrigerator for 30 minutes, then divide into sealable freezer bags in the portions desired.

When ready to heat, run the bag under hot water for 30 seconds to release the frozen soup from the bag. Then place it in a saucepan, cover, and heat over medium heat, breaking it up occasionally with a spoon, until thawed and warmed through, 15 to 50 minutes, depending on the amount.

Alternatively, after releasing the soup from the bag, transfer it to a microwave-safe bowl, cover with a splatter guard, and microwave on the defrost setting for about 12 minutes, then continue to microwave on high for about 2 minutes for one portion.

---

* **Serving size:** About 1½ cups; **Per serving:** Calories 120; Total Fat 5g (Mono Fat 3.3g, Poly Fat 0.6g, Sat Fat 0.7g); Protein 4g; Carb 14g; Fiber 3g; Cholesterol 0mg; Sodium 630mg; **Excellent source of:** Vitamin A, Vitamin C, Vitamin K; **Good source of:** Copper, Fiber, Folate, Manganese, Vitamin B6

Chilled Honeydew and Toasted Almond Milk Soup • MAKES 4 SERVINGS •

THIS REFRESHING SUMMER SOUP HAS a delightful sweetness and stunning pale green hue from the melon, enhanced with a little honey and balanced with lime juice. It gets a lightly nutty taste and creamy body from almond milk, which can be made easily as written here, with toasted almonds, a step I think is well worth it, but for a shortcut, you can also use store-bought. Coconut or cashew milk would work nicely too. The garnish of sweet-tart green grapes and floral, fresh basil ribbons adds a beautiful crown of flavor and texture.

¾ CUP SLICED ALMONDS, DIVIDED, OR ¼ CUP SLICED ALMONDS AND 1¼ CUPS STORE-BOUGHT UNSWEETENED ALMOND MILK

½ HONEYDEW MELON, SEEDED, RIND REMOVED, AND CUT INTO CHUNKS (ABOUT 6 CUPS)

2 TABLESPOONS FRESH LIME JUICE

1 TABLESPOON HONEY

PINCH SALT

FOR SERVING:

⅓ CUP GREEN GRAPES, QUARTERED

2 TABLESPOONS FRESH BASIL LEAVES, CUT INTO RIBBONS

1 Toast the almonds in a large, dry skillet over medium-high heat, stirring frequently, until they are golden and fragrant, about 3 minutes. Set aside to cool, 5 minutes.

2 If making the almond milk, place ½ cup of the toasted almonds in a blender with 1½ cups cold water. Blend on high until the almonds are finely ground, about 20 seconds. Strain the mixture through a fine-mesh strainer set over a bowl, pressing down on the solids to release as much of the almond milk as possible. Discard the solids and rinse out the blender.

3 Place the almond milk, melon, lime juice, honey, and salt in the blender and blend until smooth. Transfer the soup to a bowl and chill for at least 1 hour, and up to 1 day. The soup may be frozen at this stage.

4 Serve the soup garnished with the grapes, remaining toasted almonds, and the basil.

TO REFRIGERATE

The soup will keep in an airtight container in the refrigerator for up to 1 day. Stir before serving chilled, with the garnishes.

TO FREEZE

Place in an airtight container or sealable plastic freezer bags in the portions desired and freeze for up to 3 months. Thaw in the refrigerator for 24 to 36 hours. Stir before serving chilled, with the garnishes.

* **Serving size:** 1¼ cups; **Per serving:** Calories 220; Total Fat 9g (Mono Fat 5.5g, Poly Fat 2.3g, Sat Fat 0.8g); Protein 5g; Carb 34g; Fiber 4g; Cholesterol 0mg; Sodium 120mg; **Excellent source of:** Manganese, Potassium, Vitamin C, Vitamin E; **Good source of:** Copper, Fiber, Folate, Magnesium, Phosphorus, Protein, Riboflavin, Vitamin B6, Vitamin K

Creamy Tomato Soup   • MAKES 6 SERVINGS •

MY HUSBAND WAS SHOCKED WHEN I told him there was no cream in this velvety tomato soup. He was also surprised at how well it satisfied his hunger. What makes all that rich taste and contentment is cashews, which have a mild, creamy flavor and easily puree to a smooth consistency, so they are perfect to add to soups when you want extra body and creaminess, as well as the extra satisfaction from their protein, fiber, and healthy fats.

2 TABLESPOONS OLIVE OIL

2 MEDIUM ONIONS, CHOPPED

2 LARGE STALKS CELERY, CHOPPED

1 TABLESPOON CHOPPED FRESH THYME

2 CLOVES GARLIC, CHOPPED

1 TEASPOON SALT

½ TEASPOON FRESHLY GROUND BLACK PEPPER

TWO 28-OUNCE CANS NO-SALT-ADDED DICED TOMATOES

¾ CUP RAW CASHEWS

2 TABLESPOONS TOMATO PASTE

1 Heat the oil in a large pot over medium heat. Add the onions, celery, thyme, garlic, salt, and pepper and cook, stirring occasionally, until softened, about 5 minutes. Stir in the tomatoes with their juices, 1½ cups of water, the cashews, and tomato paste. Bring to a boil, then lower the heat to medium-low and simmer, stirring occasionally, until the soup begins to thicken, about 20 minutes. Allow to cool slightly, for about 15 minutes, then puree in 3 batches until smooth, transferring the puree to a pot or storage container as it is pureed.

2 To continue, reheat the soup in a pot over medium heat until it comes to a simmer.

TO REFRIGERATE AND REHEAT
Place in an airtight container and store in the refrigerator for up to 4 days. To reheat, ladle the amount to be warmed into a saucepan, cover, and heat over medium heat for 6 to 30 minutes, depending on the amount. Or in a microwave-safe bowl, cover with a splatter guard, and microwave on high for 90 seconds to 2 minutes for one portion.

TO FREEZE AND REHEAT
Chill in the refrigerator for 30 minutes, then divide into sealable plastic freezer bags in the portions desired.

When ready to heat, run the bag under hot water for 30 seconds to release the frozen soup from the bag. Then place it in a saucepan, cover, and heat over medium heat, breaking it up occasionally with a spoon, until thawed and warmed through, 15 to 45 minutes, depending on the amount. Add 1 to 2 tablespoons of water if the pan appears dry.

Alternatively, after releasing the soup from the bag, transfer it to a microwave-safe bowl, cover with a splatter guard, and microwave on the defrost setting for about 12 minutes, then continue to microwave on high for 90 seconds to 2 minutes for a single portion.

＊ **Serving size:** 1½ cups; **Per serving:** Calories 210; Total Fat 11g (Mono Fat 6.8g, Poly Fat 1.5g, Sat Fat 1.7g); Protein 5g; Carb 22g; Fiber 4g; Cholesterol 0mg; Sodium 480mg; **Excellent source of:** Vitamin A, Vitamin C; **Good source of:** Fiber, Iron, Protein, Vitamin K

Meat

Beef and Bean Burrito • MAKES 6 SERVINGS •

WHEN A DEEP HUNGER STRIKES on a crazy-busy day, what a comfort to know you have these deliciously filling burritos tucked away in the freezer! They are stuffed to the brim with chili-seasoned beef, smashed beans, and sharp cheese, and will satisfy you completely, without slowing you down.

1 POUND LEAN GROUND BEEF

1 MEDIUM ONION, CHOPPED

3 CLOVES GARLIC, MINCED

TWO 15-OUNCE CANS LOW-SODIUM PINTO BEANS, DRAINED AND RINSED

1 CUP NO-SALT-ADDED BEEF BROTH

1 TABLESPOON ANCHO CHILI POWDER OR REGULAR CHILI POWDER

2 TEASPOONS GROUND CUMIN

1 TEASPOON GROUND CORIANDER

½ TEASPOON SALT

⅛ TEASPOON CAYENNE PEPPER

SIX 8-INCH WHOLE-WHEAT TORTILLAS

¾ CUP SHREDDED SHARP CHEDDAR OR MONTEREY JACK CHEESE (3 OUNCES)

FOR SERVING:

½ CUP PLAIN LOW-FAT GREEK YOGURT OR REDUCED-FAT SOUR CREAM

½ CUP PREPARED TOMATO SALSA

1 Heat a large skillet over medium heat, add the meat and onions, and cook, stirring and breaking the meat up with a spoon, until the meat is browned and the onion is softened, 4 minutes. Add the garlic and cook, stirring, for 30 seconds more. Stir in the beans, broth, chili powder, cumin, coriander, salt, and cayenne, and bring to a boil. Cook, stirring occasionally and mashing the beans a bit with the spoon, until the mixture is creamy and thickened, about 10 minutes. If planning to freeze or refrigerate, remove the mixture from the heat and allow it to cool for 20 minutes. Then skip to step 3 and make the burritos with unwarmed tortillas.

2 To continue now, warm the tortillas on a hot, ungreased griddle or directly over a gas burner, one at a time, for 30 seconds each, turning once. Alternatively, wrap the tortillas in a slightly damp paper towel and heat in the microwave for 30 to 40 seconds.

3 To make the burritos, sprinkle each tortilla with 2 tablespoons of the cheese, then mound ⅔ cup of the mixture in the middle and roll up burrito style, with both ends folded under so the burrito is closed. Refrigerate or freeze at this stage.

4 To serve, top each burrito with a dollop of the yogurt or sour cream and a heaping tablespoon of the salsa.

TO REFRIGERATE AND SERVE

Wrap the burritos individually in plastic wrap or foil and store in the refrigerator in an airtight container where they will keep for up to 4 days.

To heat, unwrap completely, place on a baking sheet or piece of foil in a 350°F oven until warmed through, 20 to 25 minutes. Alternatively, unwrap the burrito, rewrap in a paper towel, and microwave for about 1 minute, for one burrito. Then follow the "to serve" directions in the recipe.

TO FREEZE AND SERVE

Wrap the burritos individually in plastic wrap or foil and place in an airtight container or sealable freezer bag and freeze for up to 3 months.

There is no need to thaw. To heat, unwrap completely and place on a piece of foil in a cold oven set to 350°F. Once the oven reaches temperature, continue to cook for 30 to 35 minutes, until warmed through. Alternatively, unwrap the frozen burrito completely, then rewrap it in a paper towel and microwave on the defrost setting for 6 minutes and then on full power for 90 seconds, for one burrito. Once the burrito is warmed, continue with the "to serve" directions in the recipe.

✳ **Serving size:** 1 burrito; **Per serving:** Calories 420; Total Fat 13g (Mono Fat 2g, Poly Fat 0.3g, Sat Fat 7g); Protein 30g; Carb 46g; Fiber 9g; Cholesterol 65mg; Sodium 620mg; **Excellent source of:** Calcium, Fiber, Iron, Magnesium, Phosphorus, Protein, Thiamin, Vitamin B12, Zinc; **Good source of:** Niacin, Potassium, Riboflavin, Selenium, Vitamin A, Vitamin B6

Cheeseburger-Stuffed Twice-Baked Potatoes

• MAKES 8 SERVINGS •

THIS RECIPE IS THE LUSCIOUS love-child of a stuffed potato skin and a cheeseburger, where Russet potatoes are scooped out and twice-baked to make crispy carriers for a generous helping of beefy filling that's smothered in melted cheddar cheese. It tastes as decadent as it sounds, but it is actually quite healthy, because hollowing out the potatoes keeps carbs in check (and gives you the makings of mashed potatoes for the next day) and amping up lean beef with chopped mushrooms, broccoli, and tomatoes gives you a big portion with a sensible amount of meat.

8 LARGE RUSSET POTATOES (12 OUNCES EACH)

1 TABLESPOON OLIVE OIL

1 TEASPOON SALT, DIVIDED

½ TEASPOON FRESHLY GROUND BLACK PEPPER, DIVIDED

2 POUNDS LEAN GROUND BEEF

1 LARGE ONION, CHOPPED

3 CLOVES GARLIC, MINCED

1 TEASPOON ONION POWDER

½ TEASPOON PAPRIKA

1 POUND BUTTON MUSHROOMS, CHOPPED

ONE 15-OUNCE CAN NO-SALT-ADDED TOMATO SAUCE

ONE 14.5-OUNCE CAN NO-SALT-ADDED DICED TOMATOES

2 CUPS BROCCOLI FLORETS (8 OUNCES), CHOPPED INTO ½-INCH PIECES

FOR SERVING:

1 CUP GRATED CHEDDAR CHEESE

KETCHUP, OPTIONAL

1 Preheat the oven to 400°F.

2 Pierce each potato in several places with a fork and bake until tender, 80 to 90 minutes. Allow potatoes to cool at room temperature until they can be comfortably handled, then cut each potato in half lengthwise and scoop out most of the flesh from each half. Reserve the potato flesh for another use, such as mashed potatoes.

3 Brush the scooped potato skins lightly all over with the oil and sprinkle the cut sides with ¼ teaspoon of the salt and ¼ teaspoon of the pepper. Place on a baking tray, cut-side up, and return to the oven. Bake until golden and crisped, 15 to 20 minutes.

4 Meanwhile, heat a large skillet over medium-high heat. Add the meat and cook, breaking it up with a spoon, until browned, 5 to 6 minutes. Transfer the meat to a plate with a slotted spoon, leaving the liquid in the pan.

5 Add the onions to the pan and cook, stirring, until softened, 6 to 7 minutes. Add the garlic, onion powder, and paprika and cook, stirring, 1 minute more. Add the mushrooms and cook, stirring,

Recipe continues

until they release their water, 5 to 6 minutes. Add the tomato sauce, diced tomatoes with their juices, remaining ¾ teaspoon salt and ¼ teaspoon pepper, and return the meat to the pan and cook, stirring occasionally, until the mixture has thickened but is still very moist, 3 to 4 minutes. Add the broccoli and cook, stirring, until it is crisp-tender and bright green, 3 to 4 minutes.

6 Place each potato half on a plate and fill with ½ cup filling. The stuffed potatoes may be refrigerated or frozen at this stage.

7 To continue, preheat the broiler on high. Place the stuffed potatoes on a baking tray, sprinkle each with 1 tablespoon of the cheese, and broil until the cheese is melted, about 1 minute. Serve with ketchup, if desired.

TO REFRIGERATE AND SERVE

Place in an airtight container and refrigerate for up to 4 days.

To reheat, allow to sit at room temperature as the oven preheats to 350°F. Place on a baking tray or piece of foil, uncovered, for 15 minutes, then follow the "to continue" directions in the recipe.

Alternatively, unwrap completely, place on a microwave-safe dish, sprinkle with the cheese, cover with a splatter guard, and microwave on high for about 2 minutes for one two-piece portion.

TO FREEZE AND SERVE

Allow the stuffed potatoes to chill in the refrigerator for 30 minutes, then wrap individual portions in foil or plastic wrap and place in a sealable freezer bag in the freezer for up to 3 months.

There is no need to thaw. To reheat, place on a baking sheet or foil, uncovered, in a cold oven and set it to 350°F. When the oven reaches temperature, continue to cook for 30 minutes, until warmed through. Then follow the "to continue" directions in the recipe.

Alternatively, unwrap completely, place in a microwave-safe dish, sprinkle with cheese, cover with a splatter guard, and microwave on the defrost setting for 10 minutes and then sprinkle with cheese and microwave on high for 2 minutes for a single portion.

∗ **Serving size:** 2 stuffed potato halves; **Per serving:** Calories 410; Total Fat 12g (Mono Fat 3.5g, Poly Fat 0.6g, Sat Fat 5.8g); Protein 32g; Carb 47g; Fiber 6g; Cholesterol 75mg; Sodium 470mg; **Excellent source of:** Copper, Fiber, Folate, Iron, Magnesium, Manganese, Niacin, Pantothenic Acid, Phosphorus, Potassium, Protein, Riboflavin, Selenium, Vitamin C, Vitamin B6, Vitamin B12, Vitamin K, Zinc; **Good source of:** Thiamin, Vitamin A

East Meets West Brisket

THIS SUPREMELY SAVORY, TENDER BRISKET tastes like one my Eastern European grandmother would have made if she had access to an Asian pantry. It has the deep tomato essence and piles of sweet caramelized onions that made hers so tasty, but this recipe layers that flavor with a Chinese five-spice rub, and a distinctively Asian soy-ginger-garlic sauce that clings luxuriously to the meat. Try it with the Asian Slaw, page 65.

FOR THE RUB:

- 1 TABLESPOON GRANULATED SUGAR
- 2 TEASPOONS ONION POWDER
- 1 TEASPOON SALT
- 1 TEASPOON FRESHLY GROUND BLACK PEPPER
- ½ TEASPOON CHINESE FIVE-SPICE POWDER
- ¼ TEASPOON CAYENNE PEPPER
- ONE 3½-LB BRISKET, FIRST-CUT OR FLAT-HALF, TRIMMED OF ALL EXCESS FAT

FOR THE SAUCE:

- 3 TABLESPOONS TOMATO PASTE
- 3 TABLESPOONS UNSEASONED RICE VINEGAR
- 3 TABLESPOONS REDUCED-SODIUM SOY SAUCE
- 2 TABLESPOONS HONEY
- 1 TABLESPOON CHILI-GARLIC SAUCE, SUCH AS SRIRACHA
- 1 TABLESPOON CHOPPED FRESH GARLIC
- 1 TABLESPOON CHOPPED FRESH GINGER
- 2 TEASPOONS CHINESE MUSTARD OR DIJON MUSTARD
- 2 TEASPOONS TOASTED SESAME OIL
- 2 TABLESPOONS CANOLA OIL, OR OTHER NEUTRAL TASTING OIL
- 1 LARGE ONION, SLICED INTO HALF-MOONS

1 Preheat the oven to 325°F.

2 To make the rub, in a small bowl combine the sugar, onion powder, salt, pepper, Chinese five-spice powder, and cayenne pepper. Rub it all over the brisket and set it aside as you prepare the sauce.

3 In a medium bowl, whisk together 3 tablespoons of water, the tomato paste, rice vinegar, soy sauce, honey, chili-garlic sauce, garlic, ginger, mustard, and sesame oil.

4 Heat the canola oil in a large Dutch oven or heavy roasting pan over medium heat. Add the brisket and cook until golden, about 6 minutes per side, turning once. (It is fine, good even, if the meat becomes slightly charred.) Transfer the meat to a large plate or board.

5 Add the onion to the pot and cook, scraping the bottom of the pan to incorporate browned bits, until the onions are softened, 7 to 8 minutes. Return the brisket to the pot and add the sauce along with ½ cup water. Cover tightly, transfer to the oven, and cook until the meat is tender, 2½ to 3 hours.

6 Transfer the meat to a cutting board and allow to cool for 30 minutes at room temperature, or it may be refrigerated at this stage for up to 4 days.

Recipe continues

7 To continue, cut the meat against the grain into ¼-inch slices. Return the sliced brisket to the sauce and cook, covered, over medium-low heat until warmed through, 10 to 20 minutes. Add water by the tablespoonful to the sauce to loosen it if necessary.

TO REFRIGERATE AND REHEAT

Prior to being sliced, the meat and sauce may be stored separately in airtight containers in the refrigerator for up to 4 days. Follow the "to continue" directions above to serve.

Already-sliced meat may be stored together with the sauce in an airtight container in the refrigerator. Total refrigeration time for the cooked meat, sliced or unsliced, should not exceed 4 days.

To reheat the sliced meat and sauce, place in a saucepan, cover, and cook over medium-low heat until warmed through, 10 to 30 minutes, depending on the amount. Alternatively, place in a microwave-safe dish, cover with a spatter guard, and microwave on high for about 1 minute for a single portion.

TO FREEZE AND REHEAT

Transfer the sliced meat and sauce to sealable freezer bags in the portions desired and freeze for up to 3 months.

Thaw in the refrigerator for 24 to 36 hours, then reheat as above. Or, to thaw quickly, run the bag under hot water for 30 seconds to release the food, transfer it to a microwave-safe dish, cover with a splatter guard, and microwave on the defrost setting for about 6 minutes, then microwave another 1 minute on high to warm through for a single serving.

---

* **Serving size:** About 4 slices meat and 3 tablespoons sauce; **Per serving:** Calories 350; Total Fat 15g (Mono Fat 8.1g, Poly Fat 2g, Sat Fat 4.1g); Protein 43g; Carb 11g; Fiber 1g; Cholesterol 135mg; Sodium 720mg; **Excellent source of:** Iron, Niacin, Phosphorus, Potassium, Protein, Selenium, Vitamin B6, Vitamin B12, Zinc; **Good source of:** Magnesium, Pantothenic Acid, Riboflavin, Thiamin

Hungarian Beef Stew • MAKES 6 SERVINGS •

THIS HOMEY ONE-POT MEAL HAS everything you expect and crave in a beef stew: chunks of tender meat, carrots, and potatoes in a sauce made with beef stock and red wine. But it has several elements that take it out of the ordinary and into deep flavor territory: a generous amount of sweet paprika infuses the broth with a rich depth of flavor and color, slices of red bell pepper add a tender brightness, and caraway seeds bring a deliciously unexpected note to each bite.

If you are planning to freeze this dish, be sure to use the fingerling potatoes called for here because they tend to hold up well, which is not so with many other potato varieties.

1½ POUNDS LEAN BONELESS CHUCK ROAST, TRIMMED AND CUT INTO 1-INCH PIECES

¾ TEASPOON SALT, PLUS MORE TO TASTE

½ TEASPOON FRESHLY GROUND BLACK PEPPER, PLUS MORE TO TASTE

2 TABLESPOONS OLIVE OIL

2 MEDIUM ONIONS, CHOPPED

3 CLOVES GARLIC, MINCED

2 TABLESPOONS ALL PURPOSE FLOUR

1 TABLESPOON PAPRIKA

1 TEASPOON CARAWAY SEEDS

1 CUP DRY RED WINE, SUCH AS PINOT NOIR OR MERLOT

1½ CUPS LOW-SODIUM BEEF BROTH

1 POUND FINGERLING POTATOES, UNPEELED, CUT INTO 1-INCH CHUNKS

3 MEDIUM CARROTS, COARSELY CHOPPED

2 MEDIUM RED BELL PEPPERS, SLICED

1 Sprinkle the beef with the salt and pepper. Heat the oil in a large heavy pot, such as a Dutch oven, over medium-high heat and cook the beef in 2 to 3 batches, until golden brown on both sides, about 6 minutes per batch. Using tongs, transfer the meat to a plate as it is browned.

2 Lower the heat to medium, add the onions to the pot, and cook until softened, about 5 minutes. Add the garlic, flour, paprika, and caraway seeds, stirring for 1 minute. Add the wine and cook, stirring occasionally, scraping up any browned bits, until thickened, about 2 minutes.

3 Add the broth, return the browned meat to the pot, and bring to a simmer. Lower the heat to low, cover, and cook for 1¼ hours. Stir in the potatoes, carrots, and peppers and simmer, partially covered for 20 minutes. Then uncover and cook until the meat and vegetables are fork-tender and the liquid has thickened, stirring occasionally, 25 to 40 minutes more. Season with additional salt and pepper to taste. Serve over noodles.

Recipe continues

TO REFRIGERATE AND REHEAT

Transfer the stew to an airtight container and refrigerate for up to 4 days.

To reheat, place in a saucepan over medium-low heat, cover, and cook, stirring occasionally, until warmed through, 8 to 25 minutes, depending on the amount. Alternatively, place in a microwave-safe bowl, cover with a splatter guard, and microwave on full power for about 2 minutes for a single portion.

TO FREEZE AND REHEAT

Chill in the refrigerator for 30 minutes. Transfer the stew to sealable plastic freezer bags in the portions desired and freeze for up to 3 months.

Thaw in the refrigerator for 24 to 36 hours and reheat as above. Or, to thaw quickly, run the bag under hot water for 30 seconds to release the stew from the bag, then transfer it to a pot along with 1 to 2 tablespoons of water per portion. Cover and cook over medium-low heat, stirring occasionally, until warmed through, 10 to 40 minutes, depending on the amount. Add more water to the pot if the bottom is getting dry.

Alternatively, after running the bag under hot water, transfer the stew to a microwave-safe bowl, cover with a splatter guard, and microwave on the defrost setting for about 7 minutes, then heat through on full power for 2 minutes for a single portion.

---

* **Serving size:** 1⅓ cups; **Per serving:** Calories 400; Total Fat 19g (Mono Fat 9.4g, Poly Fat 1.1g, Sat Fat 6.2g); Protein 25g; Carb 25g; Fiber 4g; Cholesterol 85mg; Sodium 390mg; **Excellent source of:** Protein, Selenium, Vitamin A, Vitamin B6, Vitamin B12, Vitamin C, Zinc; **Good source of:** Fiber, Folate, Iron, Niacin, Phosphorus, Potassium, Riboflavin, Vitamin K

Lettuce Wraps with Beef and Tofu
in Ginger-Scallion-Peanut Sauce • MAKES 8 SERVINGS •

THESE WRAPS ARE NOT ONLY fun to eat, they are bundles of exciting flavors and textures that make for an unforgettable meal. The filling is a blend of ground beef and tofu (who says you have to choose!?) with a crunch of water chestnuts, all enveloped in a luxuriously rich, ginger infused, sweet-spicy peanut sauce. The intensity of the filling is balanced by the light freshness of the lettuce leaves it is piled in, and the crisp confetti of bell pepper sprinkled on top. You can serve them already compiled on individual plates, or just put out bowls of the lettuce, filling, and toppings for diners to build their own, taco-style.

⅓ CUP REDUCED-SODIUM SOY SAUCE

¼ CUP UNSEASONED RICE VINEGAR

¼ CUP CHINESE RICE WINE OR DRY SHERRY

2 TABLESPOONS NATURAL PEANUT BUTTER

2 TABLESPOONS CHILI-GARLIC SAUCE, SUCH AS SRIRACHA

2 TABLESPOONS TOASTED SESAME OIL

1 TABLESPOON MOLASSES

14 OUNCES EXTRA-FIRM TOFU

1 TABLESPOON CANOLA OIL, OR OTHER NEUTRAL TASTING OIL

6 SCALLIONS, THINLY SLICED, GREEN AND WHITE PARTS SEPARATED

1 POUND LEAN GROUND BEEF

2 TABLESPOONS FRESH MINCED GINGER

1 CUP FINELY DICED WATER CHESTNUTS

FOR SERVING:

2 LARGE HEADS BIBB OR BOSTON LETTUCE, OUTER LEAVES DISCARDED, LEAVES SEPARATED

1 RED BELL PEPPER, FINELY DICED

½ CUP COARSELY CHOPPED, UNSALTED, ROASTED PEANUTS

1 In a medium bowl, whisk together the soy sauce, vinegar, rice wine, peanut butter, chili-garlic sauce, sesame oil, and molasses.

2 Slice the tofu into ½-inch thick slabs and lay the slices on top of paper towels. Use more paper towels to firmly pat the tofu in order to remove as much water as possible. This should take about 2 minutes and use about 3 paper towels. Finely mince the dried tofu and set aside.

3 Heat the oil in a wok or extra-large skillet over medium-high heat. Add the scallion whites and cook, stirring, until they are translucent, 1 to 2 minutes. Add the ground beef and ginger and cook, stirring and breaking up the meat with a spoon, until the beef is browned and just cooked through, about 4 to 5 minutes. Stir in the tofu and reserved sauce. Lower the heat to medium-low and cook, stirring occasionally, until the sauce has thickened and the ingredients have melded, about 3 minutes. Add the water chestnuts and stir to incorporate. The filling may be refrigerated or frozen at this stage.

4 To continue, top each lettuce leaf with about 1 cup of the meat mixture. Garnish with the red pepper, scallion greens, and peanuts.

TO REFRIGERATE AND SERVE

Pack the beef-tofu mixture, peanuts, chopped peppers, and scallion into separate airtight containers where they will keep for up to 3 days.

Reheat the beef-tofu mixture in a pot, covered, over low heat, stirring occasionally, for 5 to 20 minutes, depending on the amount. Add 1 to 2 tablespoons of water if the pan appears dry. Alternatively, place in a microwave-safe dish, cover with a splatter guard, and microwave for about 40 seconds for one serving. Then follow the "to continue" directions in the recipe.

TO FREEZE AND SERVE

Chill the filling in the refrigerator for 30 minutes, then transfer it to sealable freezer bags in the portions desired and freeze for up to 3 months.

Allow to thaw in the refrigerator for 18 to 24 hours, then reheat as above, or place in a microwave-safe container, cover with a splatter guard, and microwave on the defrost setting for 2 to 3 minutes and then on high for 40 seconds, for one serving. Continue with the freshly prepared "for serving" ingredients.

∗ **Serving size:** ⅔ cup filling and 2 large or 4 small lettuce leaves; **Per serving:** Calories 330; Total Fat 18g (Mono Fat 7.1g, Poly Fat 5.2g, Sat Fat 3.6g); Protein 25g; Carb 15g; Fiber 3g; Cholesterol 45mg, Sodium 430mg, **Excellent source of:** Iron, Manganese, Niacin, Protein, Potassium, Selenium, Vitamin A, Vitamin B6, Vitamin B12, Vitamin C, Vitamin K, Potassium, Zinc; **Good source of:** Copper, Fiber, Folate, Magnesium, Phosphorus, Riboflavin, Thiamin

Sunday Sauce Beef Stew · MAKES 8 SERVINGS ·

MY ITALIAN NEIGHBORS GROWING UP called the long-cooking, Chianti-infused, meaty tomato sauce they served for dinner after church each week, Sunday sauce. This dish takes the flavor and spirit of that sauce, and adds extra chunks of lean, tender beef, as well as mushrooms and carrot coins, turning it into a true comfort food stew. I like to serve it in big bowls with a hunk of crusty whole-grain bread, or over farro, on Sunday, or any day.

2 POUNDS LEAN STEW BEEF (SUCH AS ROUND OR CHUCK SHOULDER), CUT INTO 1½-INCH CUBES

½ TEASPOON SALT

¼ TEASPOON FRESHLY GROUND BLACK PEPPER

3 TABLESPOONS OLIVE OIL, DIVIDED

1 JUMBO ONION, CHOPPED

8 OUNCES WHITE BUTTON MUSHROOMS, QUARTERED

4 CLOVES GARLIC, MINCED

1 CUP DRY RED WINE, SUCH AS CHIANTI

2 TABLESPOONS TOMATO PASTE

2 TEASPOONS DRIED OREGANO

2 TEASPOONS DRIED BASIL

½ TEASPOON DRIED ROSEMARY

¼ TEASPOON CRUSHED RED PEPPER FLAKES

ONE 28-OUNCE CAN NO-SALT-ADDED DICED TOMATOES

ONE 15-OUNCE CAN NO-SALT-ADDED TOMATO SAUCE

1 POUND CARROTS, CUT INTO ¼-INCH-THICK COINS

FOR SERVING:

CHOPPED FRESH ITALIAN PARSLEY LEAVES, OPTIONAL

1 Season the meat with the salt and pepper. Heat 1½ tablespoons of the oil in a large (6-quart) pot over medium-high heat. Add half the meat and cook, turning once, until browned, 5 to 6 minutes. Transfer the browned meat to a plate, then add the remaining 1½ tablespoons oil and repeat with the remaining meat.

2 Add the onion and cook, stirring, until translucent, 6 to 7 minutes. Add the mushrooms and cook, stirring, until they have released their liquid, about 5 minutes. Add the garlic and cook, stirring, 1 minute more.

3 Add the wine and cook, scraping the bottom of pan to release any brown bits, until the wine is mostly evaporated, 4 to 5 minutes. Stir in the tomato paste, oregano, basil, rosemary, and crushed red pepper flakes and cook, stirring, for 2 minutes. Add the diced tomatoes with their juices, tomato sauce, and carrots and bring to a boil over high heat, then decrease the heat to low, cover, and simmer until the meat is tender, about 2 hours.

4 Serve in bowls topped with a sprinkle of fresh parsley over cooked pasta or farro, or with a hunk of whole-grain Italian bread.

TO REFRIGERATE AND REHEAT

Transfer the stew to an airtight container and refrigerate for up to 4 days.

To reheat, place in a saucepan over medium-low heat, cover, and cook, stirring occasionally, until warmed through, 8 to 25 minutes, depending on the amount. Alternatively, place in a microwave-safe bowl, cover with a splatter guard, and microwave on full power for about 2 minutes for a single portion.

TO FREEZE AND REHEAT

Chill in the refrigerator for 30 minutes. Transfer the stew to sealable plastic freezer bags in the portions desired and freeze for up to 3 months.

Thaw in the refrigerator for 24 to 36 hours and reheat as above. Or, to thaw quickly, run the bag under hot water for 30 seconds to release the stew from the bag, then transfer it to a pot along with 1 to 2 tablespoons of water per portion. Cover and cook over medium-low heat, stirring occasionally, until warmed through, 10 to 40 minutes, depending on the number of portions being thawed. Add more water to the pot if the bottom is getting dry.

Alternatively, after running the bag under hot water, transfer the stew to a microwave-safe bowl, cover with a splatter guard, and microwave on the defrost setting for about 7 minutes, then heat through on full power for 2 minutes for a single portion.

---

* **Serving size:** 1¼ cups; **Per serving:** Calories 410; Total Fat 23g (Mono Fat 11.5g, Poly Fat 1.3g, Sat Fat 7.9g); Protein 25g; Carb 19g; Fiber 4g; Cholesterol 75mg; Sodium 280mg; **Excellent source of:** Iron, Phosphorus, Potassium, Protein, Riboflavin, Selenium, Vitamin A, Vitamin B6, Vitamin B12, Vitamin C, Vitamin K, Zinc; **Good source of:** Fiber, Copper, Magnesium, Manganese, Pantothenic Acid, Thiamin

Tapas-Style Meatballs · MAKES 8 SERVINGS ·

A LITTLE WINE AND TAPAS bar with a bright red awning on the Upper West Side of Manhattan has become a favorite local spot for my husband, Thom, and me. One of the dishes we always get there is "albondigas," little meatballs simmered in a garlicky, smoked paprika-infused tomato sauce. They are satisfying but tender and light, just like these, which are made with lean beef and homemade whole-grain bread crumbs. With a salad and some bread they are a lovely light supper, but they are also a fabulous party food that you can eat with a toothpick. I am always glad to have some in my freezer to thaw quickly and serve to pop-in guests.

1 SMALL SLICE WHOLE-GRAIN SANDWICH BREAD (1 OUNCE)

1½ POUNDS LEAN GROUND BEEF

1 LARGE ONION, FINELY DICED, DIVIDED

6 CLOVES GARLIC, FINELY MINCED, DIVIDED

1 LARGE EGG

1 LARGE EGG WHITE

2 TABLESPOONS FINELY CHOPPED FRESH ITALIAN PARSLEY LEAVES

2 TEASPOONS SMOKED PAPRIKA, DIVIDED

1½ TEASPOONS SALT, DIVIDED

½ TEASPOON FRESHLY GROUND BLACK PEPPER, DIVIDED

3 TABLESPOONS OLIVE OIL

THREE 8-OUNCE CANS NO-SALT-ADDED TOMATO SAUCE

1 TABLESPOON SHERRY VINEGAR

1 Place the bread in the small bowl of a food processor and process until fine crumbs form. You should wind up with about ½ cup of crumbs. Transfer to a large bowl and add the beef, half the onion, half the garlic, the egg, egg white, parsley, 1 teaspoon of the smoked paprika, ½ teaspoon of the salt, and ¼ teaspoon of the pepper and mix to combine. Form into small meatballs (about 1-inch in diameter).

2 Heat the oil in a medium saucepan over medium-high heat. Add the remaining onion and cook, stirring, until lightly golden, 7 to 8 minutes. Add the remaining garlic and cook, stirring, 1 additional minute. Add the tomato sauce, vinegar, remaining 1 teaspoon each paprika and salt, and remaining ¼ teaspoon pepper and bring to a simmer. Gently add the meatballs and cook, uncovered, until cooked through and tender, 30 minutes.

Recipe continues

TO REFRIGERATE AND REHEAT

Place in an airtight container and refrigerate for up to 4 days.

To reheat, ladle the amount to be warmed into a saucepan, cover, and heat over medium-low heat, stirring occasionally, for 8 to 25 minutes, depending on the amount. Add 1 to 2 tablespoons of water if the pan seems dry. Alternatively, place in a microwave-safe bowl, cover with a splatter guard, and microwave on high for about 90 seconds for one portion.

TO FREEZE AND REHEAT

Chill in the refrigerator for 30 minutes, then divide into sealable plastic freezer bags in the portions desired.

Thaw in the refrigerator for 24 to 36 hours. Or to thaw quickly, run the bag under hot water for 30 seconds to release the food from the bag. Then place it in a saucepan, with 1 to 2 tablespoons of water per portion, cover, and heat over medium-low heat, breaking it up occasionally with a spoon until thawed and warmed through, 15 to 45 minutes, depending on the amount. Add more water as needed if the pan is getting dry.

Alternatively, after running the bag under water to release the food, place it into a microwave-safe bowl, cover with a splatter guard, and microwave on the defrost setting for 5 minutes, then on high for about 1 minute for a single portion.

＊**Serving size:** About 8 meatballs and 1 cup of sauce; **Per serving:** Calories 210; Total Fat 10g (Mono Fat 5.6g, Poly Fat 1g, Sat Fat 2.8g); Protein 19g; Carb 10g; Fiber 2g; Cholesterol 70mg; Sodium 520mg; **Excellent source of:** Niacin, Protein, Vitamin B6, Vitamin B12, Zinc; **Good source of:** Iron, Phosphorus, Potassium, Riboflavin, Vitamin C, Vitamin E

Tuscan Beef Pot Pie
with Olive Oil Crumble Crust · MAKES 6 SERVINGS ·

THIS RUSTIC POT PIE IS a bounty of beef and vegetables in a sumptuous gravy, just like you'd expect, but this one has the extraordinary taste of the Italian wine country, thanks to the addition of the nutty ancient grain farro, some red wine and rosemary, and a crumble crust made with fruity, fragrant olive oil.

1½ POUNDS LEAN ROUND OR CHUCK SHOULDER STEW BEEF, CUT INTO 1 × ½-INCH PIECES

1 TEASPOON SALT

½ TEASPOON FRESHLY GROUND BLACK PEPPER

2½ TABLESPOONS OLIVE OIL

1¼ CUPS FROZEN, PEELED PEARL ONIONS, THAWED AND PATTED DRY (7 OUNCES)

5 MEDIUM CARROTS, SLICED INTO COINS

3 CLOVES GARLIC, MINCED

3 TABLESPOONS WHOLE-WHEAT PASTRY FLOUR OR ALL-PURPOSE FLOUR

1½ TABLESPOONS FINELY CHOPPED FRESH ROSEMARY

1 CUP DRY RED WINE, SUCH AS CHIANTI

3 CUPS LOW-SODIUM BEEF BROTH

ONE 10-OUNCE BOX FROZEN PEAS (2 CUPS)

1 CUP COOKED FARRO (SEE GRAIN FREEZE, PAGE 149)

1 RECIPE MELT-IN-YOUR-MOUTH, NO-ROLL OLIVE OIL PIE CRUST, PAGE 35, DOUGH ONLY, UNBAKED

1 Toss the beef with the salt and pepper. Heat the oil in a large pot over medium-high heat and brown the beef in 2 batches, turning once or twice, about 3 to 5 minutes per batch. Transfer to a plate as browned.

2 Lower the heat to medium, add the onions, and cook, stirring, until golden brown, about 6 minutes. Add the carrots and cook, stirring, 3 minutes more. Stir in the garlic, flour, and rosemary and cook, stirring constantly, for 1 minute more.

3 While stirring, pour in the wine and then the broth in a slow stream and bring to a boil. Return the beef to the pot. Cover and simmer, stirring occasionally, until the beef is tender, about 1½ to 2 hours. Stir in the peas and the farro. The beef mixture may be refrigerated at this stage.

4 To continue, divide the mixture among 6 (1½- to 2-cup) capacity baking dishes or crocks. Divide the dough into 6 rounds, place on a clean work surface and, using the heel of your hand, press each ball out to flatten it as thinly as possible. Tear flake-like pieces of the dough, using one round per dish, and arrange on top of the beef mixture to make a rustic, flaky, crumble-like crust. The pot pies may be frozen at this stage.

5 Preheat the oven to 400°F. Bake the pot pies in the middle of the oven until the mixture is bubbling and the crust is golden brown, 20 to 30 minutes. Let cool slightly before serving.

Recipe continues

TO REFRIGERATE AND SERVE

The beef mixture may be made ahead and refrigerated in an airtight container for up to 4 days. When ready to cook follow the "to continue" directions in the recipe, adding 5 minutes to the cooking time for a total of 25 to 35 minutes.

TO FREEZE AND SERVE

Chill the unbaked pies, uncovered, in the refrigerator for 30 minutes, then cover tightly with an airtight lid or with plastic wrap and then foil. Freeze for up to 3 months.

When ready to serve, uncover the pies completely and place in a cold oven set for 400°F. Once the oven comes to temperature, continue to cook for 40 minutes, until the mixture is bubbling and the crust is golden brown. Let cool slightly before serving.

Microwave heating is not recommended.

GRAIN FREEZE

Cooked grains freeze very well, and are better when reheated from frozen than from refrigerated. Having them on hand can make it easy to get a healthy meal on the table fast. Here are the how-tos:

TO COOK AND FREEZE:

* Cook the grain (rice, farro, wheat berries, barley, bulgur) according to the package directions.

* Once cooked, uncover and allow to cool just long enough for it to stop steaming, about 10 minutes.

* Divide the still-hot grain into 1 cup portions and place into sealable freezer bags, removing as much air as possible.

* Store in the freezer for up to 3 months.

TO THAW AND HEAT (PER 1 CUP BAG OF GRAIN):

* Run the bag under hot water for 30 seconds to release the frozen grain from the bag.

* Place in a small pot with 2 tablespoons of water, cover, and heat over low heat, turning once or twice, until it is thawed and warmed through, 15 minutes. (Use a larger pot and more water, 2 tablespoons per cup of grain, and allow more time if reheating more than one bag at a time.)

OR

* Once released from the bag, place in a microwave-safe dish, cover tightly with plastic wrap, leaving just a small vent hole and microwave on high for 2½ minutes, for 1 cup of grain.

* Fluff with a fork and serve.

Beef Picadillo • MAKES 6 SERVINGS •

THIS GROUND BEEF SKILLET DISH is what I imagine taco filling aspires to be. It has the same savory, moist, ground beef and cumin-garlic scented flavor, but it is layered with warm spices (cinnamon and cloves) and a trio of raisins, olives, and pine nuts gives it a sweet-salty-nuttiness that makes it officially heavenly. Like taco filling, you can eat it with corn tortillas or with baked tortilla chips, serve it with rice, or over a salad.

- 1 TABLESPOON CANOLA OIL, OR OTHER NEUTRAL TASTING OIL
- 1 POUND LEAN GROUND BEEF
- 2 MEDIUM ONIONS, FINELY CHOPPED
- 4 CLOVES GARLIC, MINCED
- 2 TEASPOONS GROUND CUMIN
- ¾ TEASPOON SALT
- ½ TEASPOON DRIED OREGANO
- ¼ TEASPOON GROUND CINNAMON
- ⅛ TEASPOON GROUND CLOVES
- ONE 14.5-OUNCE CAN CRUSHED TOMATOES
- 1 CUP LOW-SODIUM BEEF BROTH
- ⅓ CUP RAISINS, CHOPPED
- ¼ CUP PINE NUTS, TOASTED
- ONE 15-OUNCE CAN NO-SALT-ADDED BLACK BEANS, DRAINED AND RINSED
- ½ CUP PIMIENTO STUFFED GREEN OLIVES, CHOPPED
- ⅓ CUP CHOPPED FRESH CILANTRO

1 Heat the oil in a large deep skillet over medium-high heat. Cook the beef, stirring to break up clumps, until browned, about 5 minutes. Transfer the meat with a slotted spoon to a bowl, leaving the juices in the pan.

2 Add the onions, lower the heat to medium, and cook, stirring, until softened, about 4 minutes. Add the garlic, cumin, salt, oregano, cinnamon, and cloves and cook, stirring, 1 minute more. Stir in the tomatoes with their juices, broth, and raisins and return the browned beef to the pan. Bring to a boil, then lower the heat to medium-low and simmer, stirring occasionally, until the liquid is reduced and the mixture is somewhat thickened, about 8 minutes.

3 Meanwhile, toast the pine nuts in a dry skillet over medium-high heat, stirring frequently, until fragrant and golden brown, 3 to 5 minutes.

4 Stir the beans, olives, and cilantro into the beef mixture and cook until heated through, for 2 to 3 minutes more. Stir in the pine nuts.

TO REFRIGERATE AND REHEAT

Place in an airtight container in the refrigerator for up to 4 days.

To reheat, place in a saucepan, cover, and warm over low heat, stirring occasionally, until warmed through, 5 to 15 minutes, depending on the amount being reheated. Add a few tablespoons of water if needed to loosen. Alternatively, place in a microwave-safe bowl, cover with a splatter guard, and microwave for about 60 seconds for one portion.

TO FREEZE AND REHEAT

Allow to cool in the refrigerator for 30 minutes, then place in sealable freezer bags in the quantities desired.

Thaw in the refrigerator for 18 to 24 hours, then reheat following the "to refrigerate" directions. Or, to thaw quickly, run hot water over the bag for 30 seconds to release the food, then place in a covered saucepan on the stove with about 1 tablespoon water per portion, and warm over medium-low heat, stirring occasionally and breaking the mixture up with a spoon, for 12 to 40 minutes, depending on the amount. Alternatively, after releasing from the bag, place in a microwave-safe dish and microwave on the defrost setting for 4 minutes and then on high for 2 minutes for one portion.

---

* **Serving size:** about 1 cup; **Per serving:** Calories 330; Total Fat 16g (Mono Fat 5.8g, Poly Fat 2.9g, Sat Fat 3.6g); Protein 22g; Carb 27g; Fiber 6g; Cholesterol 50mg; Sodium 630mg; **Excellent source of:** Fiber, Iron, Niacin, Phosphorus, Protein, Vitamin B12, Zinc; **Good source of:** Magnesium, Potassium, Riboflavin, Vitamin C, Vitamin B6

Lamb and Bulgur Stuffed Zucchini

• MAKES 4 SERVINGS •

IN THIS EASTERN MEDITERRANEAN INSPIRED dish, rich lamb and nutty bulgur are paired with aromatic spices, raisins, parsley, and pine nuts, then packed into fresh zucchini boats and baked in a simple but savory tomato sauce until the vegetable has softened and the flavors have melded.

The zucchini itself doesn't freeze well, but the stuffing does, so you can make that ahead to be thawed and piled into freshly scooped zucchini when you want to serve it. The stuffed zucchini will keep in the refrigerator before and after baking.

- 3 TABLESPOONS PINE NUTS
- 1 TABLESPOON OLIVE OIL
- 1 SMALL ONION, CHOPPED
- 3 CLOVES GARLIC, MINCED
- ½ POUND GROUND LAMB
- 2 TEASPOONS GROUND CUMIN
- 1 TEASPOON GROUND CORIANDER
- ¼ TEASPOON CRUSHED RED PEPPER FLAKES
- ONE 14.5-OUNCE CAN NO-SALT-ADDED DICED TOMATOES, JUICES STRAINED
- 1 CUP COOKED BULGUR (⅓ CUP UNCOOKED)
- ¼ CUP CHOPPED FRESH ITALIAN PARSLEY LEAVES
- 2 TABLESPOONS CHOPPED RAISINS
- ½ TEASPOON SALT
- ¼ TEASPOON FRESHLY GROUND BLACK PEPPER

FOR SERVING:

- 4 MEDIUM ZUCCHINI (ABOUT 8 OUNCES EACH)
- ½ TEASPOON SALT
- ONE 15-OUNCE CAN NO-SALT-ADDED TOMATO SAUCE

1 Toast the pine nuts in a dry skillet over medium-high heat, stirring frequently, until lightly browned and fragrant, 2 to 3 minutes.

2 Heat the oil in a heavy skillet over medium-high heat. Add the onion and cook, stirring, until soft and translucent, about 3 minutes. Add the garlic and cook, stirring, for 30 seconds more. Add the ground lamb, cumin, coriander, and red pepper flakes and cook, stirring and breaking the meat up with a spoon until it is in small pieces and no longer pink, 4 to 5 minutes. Remove from the heat. Add the diced tomatoes, bulgur, parsley, pine nuts, raisins, salt, and pepper, and stir to combine. The filling may be refrigerated or frozen at this stage.

3 To serve, cut each zucchini in half lengthwise. Use a small spoon or melon baller to scoop out the seeds and some of the flesh, leaving about ¼-inch thick zucchini boats. Using a small spoon or your hands, stuff the zucchini halves generously with the lamb mixture. Stir the salt into the tomato sauce and spread the sauce on the bottom of a 9 × 13-inch baking dish. Place the stuffed zucchini into the dish and cover tightly with foil. The stuffed zucchini may be refrigerated at this stage.

4 To continue, preheat the oven to 375°F, then bake, covered, until the zucchini is tender and the stuffing is warmed through, about 40 minutes. Serve drizzled with the sauce.

Before baking:

TO REFRIGERATE THE STUFFED ZUCCHINI OR THE FILLING

Stuffed, prebaked zucchini, or the filling alone, may be stored in the refrigerator for up to 4 days. When ready to serve, bake the stuffed zucchini, covered, in a 375°F oven until the zucchini is tender and the filling is warmed through, 55 to 65 minutes.

TO FREEZE THE FILLING

Chill the filling in the refrigerator for 30 minutes, then place it in a sealable plastic bag and freeze for up to 3 months.

Thaw in the refrigerator for 18 to 24 hours, or to thaw quickly, run the bag under hot water to release the food, then transfer it to a microwave-safe bowl and microwave on the defrost setting for about 20 minutes. Then follow the "to serve" instructions in the recipe.

Once baked:

TO REFRIGERATE AND REHEAT THE STUFFED ZUCCHINI

Cover tightly and refrigerate for up to 4 days.

To reheat, cover with foil and place in a 375°F oven for 30 to 45 minutes. To reheat in the microwave, place on a microwave-safe plate, cover with a splatter guard, and microwave on high for about 2 minutes for one portion.

Freezing the zucchini before or after baking is not recommended.

＊ **Serving size:** 2 stuffed zucchini halves; **Per serving:** Calories 330; Total Fat 20g (Mono Fat 8.2g, Poly Fat 3.3g, Sat Fat 6.5g); Protein 15g; Carb 27g; Fiber 4g; Cholesterol 40mg; Sodium 650mg; **Excellent source of:** Manganese, Protein, Vitamin A, Vitamin C, Vitamin K; **Good source of:** Fiber, Copper, Iron, Magnesium, Phosphorus, Potassium, Vitamin B6, Vitamin E

Savory Lamb and Chickpea Stew • MAKES 8 SERVINGS •

THIS SUMPTUOUS STEW HAS A double dose of heartiness from both tender chunks of lamb and meaty chickpeas, which are married in a thick, fragrant tomato sauce laced with fresh spinach. I can't think of a tastier way to find fulfillment on a cold winter's evening.

- 2 POUNDS BONELESS LAMB STEW MEAT, CUT INTO 1-INCH CUBES
- 1½ TEASPOONS SALT, DIVIDED
- ½ TEASPOON FRESHLY GROUND BLACK PEPPER, DIVIDED
- 3 TABLESPOONS OLIVE OIL, DIVIDED
- 1 VERY LARGE ONION (1 POUND), CHOPPED
- 4 CLOVES GARLIC, MINCED
- 1 TEASPOON GROUND CUMIN
- ½ TEASPOON GROUND CORIANDER
- ¼ TEASPOON CRUSHED RED PEPPER FLAKES
- ONE 15-OUNCE CAN NO-SALT-ADDED TOMATO SAUCE
- ONE 15-OUNCE CAN NO-SALT-ADDED DICED TOMATOES
- TWO 15-OUNCE LOW-SODIUM CHICKPEAS, DRAINED AND RINSED
- 4 CUPS LIGHTLY PACKED, CHOPPED FRESH SPINACH

1 Season the meat with ½ teaspoon of the salt and ¼ teaspoon of the pepper. Heat 1 tablespoon of the oil in a wide-bottomed, 6-quart pot over medium-high heat. Add half of the meat and cook, turning once, until browned, 5 to 6 minutes total. Transfer the meat to a plate, then repeat with an additional 1 tablespoon of the oil and the rest of the meat, transferring it to the plate when it is browned.

2 Add the remaining 1 tablespoon oil to the pot, then add the onion and cook, stirring, until translucent, 6 to 7 minutes. Add the garlic, cumin, remaining 1 teaspoon of salt, the coriander, crushed red pepper flakes, and the remaining ¼ teaspoon pepper and cook, stirring, 1 minute more. Return the meat to the pan along with any accumulated juices and add the tomato sauce, diced tomatoes with their juices, and chickpeas and bring to a boil. Lower the heat to low, cover, and simmer until the lamb is tender, 90 minutes to 2 hours. Stir in the spinach and cook until it is wilted, 1 minute.

Recipe continues

TO REFRIGERATE AND REHEAT

Transfer the stew to an airtight container and refrigerate for up to 4 days.

To reheat, place in a saucepan over medium-low heat, cover, and cook, stirring occasionally, until warmed through, 8 to 25 minutes, depending on the amount. Alternatively, place in a microwave-safe bowl, cover with a splatter guard, and microwave on full power for about 90 seconds to 2 minutes for a single portion.

TO FREEZE AND REHEAT

Chill in the refrigerator for 30 minutes. Transfer to sealable plastic freezer bags in the portions desired, and freeze for up to 4 months.

Thaw in the refrigerator for 24 to 36 hours and reheat as above. Or, to thaw quickly, run the bag under hot water for 30 seconds to release the stew from the bag, then transfer it to a pot along with 1 to 2 tablespoons of water per portion. Cover and cook over medium-low heat, stirring occasionally, until warmed through, 15 to 45 minutes, depending on the number of portions being thawed. Add more water to the pot if the bottom is getting dry.

Alternatively, after running the bag under hot water, transfer the stew to a microwave-safe bowl, cover with a splatter guard, and microwave on the defrost setting for about 7 minutes, then heat through on full power for 90 seconds to 2 minutes for a single portion.

∗ **Serving size:** About 1⅓ cups; **Per serving:** Calories 360; Total Fat 12g (Mono Fat 6.1g, Poly Fat 1.2g, Sat Fat 2.9g); Protein 31g; Carb 31g; Fiber 7g; Cholesterol 75mg; Sodium 560mg; **Excellent source of:** Copper, Fiber, Iron, Magnesium, Niacin, Phosphorus, Potassium, Protein, Riboflavin, Selenium, Vitamin A, Vitamin C, Vitamin B12, Vitamin K, Zinc; **Good source of:** Folate, Manganese, Pantothenic Acid, Thiamin, Vitamin B6, Vitamin E

Jerk Pork Loin
with Mango Cucumber Salsa
• MAKES 6 SERVINGS •

THIS JERK-MARINATED PORK HAS LOTS of island flavor and just enough heat, which is offset by the cool, fruity salsa to serve alongside it.

The make-ahead idea here is that you can marinate the pork in the refrigerator for a couple of days, or in the freezer for months, so all you need to do when you want it is thaw if frozen, and pop it in the oven. Any leftover cooked meat can also be reheated or served at room temperature as part of a cold plate, or in sandwiches.

1 SMALL ONION, ROUGHLY CHOPPED

⅓ CUP WHITE VINEGAR

3 TABLESPOONS CANOLA OIL, OR OTHER NEUTRAL TASTING OIL

8 CLOVES GARLIC

1 MEDIUM JALAPEÑO PEPPER, TOP TRIMMED, WITH SEEDS

2 TEASPOONS DRIED THYME

1 TEASPOON GROUND ALLSPICE

1 TEASPOON GROUND NUTMEG

½ TEASPOON GROUND CLOVES

¼ TEASPOON FRESHLY GROUND BLACK PEPPER

ONE 2-POUND PORK LOIN

1 BAY LEAF

FOR SERVING:

1 RECIPE MANGO CUCUMBER SALSA (RECIPE FOLLOWS)

1 Place the onion, vinegar, oil, garlic, jalapeño pepper, thyme, all-spice, nutmeg, cloves, and black pepper into a food processor and process until smooth.

2 Place the pork into a large (2-gallon) sealable plastic bag. Add the marinade and bay leaf, toss to coat, and seal the bag, removing as much air as possible. Place in the refrigerator for up to 2 days or freeze for up to 2 months. Thaw in the refrigerator for 36 to 48 hours to be ready to cook.

3 To continue, preheat the oven to 400°F. Drain the liquid from the bag, maintaining any marinade solids but discarding the bay leaf. Transfer the pork to a roasting pan and rub the solids onto the surface of the pork. Roast until the internal temperature reaches 145°F for medium rare, about 45 minutes, or 160°F for medium, about 1 hour.

4 Allow to rest at room temperature for 15 minutes before slicing into ¼-inch-thick slices. Serve with the Mango Cucumber Salsa.

Recipe continues

TO REFRIGERATE AND REHEAT

Once cooked and sliced, the meat will keep in an airtight container in the refrigerator for up to 3 days.

Serve at room temperature, or to reheat, wrap in foil and place in a 350°F oven for about 10 to 15 minutes. Alternatively, place on a microwave-safe plate, cover with a splatter guard, and microwave for about 30 seconds per portion.

TO FREEZE AND REHEAT

If the pork has been marinated in the freezer, refreezing is not recommended.

Otherwise, to freeze the cooked pork, slice and wrap in individual portions in plastic wrap or foil, place in a sealable plastic bag, and freeze for up to 3 months.

Thaw in the refrigerator for 24 to 36 hours, then reheat following the "to refrigerate" directions. Or, to thaw more quickly, unwrap the quantity desired, wrap in foil, and place in a cold oven set to 350°F. Once the oven has reached temperature, continue to cook for about 25 minutes, until warmed through. Alternatively, unwrap, place on a microwave-safe plate, cover with a splatter guard, and microwave on the defrost setting for 3 minutes, then continue to heat through on high for about 30 seconds for a single portion.

❋ **Serving size:** 3 to 4 slices; **Per serving:** Calories 260; Total Fat 10g (Mono Fat 5.7g, Poly Fat 2.6g, Sat Fat 1.6g); Protein 33g; Carb 9g; Fiber 1g; Cholesterol 100mg; Sodium 180mg; **Excellent source of:** Niacin, Phosphorus, Potassium, Protein, Riboflavin, Selenium, Thiamin, Vitamin B6, Vitamin C, Zinc; **Good source of:** Copper, Magnesium, Pantothenic Acid, Vitamin B12, Vitamin K

MANGO CUCUMBER SALSA • MAKES 6 SERVINGS •

THIS COOL, FRUITY SALSA NOT only goes with the Jerk Pork Loin above, it's great with just about any grilled or roasted protein that has a spicy kick to it. You can also add some chopped jalapeño and serve it alongside more simply seasoned chicken, pork, or shrimp, or put it out as a dip with chips or vegetables.

1 CUP FINELY DICED MANGO

1 CUP FINELY DICED, SEEDED ENGLISH CUCUMBER

3 TABLESPOONS FINELY DICED RED ONION

1½ TABLESPOONS FRESH LIME JUICE

¼ TEASPOON SALT

⅛ TEASPOON FRESHLY GROUND BLACK PEPPER

FOR SERVING:

2 TABLESPOONS FRESH CILANTRO LEAVES

FRESH LIME JUICE TO TASTE, OPTIONAL

In a medium bowl, toss the mango, cucumber, onion, lime juice, salt, and pepper together to combine. The salsa may be made ahead at this stage. Toss the cilantro leaves in and additional lime juice to taste, right before serving.

TO REFRIGERATE

The salsa may be stored in an airtight container in the refrigerator for up to 3 days. Stir well before serving.

❋ **Serving size:** ⅓ cup; **Per serving:** Calories 25; Total Fat 0g (Mono Fat 0g, Poly Fat 0g, Sat Fat 0g); Protein 0g; Carb 6g; Fiber 1g; Cholesterol 0mg; Sodium 100mg; **Excellent source of:** Vitamin C

Pork Tenderloin
with Creamy Pumpkin Seed–Tomatillo Sauce

• MAKES 6 SERVINGS •

THIS GLORIOUSLY GREEN SAUCE IS a Mexican *pepian*, which means it's made with pepitas, aka pumpkin seeds. Here they are whirred in the blender, for a luxuriously creamy effect, with tangy tomatillos; poblano and jalapeño peppers, which add lots of flavor and a little heat; aromatic garlic, cumin, and allspice; and a cool fresh burst of cilantro.

   You can make the sauce ahead and refrigerate or freeze it, to have it ready for simmering just-browned pork (as in this recipe) or, if you'd like, chicken breast. You could also turn it into a vegetarian meal by subbing vegetable broth or water for the chicken broth in the sauce, and simmering it with some white beans or tofu.

FOR THE SAUCE:

- 6 FRESH TOMATILLOS (ABOUT 1 POUND)
- 1 LARGE POBLANO PEPPER, SEEDED AND QUARTERED
- 2 TABLESPOONS CANOLA OIL OR OTHER NEUTRAL TASTING OIL, DIVIDED
- ½ CUP HULLED UNSALTED PUMPKIN SEEDS
- 5 PEPPERCORNS
- 2 WHOLE ALLSPICE
- ½ TEASPOON WHOLE CUMIN SEEDS
- 1 MEDIUM ONION, CHOPPED
- 4 CLOVES GARLIC, MINCED
- 1 CUP FRESH CILANTRO LEAVES
- 1 CUP LOW-SODIUM CHICKEN BROTH
- 1 MEDIUM JALAPEÑO PEPPER, SEEDED AND ROUGHLY CHOPPED
- ½ TEASPOON SALT

1 Preheat the broiler. Remove the papery outer layer from the tomatillos and rinse them in warm water. Pat dry and cut into quarters. Toss the tomatillos and poblano pepper with 1 tablespoon of the oil, place on a baking sheet, and broil on high 4 to 5 inches from the flame until charred and collapsed, stirring once or twice, about 10 minutes.

2 Meanwhile, heat a large skillet over medium heat. Add the pumpkin seeds, peppercorns, allspice, and cumin seeds and toast, stirring, until fragrant, 3 to 4 minutes. Transfer to a plate.

3 In the same pan, heat the remaining 1 tablespoon oil over medium heat. Add the onion and cook, stirring, until soft and translucent, about 3 minutes. Add the garlic and cook, stirring, for 30 seconds more.

4 Place the charred tomatillos and poblanos into a blender with the onion and garlic, cilantro, chicken broth, jalapeño, toasted seeds and spices, and salt into a blender and blend on high until smooth. The sauce may be refrigerated or frozen at this stage.

FOR SERVING:

- 2 MEDIUM PORK TENDERLOINS (2 POUNDS) SLICED INTO ½-INCH MEDALLIONS
- ¼ TEASPOON SALT
- ⅛ TEASPOON FRESHLY GROUND BLACK PEPPER
- 1 TABLESPOON CANOLA OIL, OR OTHER NEUTRAL TASTING OIL
- ¼ CUP COARSELY CHOPPED FRESH CILANTRO LEAVES
- 6 LIME WEDGES

5 To continue, season the pork with the salt and pepper. Heat the 1 tablespoon oil in a large skillet over high heat. Add half the pork and cook, turning once, until it is browned on both sides, 4 minutes total. Transfer the meat to a plate and repeat with the remaining pork. Return all the meat to the skillet and add the sauce. Bring to a low boil, then lower the heat to medium-low and cook until the pork is just blush in the center, about 3 minutes more. Serve the meat topped with the sauce, garnished with some cilantro and a wedge of lime.

Make the sauce ahead:

TO REFRIGERATE AND REHEAT

Place the sauce in an airtight container in the refrigerator for up to 4 days. When ready to cook, follow the "to continue" directions in the recipe, using half of the "for serving" ingredients to make half a batch.

TO FREEZE AND REHEAT

Place the full batch or separate half-batches of sauce into sealable freezer bags and freeze for up to 3 months.

Thaw in the refrigerator for 24 to 36 hours, or, to thaw quickly, run the bag(s) under hot water for 30 seconds to release, then place in a saucepan, cover, and cook over medium-low heat for 15 to 30 minutes, depending on the amount. Alternatively, once released from the bag, place the sauce in a microwave-safe bowl, cover with a splatter guard, and microwave on the defrost setting for 7 to 10 minutes, depending on the amount. Once thawed, continue to cook following the "to continue" directions in the recipe, using half the "for serving" ingredients for a half batch of sauce.

∗ **Serving size:** About 5 slices of pork and ½ cup sauce; **Per serving:** Calories 330; Total Fat 16g (Mono Fat 7.5g, Poly Fat 5.1g, Sat Fat 2.6g); Protein 36g; Carb 9g; Fiber 3g; Cholesterol 100mg; Sodium 390mg; **Excellent source of:** Magnesium, Manganese, Niacin, Phosphorus, Potassium, Protein, Riboflavin, Selenium, Thiamin, Vitamin B6, Vitamin C, Vitamin K, Zinc; **Good source of:** Copper, Fiber, Iron, Pantothenic Acid, Vitamin A, Vitamin B12, Vitamin E

Pork Tenderloin
with Mustard-Apricot Sauce

HERE, PORK IS PAIRED WITH its old-world flavor accompaniments—mustard, herbs, and fruit—in a fresh, modern way, with simmer sauce that can be made ahead and simply poured over the browned meat in the skillet at dinnertime. The quick-cooking, lean pork tenderloin in a sauce of tangy whole-grain mustard, dried apricots, sweet, earthy root vegetables, and fresh apple cider makes for a deeply delicious meal that's convenient and healthy too.

FOR THE SAUCE:

- 1 TABLESPOON OLIVE OIL
- 1 SMALL ONION, CHOPPED
- 1 STALK CELERY, CHOPPED
- 1 MEDIUM CARROT, CHOPPED
- 1 MEDIUM PARSNIP, CHOPPED
- ¼ TEASPOON SALT
- ¼ TEASPOON FRESHLY GROUND BLACK PEPPER
- 1 LARGE CLOVE GARLIC, MINCED
- 1 TABLESPOON CHOPPED FRESH SAGE OR THYME
- 1 BAY LEAF
- 1½ TABLESPOONS ALL-PURPOSE FLOUR
- 1¼ CUPS LOW-SODIUM CHICKEN BROTH
- ¾ CUP APPLE CIDER (NOT APPLE JUICE)
- ¼ CUP DRIED APRICOTS, CHOPPED
- 1 TABLESPOON WHOLE-GRAIN MUSTARD

FOR SERVING:

- TWO ¾-POUND PORK TENDERLOINS, TRIMMED OF FAT, SLICED INTO ½-INCH MEDALLIONS
- ¼ TEASPOON SALT
- ¼ TEASPOON FRESHLY GROUND BLACK PEPPER
- 1 TABLESPOON OLIVE OIL

1 To make the sauce, heat the oil in a large saucepan over medium heat. Add the onion, celery, carrot, parsnip, ¼ teaspoon each salt and pepper and cook, stirring occasionally, until the vegetables are softened, about 8 minutes. Add the garlic, sage or thyme, and bay leaf and cook, stirring, 1 minute.

2 Add the flour and cook, stirring constantly, for 1 minute. Then, stirring all the while, add the broth in a slow stream and then the apple cider, stirring until the flour is incorporated completely. Add the apricots and mustard and simmer until thickened, 4 to 6 minutes. Remove the pot from the heat and discard the bay leaf. You can refrigerate or freeze the sauce at this stage.

3 To continue, season the pork with the ¼ teaspoon salt and ¼ teaspoon pepper. Heat the 1 tablespoon oil in a large skillet over high heat. Add half the pork and cook, turning once, until it is browned on both sides, 4 minutes total. Transfer the meat to a plate and repeat with the remaining pork. Return all the meat to the skillet and add the sauce. Bring to a simmer, lower the heat to medium-low, and cook until the pork is just blush in the center, about 3 minutes more.

Make the sauce ahead:

TO REFRIGERATE AND REHEAT

Place the sauce in an airtight container in the refrigerator for up to 4 days. When ready to cook, follow the "to continue" directions in the recipe, using half of the "for serving" ingredients if making a half-batch.

TO FREEZE AND REHEAT

Chill the sauce in the refrigerator for 30 minutes, then place the full batch or separate half-batches of sauce into sealable freezer bags and freeze for up to 3 months.

Thaw in the refrigerator for 24 to 36 hours, or, to thaw quickly, run the bag(s) under hot water for 30 seconds to release, then place in a saucepan, cover, and cook over medium-low heat for 15 to 30 minutes, depending on the amount. Alternatively, once released from the bag, place the sauce in a microwave-safe bowl, cover with a splatter guard, and microwave on the defrost setting for 7 to 10 minutes, depending on the amount. Once thawed, continue to cook following the "to continue" directions in the recipe, using half the "for serving" ingredients for a half-batch of sauce.

∗ **Serving size:** ½ cup sauce and about 5 pork medallions; **Per serving:** Calories 260; Total Fat 7g (Mono Fat 4.3g, Poly Fat 1g, Sat Fat 1.5g); Protein 26g; Carb 23g; Fiber 3g; Cholesterol 75mg; Sodium 390mg; **Excellent source of:** Niacin, Phosphorus, Riboflavin, Selenium, Thiamin, Vitamin A, Vitamin B6; **Good source of:** Iron, Magnesium, Pantothenic Acid, Potassium, Vitamin C, Zinc

Pulled Pork Tacos with Pineapple and Pickled Onions

• MAKES 10 SERVINGS •

PULLED PORK IS ONE OF those craveable, low-and-slow braised meats that you typically wouldn't count as healthy since it is made from the pork shoulder, a high-fat cut. But by refrigerating the meat and sauce before serving, you are able to skim off most of the fat, and allow the flavors to develop further, leaving you with a lean and luscious taco filling. Here it's piled on warm corn tortillas with pineapple, onion, red cabbage, fresh cilantro and lime. It's a perfect make-ahead meal for feeding a crowd, or for dividing up to have on hand for a couple of irresistible family meals.

FOR THE PORK:

1 (3½ POUNDS) BONELESS PORK SHOULDER, TRIMMED

1 TEASPOON SALT

1 TEASPOON FRESHLY GROUND BLACK PEPPER

1 TABLESPOON CANOLA OIL, OR OTHER NEUTRAL TASTING OIL

1 LARGE ONION, CHOPPED

¼ CUP CHILI POWDER

4 CLOVES GARLIC, MINCED

1 TEASPOON GROUND CUMIN

1 TEASPOON DRIED OREGANO

¼ TEASPOON CAYENNE PEPPER

ONE 14.5-OUNCE CAN NO-SALT-ADDED CRUSHED TOMATOES

FOR SERVING:

TWENTY 6-INCH CORN TORTILLAS

5 CUPS THINLY SLICED RED CABBAGE

1¼ CUPS FINELY DICED FRESH PINEAPPLE

¼ CUP CHOPPED FRESH CILANTRO

1 RECIPE PICKLED RED ONIONS (RECIPE FOLLOWS), OR 1 SMALL RED ONION, THINLY SLICED

LIME WEDGES

HOT SAUCE, OPTIONAL

1 Preheat the oven to 350°F.

2 Sprinkle the meat all over with the salt and black pepper. Heat the oil in a large heavy pot, such as a Dutch oven, over medium-high heat and brown the meat, turning two or three times, for 8 to 10 minutes total. Transfer the meat to a plate and pour off all the fat except for about 1 tablespoon.

3 Lower the heat to medium, add the onion, and cook, stirring occasionally, until softened, about 6 minutes. Add the chili powder, garlic, cumin, oregano, and cayenne pepper and cook, stirring, 1 minute more. Stir in the tomatoes with their juices and a half cup of water and return the meat to the pot. Bring to a boil, then cover and place in the oven. Cook until the meat is fork-tender, for 2½ to 3 hours.

4 Let the pork cool in the pot at room temperature for 30 minutes, then place the pot in the refrigerator for at least 8 hours or up to 4 days. Remove the pork from the pot, skim the fat that has solidified on the surface of the sauce, and discard. Shred the meat, return it to the pot, and stir it into the sauce to combine. The pork may be re-refrigerated or frozen at this stage. (Pork should not be refrigerated for more than 4 days total.)

Recipe continues

5 To continue, bring the pork to a simmer in a covered pot over medium heat and cook until warmed through. Cover and keep warm.

6 Warm the tortillas on a hot, ungreased griddle or directly over a gas burner, one at a time, for 30 seconds each, turning once. Alternatively, wrap the tortillas in a slightly damp paper towel and heat in the microwave for 30 to 40 seconds.

7 Pile each tortilla with about ⅓ cup of the pork, ¼ cup of the cabbage, 1 tablespoon of the pineapple, some of the cilantro, and a few of the onion slices. Serve with lime wedges alongside and hot sauce, if desired.

TO REFRIGERATE AND SERVE

The pulled pork will keep in the refrigerator, covered, for up to 4 days, if not previously stored. To reheat and serve, follow the "to continue" directions in the recipe. Alternatively, to reheat a single portion of the pork in the microwave, place in a microwave-safe dish, cover with a splatter guard, and microwave for 60 to 90 seconds.

TO FREEZE AND SERVE

Place the pulled pork in one or two batches into sealable freezer bags and freeze for up to 3 months. Thaw in the refrigerator for 24 to 36 hours, then follow the "to continue" instructions in the recipe.

To thaw quickly, run the bag under hot water for 30 seconds to release the pork from the bag, then transfer to a large pot. Add ¼ cup water, cover, and heat over medium-low heat, turning once or twice until thawed and warmed through, 20 to 40 minutes, depending on the amount. Because of the size of the batch, microwave thawing is not recommended.

✳ **Serving size:** 2 tacos; **Per serving:** Calories 400; Total Fat 9g (Mono Fat 3.7g, Poly Fat 2.1g, Sat Fat 2.1g); Protein 41g; Carb 39g; Fiber 7g; Cholesterol 95mg; Sodium 480mg; **Excellent source of:** Fiber, Magnesium, Niacin, Phosphorus, Potassium, Protein, Riboflavin, Thiamin, Vitamin A, Vitamin B12, Vitamin C, Zinc; **Good source of:** Calcium, Copper, Folate, Iron, Pantothenic Acid

PICKLED RED ONIONS • MAKES 1 CUP; 10 SERVINGS •

A QUICK VINEGAR-AND-HONEY PICKLE MELLOWS the onion's bite, and infuses it with a tangy sweetness that adds a bright punch of flavor to sandwiches, salads, tacos like the one above, and dishes like the Forbidden Rice Bowl, page 280.

⅓ CUP RED WINE VINEGAR

2 TEASPOONS HONEY

¾ CUP SLICED RED ONION

Stir together the vinegar and honey in a small bowl until combined well. Stir in the red onions and let stand, stirring occasionally, at least 20 minutes at room temperature, or for up to a week in the refrigerator.

✳ **Serving size:** 1½ tablespoons; **Per serving:** Calories 10; Total Fat 0g (Mono Fat 0g, Poly Fat 0g, Sat Fat 0g); Protein 0g; Carb 2g; Fiber 0g; Cholesterol 0mg; Sodium 0mg

Smoky Smothered Pork Chops

• MAKES 6 SERVINGS •

THIS DOWN-HOME DISH'S SMOKY AROMA lures you in even before you get a glimpse of the plump pork chops tucked into the creamy simmer sauce that's studded with savory red and green peppers and sweet onions. It gets its deep fire-roasted flavor from smoked paprika, which also lends it a stunning hue, along with crisped Canadian bacon.

FOR THE SAUCE:

- 1 TABLESPOON CANOLA OIL, OR OTHER NEUTRAL TASTING OIL
- 1 SMALL ONION, CHOPPED
- 2 SLICES CANADIAN BACON (2 OUNCES), CHOPPED
- 2 SMALL CLOVES GARLIC, MINCED
- ¾ TEASPOON SMOKED PAPRIKA
- ½ TEASPOON SALT
- ⅛ TEASPOON FRESHLY GROUND BLACK PEPPER
- 1 MEDIUM RED BELL PEPPER, SEEDED AND CHOPPED
- 1 MEDIUM GREEN BELL PEPPER, SEEDED AND CHOPPED
- 1 STALK CELERY, CHOPPED
- ½ TABLESPOON CHOPPED FRESH THYME OR ½ TEASPOON DRIED
- 2 TABLESPOONS WHOLE-WHEAT PASTRY FLOUR OR ALL-PURPOSE FLOUR
- 1¼ CUPS LOW-SODIUM CHICKEN BROTH

FOR SERVING:

- SIX 5-OUNCE CENTER-CUT BONELESS PORK LOIN CHOPS
- ¼ TEASPOON SALT
- ¼ TEASPOON FRESHLY GROUND BLACK PEPPER
- 1 TABLESPOON CANOLA OIL, OR OTHER NEUTRAL TASTING OIL

1 To make the sauce, heat the oil in a large skillet or saucepan over medium heat. Add the onion and Canadian bacon and cook, stirring occasionally, until the onion is translucent, 7 to 8 minutes. Add the garlic, paprika, salt, and pepper and cook, stirring, 30 seconds more. Add the red and green bell peppers, celery, and thyme and cook, stirring occasionally, until the vegetables are crisp-tender, 5 to 6 minutes. Sprinkle the flour over the vegetable mixture and cook, stirring, 2 minutes. Add the broth, and continue to stir as it comes to a simmer. Cook until the sauce thickens, 4 to 5 minutes. The sauce may be refrigerated or frozen at this stage.

2 To continue, season the pork chops with the salt and pepper. Heat the 1 tablespoon oil in a large skillet over medium-high heat. Add the pork chops and cook, turning once, until browned on both sides, about 3 minutes per side.

3 Pour the sauce over the chops, bring to a simmer, lower the heat to medium-low, and cook, turning once, until the chops are still slightly blush in the center and have reached an internal temperature of 145°F, about 6 minutes.

Recipe continues

Make the sauce ahead:

TO REFRIGERATE AND REHEAT

Place the sauce in an airtight container in the refrigerator for up to 4 days. When ready to cook, follow the "to continue" directions in the recipe. To make a partial batch, use 1 cup of sauce per 2 pork chops.

TO FREEZE AND REHEAT

Chill the sauce in the refrigerator for 30 minutes, then place the full batch, or divide into 1 cup portions, into sealable freezer bags and freeze for up to 3 months.

To thaw, place in the refrigerator for about 24 to 36 hours. Or run the bag(s) under hot water for 30 seconds to release, then place in a saucepan, cover, and cook over medium-low heat for 10 to 25 minutes, depending on the amount. Alternatively, once released from the bag, place into a microwave-safe bowl, cover with a splatter guard, and microwave on the defrost setting for about 6 minutes for one cup of sauce.

Once thawed, continue to cook following the "to continue" directions in the recipe. To make a partial batch, use 1 cup of sauce per 2 pork chops.

＊ **Serving Size:** 1 chop and ½ cup sauce; **Per serving:** Calories 240; Total Fat 8g (Mono Fat 4.2g, Poly Fat 1.9g, Sat Fat 1.5g); Protein 33g; Carb 6g; Fiber 2g; Cholesterol 95mg; Sodium 460mg; **Excellent source of:** Niacin, Phosphorus, Potassium, Protein, Riboflavin, Selenium, Thiamin, Vitamin B6, Vitamin C; **Good source of:** Iron, Magnesium, Manganese, Pantothenic Acid, Vitamin A, Vitamin B12, Zinc

Stout-Marinated Pork Chops · MAKES 6 SERVINGS ·

YOU WOULDN'T THINK TWICE ABOUT using wine in a marinade, so why not beer? It has a similar effect, tenderizing the meat with its gentle acidity and adding tremendous depth of flavor. Here, the bold taste of the stout is layered with maple-syrup sweetness, a tangy mustard punch, and piney fresh rosemary. Marinated for several hours in the fridge, or for months in the freezer, the pork becomes infused with these robust flavors that caramelize and come to life when they meet the flame. It's a perfect match for Sweet and Sour Red Cabbage with Caraway, page 326.

ONE 12-OUNCE BOTTLE STOUT BEER, SUCH AS GUINNESS STOUT

5 TABLESPOONS PURE MAPLE SYRUP

2 TABLESPOONS GRAINY MUSTARD

1 TABLESPOON CHOPPED FRESH ROSEMARY

3 LARGE CLOVES GARLIC, MINCED

1 TEASPOON SALT

½ TEASPOON FRESHLY GROUND BLACK PEPPER

SIX 8-OUNCE CENTER-CUT BONE-IN PORK LOIN CHOPS (ABOUT ¾-INCH THICK)

1 In a medium bowl or spouted measuring pitcher, whisk together the beer, maple syrup, mustard, rosemary, garlic, salt, and pepper.

2 Place the pork chops in sealable plastic freezer bags in the portions desired, and pour the marinade into the bag(s), dividing it evenly among them. Massage the bag to coat the pork in the marinade.

3 Marinate in the refrigerator for at least 4 hours or up to 1 day, or freeze the pork in the marinade for up to 2 months, then thaw in the refrigerator for 24 to 36 hours to be ready to serve.

4 To continue, preheat the broiler or grill. Remove the pork from the marinade, discarding the marinade. Broil on high 3-4 inches from the flame or grill the pork, turning once, until golden brown and cooked until it reaches an internal temperature of 145°F for medium-rare, or 160°F for medium, about 3 to 5 minutes per side.

TO REFRIGERATE AND REHEAT

The chops may be marinated in the refrigerator for up to 1 day before cooking. Once cooked, the chops may be stored in an airtight container in the refrigerator for up to 4 days.

To reheat cooked chops, cover with foil and place in a preheated 350°F oven for 10 to 12 minutes, or place on a microwave-safe plate and microwave on high for about 1 minute for one portion.

TO FREEZE AND REHEAT

If the pork has been marinated in the freezer, refreezing is not recommended.

Otherwise, to freeze the cooked pork, wrap each chop in plastic wrap or foil, place in a sealable plastic bag, and freeze for up to 3 months.

Thaw in the refrigerator for 24 to 36 hours, then reheat as above. Or, to thaw more quickly, unwrap the quantity desired, wrap in foil, and place in a cold oven set to 350°F. Once the oven has reached temperature, continue to cook for 25 minutes, until warmed through. Alternatively, unwrap, place on a microwave-safe plate, cover with a splatter guard, and microwave on the defrost setting for 4 minutes, then continue to heat through on high for 30 to 60 seconds for a single portion.

∗ **Serving size:** 1 chop; **Per serving:** Calories 370; Total Fat 9g (Mono Fat 3.1g, Poly Fat 1g, Sat Fat 2.5g); Protein 50g; Carb 16g; Fiber 0g; Cholesterol 155mg; Sodium 570mg; **Excellent source of:** Manganese, Niacin, Phosphorus, Potassium, Protein, Riboflavin, Selenium, Thiamin, Vitamin B6, Zinc; **Good source of:** Magnesium, Molybdenum, Pantothenic Acid, Vitamin B12

Hoppin' John Stew   • MAKES 8 SERVINGS •

THIS DISH OF RICE, BLACK-EYED peas, and greens laced with smoky pork is Southern comfort food that is said to bring good luck and prosperity when eaten on New Year's Day because the peas represent coins, and the collards or kale green, leafy dollar bills. This version also helps you kick off your healthy resolutions thanks to the lean Canadian bacon and brown rice used. And because it is so tasty, filling, and easy to make, it can help you stick to your resolutions throughout the year.

- 2 TABLESPOONS OLIVE OIL
- 4 SLICES CANADIAN BACON (4 OUNCES), CHOPPED
- 1 LARGE ONION, CHOPPED
- 2 STALKS CELERY, CHOPPED
- 1 MEDIUM GREEN BELL PEPPER, CHOPPED
- 2 TEASPOONS CHOPPED FRESH THYME
- 1½ TEASPOONS SALT
- ½ TEASPOON FRESHLY GROUND BLACK PEPPER
- 1¼ CUPS BROWN RICE (UNCOOKED)
- 7 CUPS LOW-SODIUM CHICKEN BROTH, DIVIDED
- 1 POUND FRESH COLLARD GREENS OR KALE, RIBS REMOVED AND DISCARDED, CHOPPED (ABOUT 8½ CUPS) OR ONE 10-OUNCE PACKAGE FROZEN, THAWED, COLLARDS GREENS OR KALE
- TWO 15-OUNCE CANS LOW-SODIUM BLACK-EYED PEAS, DRAINED AND RINSED
- 2 TABLESPOONS CIDER VINEGAR
- ¼ TEASPOON CRUSHED RED PEPPER FLAKES
- HOT SAUCE, OPTIONAL

1 Heat the oil in a large heavy pot, such as a Dutch oven, over medium-high heat. Add the bacon and cook, stirring, until browned, about 4 minutes.

2 Lower the heat to medium, add the onion, celery, bell pepper, thyme, salt, and black pepper and cook, stirring occasionally, until softened, for 8 to 10 minutes. Add the rice and stir until it is well coated, 1 minute. Add 4 cups of the broth and bring to a boil. Cover, lower the heat to low, and simmer until the rice is tender, about 40 minutes.

3 Stir in the collards or kale, in batches if necessary, and then cook until wilted, 3 to 5 minutes. Add the black-eyed peas, remaining 3 cups broth, vinegar, and red pepper flakes and bring to a simmer to warm through and serve with hot sauce, if desired.

TO REFRIGERATE AND REHEAT

Allow to cool at room temperature for 30 minutes, then place in an airtight container in the refrigerator for up to 4 days.

To reheat, place in a pot over medium-low heat, cover, and cook, stirring occasionally, until warmed through, 8 to 25 minutes, depending on the amount. Alternatively, place a single serving in a microwave-safe bowl, cover with a splatter guard, and microwave on full power for 90 seconds to 2 minutes.

TO FREEZE AND REHEAT

Allow to cool at room temperature for 30 minutes, then chill in the refrigerator for 30 minutes. Transfer into freezer bags in the portions desired and freeze for up to 3 months.

Thaw in the refrigerator for 24 to 36 hours, and reheat as above. Or, to thaw quickly, run the bag under hot water for 30 seconds to release the stew from the bag, then transfer it to a pot, cover, and cook over medium-low heat, stirring occasionally, until warmed though, 15 to 45 minutes, depending on the amount.

Alternatively, after running the bag under hot water, transfer the stew to a microwave-safe bowl, cover with a splatter guard, and microwave on the defrost setting for about 7 minutes, then heat through on full power for about 2 minutes for one serving.

∗ **Serving size:** 1⅔ cups; **Per serving:** Calories 260; Total Fat 6g (Mono Fat 2.9g, Poly Fat 0.8g, Sat Fat 0.8g); Protein 13g; Carb 42g; Fiber 7g; Cholesterol 5mg; Sodium 650mg; **Excellent source of:** Fiber, Folate, Magnesium, Manganese, Phosphorus, Protein, Thiamin, Vitamin A, Vitamin C, Vitamin K; **Good source of:** Calcium, Iron, Niacin, Potassium, Riboflavin, Selenium, Vitamin B6, Zinc

Poultry

Almond-Crusted Chicken Tenders
with Apricot-Mustard Dipping Sauce • MAKES 6 SERVINGS •

THIS RECIPE HOLDS THE SECRET to oven-fried chicken that is remarkably crispy outside, yet moist and tender inside. First, a quick marinade in yogurt does double duty, preventing the chicken from drying out and tenderizing it with a gentle acidity. Second, the almond-Panko coating is pretoasted in olive oil, so you avoid the risk of overcooking the chicken when you try to crisp it in the oven.

Not only is the texture just right, the subtle lemon, garlic, and herb seasoning is too, and it is elevated further when dipped in the tangy-sweet Apricot-Mustard Sauce. This chicken is not only delicious hot, but just like fried chicken it's a natural served at room temperature for, say, a picnic lunch.

1 CUP PLAIN LOW-FAT YOGURT

1 TABLESPOON FRESH THYME, DIVIDED

1 TEASPOON GARLIC POWDER

¾ TEASPOON SALT, DIVIDED

½ TEASPOON FRESHLY GROUND BLACK PEPPER

1½ POUNDS CHICKEN TENDERS OR SKINLESS, BONELESS CHICKEN BREASTS POUNDED TO AN EVEN THICKNESS AND CUT INTO 1-INCH-THICK SLICES

1½ CUPS WHOLE-WHEAT PANKO BREAD CRUMBS

½ CUP SLICED ALMONDS, COARSELY CHOPPED

2 TABLESPOONS OLIVE OIL

1 TEASPOON FINELY GRATED LEMON ZEST

FOR SERVING:

1 RECIPE APRICOT-MUSTARD SAUCE (RECIPE FOLLOWS), OPTIONAL

1 Preheat the oven to 450°F. Put a rack on top of a large baking sheet lined with foil.

2 In a large bowl, mix the yogurt with ½ tablespoon of the thyme, the garlic powder, ½ teaspoon of the salt, and ¼ teaspoon of the pepper. Add the chicken and toss to coat. Allow to marinate in the yogurt as you prepare the rest of the ingredients.

3 In a medium skillet, toss together the bread crumbs, almonds, and oil to combine. Set the skillet over medium heat and cook, stirring frequently, until the mixture is browned and well toasted, about 6 minutes. Transfer to a large shallow dish and allow to cool for 10 minutes. Stir in the remaining ½ tablespoon thyme, ¼ teaspoon each of the salt and pepper, and the lemon zest.

4 Working with one or two pieces at a time, transfer the chicken to the dish of crumbs and coat with the crumbs, pressing them well so they adhere to the chicken on all sides. Transfer to the rack on the baking sheet and bake until the chicken is cooked through, about 15 minutes. Serve with the Apricot-Mustard Sauce alongside for dipping, if desired.

Recipe continues

TO REFRIGERATE AND REHEAT

Allow the chicken to cool at room temperature for 30 minutes, then place in an airtight container in the refrigerator where it will keep for up to 3 days. The chicken may be served at room temperature or reheated.

To reheat, preheat the oven to 350°F, place the chicken on a foil-lined baking sheet, and cook for about 10 minutes, until warmed through. Alternatively, wrap the chicken in a paper towel, place on a microwave-safe plate, and microwave for about 40 seconds for one portion. (Oven reheating is preferred so that the chicken recrisps.)

TO FREEZE AND REHEAT

Allow the chicken to cool at room temperature for 30 minutes, then wrap individual servings in foil, place in sealable freezer bags, and freeze for up to 3 months.

To reheat, there is no need to thaw. Open the foil packet all the way and place on a baking tray in a cold oven set to 350°F. Once the oven comes to temperature, continue to bake until heated through, about 12 minutes more. To reheat in the microwave, wrap in a paper towel and microwave on high for 2 minutes for one portion. (Oven reheating is preferred so that the chicken recrisps.)

---

* **Serving size:** 3 to 4 pieces; **Per serving:** Calories 290; Total Fat 12g (Mono Fat 6.5g, Poly Fat 1.9g, Sat Fat 2g); Protein 32g; Carb 12g; Fiber 3g; Cholesterol 85mg; Sodium 280 mg; **Excellent source of:** Niacin, Phosphorus, Protein, Selenium, Vitamin B6; **Good source of:** Fiber, Magnesium, Pantothenic Acid, Potassium, Riboflavin, Vitamin E

APRICOT-MUSTARD DIPPING SAUCE • MAKES 6 SERVINGS •

THIS SWEET-TANGY SAUCE IS PERFECT for the chicken fingers, and appeals to the sensibilities of kids and adults alike. It is also delicious as a glaze for baked or grilled chicken, and as a sandwich spread.

½ CUP ALL-FRUIT APRICOT PRESERVES

⅓ CUP DIJON MUSTARD

Whisk the apricot preserves and mustard together in a medium bowl until well combined.

TO REFRIGERATE

Place in an airtight container in the refrigerator where the dip will keep for about 2 weeks.

TO FREEZE

Place in a sealable plastic freezer bag and freeze for up to 4 months. (Sauce will not freeze solid.) Thaw in the refrigerator for 12 to 18 hours.

---

* **Serving size:** About 2 tablespoons; **Per serving:** Calories 80; Total Fat 0g (Mono Fat 0g, Poly Fat 0g, Sat Fat 0g); Protein 0g; Carb 20g; Fiber 0g; Cholesterol 0mg; Sodium 330mg

Fragrant Chicken and Eggplant Stew

· MAKES 6 SERVINGS ·

AN AROMATIC MIX OF PERSIAN spices—paprika, turmeric, and saffron—lend a rich color and deep flavor to this tomato-based stew that is brimming with tender chunks of chicken breast and eggplant and studded with briny green olives. I like to serve it over whole-grain couscous or rice.

- 2 POUNDS SKINLESS, BONELESS CHICKEN BREASTS, CUT INTO 2-INCH CHUNKS
- 1 TEASPOON SALT, DIVIDED, PLUS MORE TO TASTE
- ½ TEASPOON FRESHLY GROUND BLACK PEPPER, DIVIDED
- 2 POUNDS EGGPLANT (6 SMALLER ITALIAN EGGPLANTS), UNPEELED, AND CUT INTO ½-INCH CUBES
- 5 TABLESPOONS OLIVE OIL, DIVIDED
- 1 LARGE ONION, CHOPPED
- 4 CLOVES GARLIC, MINCED
- 1½ TEASPOONS PAPRIKA
- 1 TEASPOON TURMERIC
- ¼ TEASPOON SAFFRON
- ONE 15-OUNCE CAN NO-SALT-ADDED TOMATO SAUCE
- ONE 15-OUNCE CAN NO-SALT-ADDED DICED TOMATOES
- ½ CUP SLICED PITTED GREEN OLIVES
- ½ CUP CHOPPED FRESH ITALIAN PARSLEY LEAVES

1 Season the chicken with ¼ teaspoon each of the salt and pepper, and the eggplant with the remaining ¾ teaspoon salt and ¼ teaspoon pepper.

2 Heat 1 tablespoon of the oil in a large skillet over medium-high heat. Add half the chicken and cook, turning once, until golden, 5 to 6 minutes total. Transfer the chicken to a medium bowl. Add another 1 tablespoon of the oil to the pan and repeat with the remaining chicken, transferring it to the bowl once browned.

3 Heat 2 more tablespoons of the oil in the same skillet. Add the eggplant and cook, turning once, until the eggplant is golden and begins to soften, 6 to 7 minutes. Lower the heat to medium, add ½ cup of water, and continue to cook the eggplant, stirring, until tender, 5 to 6 minutes more. Transfer the eggplant to the bowl with the chicken.

4 Heat the remaining 1 tablespoon oil, then add the onion and cook, stirring, until translucent and tender, 8 to 9 minutes. Add the garlic, paprika, turmeric, and saffron and cook, stirring, 1 minute more. Return the chicken and eggplant to the skillet. Add the tomato sauce, tomatoes with their juices, olives, and ¼ cup of water and bring to a boil. Cover, lower the heat to medium-low and simmer, stirring occasionally, until the chicken is cooked through and the ingredients have melded, about 15 minutes. Stir in the parsley and additional salt to taste.

Recipe continues

TO REFRIGERATE AND REHEAT

The stew will keep in the refrigerator in an airtight container for up to 4 days. To reheat, place in a pot over medium-low heat, cover, and cook, stirring occasionally, until warmed through, 8 to 25 minutes, depending on the amount. Alternatively, place in a microwave-safe bowl, cover with a splatter guard, and microwave on full power for about 90 seconds to 2 minutes for a single portion.

TO FREEZE AND REHEAT

Chill in the refrigerator for 30 minutes, then transfer to sealable plastic freezer bags in the portions desired. Freeze for up to 3 months. Thaw in the refrigerator for 18 to 24 hours and reheat following the "to refrigerate" directions.

Or, to thaw quickly, run the bag under hot water for 30 seconds to release the stew from the bag, then transfer it to a pot along with 1 to 2 tablespoons of water. Cover and cook over medium-low heat, stirring occasionally, until warmed through, 15 to 45 minutes, depending on the amount. Add more water to the pot if the bottom is getting dry.

Alternatively, after running the bag under hot water, transfer the stew to a microwave-safe bowl, cover with a splatter guard, and microwave on the defrost setting for about 7 minutes, then heat through on full power for 90 seconds to 2 minutes for a single serving.

✳ **Serving size:** 1½ cups; **Per serving:** Calories 400; Total Fat 17g (Mono Fat 9.3g, Poly Fat 2g, Sat Fat 2.5g); Protein 38g; Carb 24g; Fiber 6g; Cholesterol 110mg; Sodium 560mg; **Excellent source of:** Fiber, Magnesium, Manganese, Niacin, Pantothenic Acid, Phosphorus, Potassium, Protein, Riboflavin, Selenium, Vitamin A, Vitamin C, Vitamin B6, Vitamin K; **Good source of:** Copper, Folate, Iron, Molybdenum, Thiamin, Vitamin E, Zinc

Chicken Broccoli Brown Rice Casserole

• MAKES 6 SERVINGS •

THIS IS THE VERY DEFINITION of a comfort-food casserole. It's a homey baked chicken and rice dinner, studded with broccoli in a lightly creamy sauce with a Parmesan topping. It's a complete meal that will surely make the whole family happy.

- 2 POUNDS BONELESS, SKINLESS CHICKEN THIGHS, TRIMMED OF ANY EXCESS FAT AND CUT INTO 2-INCH PIECES
- ½ TEASPOON SALT
- ½ TEASPOON FRESHLY GROUND BLACK PEPPER
- 2 TABLESPOONS OLIVE OIL
- 1 LARGE ONION, CHOPPED
- 4 CLOVES GARLIC, MINCED
- 1 TABLESPOON CHOPPED FRESH ROSEMARY OR THYME
- 2 TABLESPOONS ALL-PURPOSE FLOUR
- ½ CUP DRY WHITE WINE, SUCH AS PINOT GRIGIO
- 1½ CUPS LOW-SODIUM CHICKEN BROTH
- ½ CUP WHOLE MILK
- 1 TEASPOON FINELY GRATED LEMON ZEST
- ½ CUP FINELY GRATED PARMESAN CHEESE, DIVIDED
- 1 CUP INSTANT (PARBOILED) BROWN RICE
- 4 CUPS SMALL (1½-INCH) BROCCOLI FLORETS

1 Preheat the oven to 400°F.

2 Sprinkle the chicken with the salt and pepper. Heat the oil in a large nonstick skillet over medium-high heat. Add half the chicken and cook, stirring once or twice, until the meat is browned, about 4 minutes total, then transfer it to a plate. Repeat with the remaining chicken.

3 Add the onion to the skillet, lower the heat to medium, and cook, stirring, until softened, about 3 minutes. Add the garlic and rosemary or thyme and cook, stirring for 1 minute more. Sprinkle the flour over and cook, stirring constantly, for 1 minute. While stirring, add the white wine, then simmer until the wine is reduced by half, about 30 seconds.

4 Add the broth, milk, and zest and cook, stirring occasionally, scraping up any browned bits in the pan, until slightly thickened, 6 to 8 minutes. Remove the pan from the heat and stir in ¼ cup of the Parmesan. Pour the mixture into a 9 × 13-inch casserole dish. Stir in the rice then add the chicken with any juices and the broccoli, nestling them into the mixture.

Recipe continues

5 Cover with foil and bake until the chicken is cooked through, the rice is tender, and most of the liquid has been absorbed by the rice, 30 to 35 minutes. Remove the foil, sprinkle the remaining cheese on top, and bake, uncovered, until golden on top, about 5 minutes. Let stand 5 minutes before serving.

TO REFRIGERATE AND REHEAT

Chill in the refrigerator, uncovered, for 30 minutes, then cover tightly and refrigerate for up to 4 days.

To reheat, allow the dish to sit at room temperature while the oven heats to 350°F. Place the casserole dish in the oven, cover with foil, and cook until warmed through, about 30 minutes, then uncover and cook for 10 to 15 minutes more. Alternatively, scoop the amount desired onto a microwave-safe plate, cover with a splatter guard, and microwave on high, 90 seconds to 2 minutes for one serving.

TO FREEZE AND REHEAT

Allow to chill in the refrigerator, uncovered, for 1 hour, then cover tightly with plastic wrap and then foil, as a full casserole, or divided into individual oven-, microwave-, and freezer-proof serving dishes and freeze for up to 3 months.

Thaw in the refrigerator for 24 to 36 hours, then reheat full casserole following the "to refrigerate" directions. Or, to reheat without thawing, remove the plastic wrap and re-cover with foil, then place the frozen dish(es) in a cold oven set to 350°F. Once the oven reaches temperature, continue to cook until warmed through, about 45 to 75 minutes, depending on the size of the dish, then cook uncovered for 10 to 15 minutes more. Alternatively, to thaw and heat a single serving dish in the microwave, uncover completely, then re-cover with a splatter guard and microwave for 6 to 8 minutes on the defrost setting, then on high for 90 seconds to 2 minutes.

✳ **Serving size:** 1¾ cups; **Per serving:** Calories 340; Total Fat 13g (Mono Fat 5.9g, Poly Fat 2.2g, Sat Fat 3.7g); Protein 33g; Carb 18g; Fiber 3g; Cholesterol 115mg; Sodium 450mg; **Excellent source of:** Manganese, Niacin, Pantothenic Acid, Phosphorus, Protein, Riboflavin, Selenium, Vitamin B6, Vitamin C, Vitamin K, Zinc; **Good source of:** Calcium, Fiber, Folate, Iron, Magnesium, Potassium, Thiamin, Vitamin B12

Grilled Chicken with Cherry Bourbon BBQ Sauce • MAKES 8 SERVINGS •

THIS FINGER-LICKING BARBECUE SAUCE HAS a classic thick, clingy texture and irresistible savory-sweet-tangy flavor, but here you get it in a healthier way, without lots of added sugar, thanks to the cherries at its base, as well as a touch of molasses, which adds a deep, distinctive taste and is as unrefined and mineral-rich as a sweetener gets. The bourbon spikes it with an exciting layer of flavor, but you can simply leave it out if you prefer.

The sauce requires no cooking, just an easy whir in the blender, and of course you can make it ahead so it's ready whenever you want it. Although I have paired it here with chicken, it also works perfectly with pork, and the cooked meat will keep in the refrigerator or freezer too, to be rewarmed or served at room temperature, piled in a sandwich or with a side, like the Asian Slaw, page 65.

1 CUP PITTED FRESH SWEET CHERRIES, OR FROZEN, THAWED

½ CUP CANNED, NO-SALT-ADDED TOMATO SAUCE

3 TABLESPOONS MOLASSES

3 TABLESPOONS CIDER VINEGAR

2 TABLESPOONS BOURBON, OPTIONAL

3 WHOLE PEELED CLOVES GARLIC

1 TEASPOON YELLOW MUSTARD

½ TEASPOON SALT

¼ TEASPOON FRESHLY GROUND BLACK PEPPER

PINCH GROUND CLOVES

FOR SERVING:

EIGHT 6-OUNCE SKINLESS, BONELESS CHICKEN BREASTS, POUNDED TO AN EVEN ½-INCH THICKNESS

COOKING SPRAY

1 Combine the cherries, tomato sauce, molasses, vinegar, bourbon, garlic, mustard, salt, pepper, and cloves in a blender and puree until almost smooth. The sauce may be refrigerated or frozen at this stage.

2 To continue, set aside about a cup of the sauce for serving. Brush the chicken breasts generously with the remaining sauce. Spray a grill or grill pan with cooking spray and preheat it over medium-high heat. Grill until the chicken is cooked through, the outside is charred, and grill marks have formed, 4 to 5 minutes per side. Serve drizzled with the reserved sauce.

Recipe continues

For the sauce:

TO REFRIGERATE AND REHEAT

The sauce will keep in an airtight container in the refrigerator for 1 week. Allow to come to room temperature, or warm slightly on the stove in a small pan over medium-low heat for 5 to 10 minutes. Alternatively, place in a microwave-safe bowl, cover with a splatter guard, and microwave on high for about 1 minute for a half-batch of the sauce.

TO FREEZE AND REHEAT

Place the sauce in full or half-batches into one or two sealable plastic freezer bags and freeze for up to 4 months. (The sauce will not freeze to a solid state.) Thaw in the refrigerator for 24 to 36 hours, or to thaw quickly, run the bag under hot water for 30 seconds to release the sauce from the bag, then transfer the sauce to a saucepan. Heat over medium-low heat, covered, for 6 to 12 minutes, until warmed through. Alternatively, place in a microwave-safe dish, cover with a splatter guard, and microwave on high for about 90 seconds for a half-batch of the sauce.

For the cooked chicken:

TO REFRIGERATE AND SERVE

Place in an airtight container in the refrigerator for up to 4 days.

The chicken may be served at room temperature, or to reheat, cover in foil and place in a 350°F oven for about 10 minutes, until warmed through. Alternatively, place on a microwave-safe plate, cover with a splatter guard, and microwave on high for 1 minute for a single portion.

TO FREEZE AND REHEAT

Chill in the refrigerator for 30 minutes, wrap the chicken pieces individually in foil or plastic wrap, and place in a sealable plastic freezer bag in the freezer for up to 3 months.

Allow to thaw in the refrigerator for about 24 hours, and reheat as above. Or to thaw and heat quickly, wrap the chicken in foil and place in a cold oven set for 350°F. Once the oven reaches temperature, continue to cook for 25 minutes, until warmed through. Alternatively, place on a microwave-safe plate, cover with a splatter guard, and microwave on the defrost setting for 3 minutes, then on high for 1 minute for a single portion.

✳ **Serving size:** 1 piece chicken breast plus 2 tablespoons additional sauce; **Per serving:** Calories 250; Total Fat 4.5g (Mono Fat 1.2g, Poly Fat 0.8g, Sat Fat 0.9g); Protein 1g; Carb 10g; Fiber 1g; Cholesterol 0mg; Sodium 160mg; **Excellent source of:** Niacin, Pantothenic Acid, Phosphorus, Potassium, Protein, Selenium Vitamin B6; **Good source of:** Magnesium, Riboflavin, Thiamin

Chicken Curry with Green Beans

• MAKES 8 SERVINGS •

THIS INDIAN-STYLE CURRY IS A sumptuous stew of moist chicken thighs, green beans, and tomatoes in a creamy coconut curry sauce. It's a one-pot meal that's easy to prepare, ready in about an hour, and uses ingredients you can find at most regular grocery stores. And it's one of those dishes that taste even better over time, so you'll want to have leftovers to pack up for later. I like to serve it over brown basmati rice.

- 1 TABLESPOON CANOLA OIL, OR OTHER NEUTRAL TASTING OIL
- 2 POUNDS SKINLESS, BONELESS CHICKEN THIGHS (8 THIGHS)
- 1½ TEASPOONS SALT, DIVIDED
- ¼ TEASPOON FRESHLY GROUND BLACK PEPPER
- 1 LARGE ONION, THINLY SLICED INTO HALF-MOONS
- ONE 2-INCH PIECE GINGER, PEELED AND MINCED (2 TABLESPOONS)
- 3 CLOVES GARLIC, MINCED
- 2 TABLESPOONS MILD CURRY POWDER
- ½ TEASPOON CRUSHED RED PEPPER FLAKES
- ¾ CUP LOW-SODIUM CHICKEN BROTH
- ONE 13.5-OUNCE CAN LIGHT COCONUT MILK
- ONE 28-OUNCE CAN NO-SALT-ADDED DICED TOMATOES
- 1 POUND GREEN BEANS, TRIMMED
- ¼ CUP CHOPPED FRESH CILANTRO

1 Heat the oil in a large (6 to 8 quart) pot with a lid over medium-high heat. Season the chicken with ½ teaspoon of the salt and the pepper. Place half the chicken in the pot and cook until lightly golden, 3 minutes per side. Transfer to a plate and repeat with the remaining chicken.

2 Lower the heat to medium, add the onion to the pot and cook, stirring, until translucent, 5 to 6 minutes. Add the ginger, garlic, curry powder, crushed red pepper flakes, and remaining 1 teaspoon salt and cook, stirring, until the spices are fragrant, 30 seconds to 1 minute.

3 Add the broth and coconut milk and stir to loosen any browned bits. Return the chicken to the pot, add the tomatoes with their juices and green beans and bring to a boil. Lower the heat to medium-low, cover, and simmer until the chicken is tender and cooked through, stirring once or twice, about 45 minutes. Serve garnished with the cilantro.

Recipe continues

TO REFRIGERATE AND REHEAT

The curry will keep in the refrigerator in an airtight container for up to 4 days. To reheat, place in a pot, cover, and heat over low heat until warmed through, 5 to 15 minutes, depending on the amount. Alternatively, place in a microwave-safe dish, cover with a splatter guard, and heat on full power, 90 seconds to 2 minutes for one portion.

TO FREEZE AND REHEAT

Allow to cool in the refrigerator for 30 minutes, and then transfer to sealable freezer bags in the portions desired. Freeze for up to 3 months.

Thaw in the refrigerator for 24 to 36 hours and reheat following the "to refrigerate" directions. Or, to thaw quickly, run the bag(s) under hot water for 30 seconds to release the food, then transfer it to a pot, cover, and heat over medium-low heat, stirring occasionally, until thawed and warmed through, 20 to 40 minutes, depending on the amount. Add 1 to 2 tablespoons of water if the pot seems dry.

Alternatively, once released from the bag, place the food in a microwave-safe bowl, cover with a splatter guard, and microwave on the defrost setting for about 7 minutes, then on full power for 90 seconds to 2 minutes for one portion.

∗ **Serving size:** 1 thigh and 1 cup vegetables and sauce; **Per serving:** Calories 250; Total Fat 10g (Mono Fat 2.9g, Poly Fat 2g, Sat Fat 3.5g); Protein 25g; Carb 14g; Fiber 4g; Cholesterol 90mg; Sodium 570mg; **Excellent source of:** Niacin, Phosphorus, Protein, Selenium, Vitamin A, Vitamin B6, Vitamin C; **Good source of:** Fiber, Iron, Magnesium, Manganese, Pantothenic Acid, Potassium, Riboflavin, Vitamin K, Zinc

Chicken Enchilada Pie · MAKES 6 SERVINGS ·

THIS DISH IS LIKE A Mexican lasagna with layers of corn tortillas, chicken, vegetables, cheese, and salsa. It is hearty, filling, and flavor-packed, but it won't weigh you down like most versions because here the tortillas are baked crispy instead of fried, chunks of zucchini are added to amp up portion size and color, and there is a generous, but not over-the-top amount of cheese. Using green salsa gives it a vibrant, fresh look and taste, and preparing it in an actual pie dish means you can slice it up attractively into wedges for serving.

- 2 TABLESPOONS CANOLA OIL, OR OTHER NEUTRAL TASTING OIL, DIVIDED
- 1 SMALL ZUCCHINI, CUT INTO ¼-INCH THICK HALF-MOONS
- 1 POBLANO PEPPER, STEMMED, SEEDED, AND FINELY CHOPPED
- 1 SMALL ONION, CHOPPED
- ½ TEASPOON SALT, DIVIDED
- 1 CUP FRESH OR FROZEN CORN KERNELS
- 2 LARGE CLOVES GARLIC, MINCED
- 1 TEASPOON GROUND CUMIN, DIVIDED
- 5 TABLESPOONS CHOPPED FRESH CILANTRO, DIVIDED, OPTIONAL
- 2 CUPS SHREDDED COOKED CHICKEN (FROM CHILLED OVEN-POACHED CHICKEN, PAGE 85 OR THE MEAT FROM A HALF OF A 2½ POUND ROTISSERIE CHICKEN)
- 1½ TABLESPOONS FRESH LIME JUICE
- 1 TABLESPOON CHILI POWDER
- ELEVEN 6-INCH CORN TORTILLAS
- COOKING SPRAY
- 2 CUPS STORE-BOUGHT TOMATILLO SALSA OR SALSA VERDE
- 1⅓ CUPS SHREDDED SHARP CHEDDAR OR MONTEREY JACK CHEESE
- ½ CUP LOW-FAT PLAIN GREEK YOGURT

1 Heat 1 tablespoon of the oil in a large nonstick skillet over medium-high heat. Add the zucchini, poblano pepper, onion, and ¼ teaspoon of the salt, and cook stirring, until the vegetables have softened, about 6 minutes. Stir in the corn, garlic, and ½ teaspoon of the cumin and cook, stirring, for 2 minutes more. Remove from the heat and stir in 2 tablespoons of the cilantro, if using.

2 In a medium bowl, toss together the chicken, remaining 3 tablespoons of the cilantro, the lime juice, chili powder, remaining ½ teaspoon cumin, and remaining ¼ teaspoon salt.

3 Preheat the broiler. Brush the tortillas with the remaining 1 tablespoon oil on one side. Place in one layer, oil side up, onto 2 baking sheets and broil, one pan at a time, about 6 inches from the heat, until golden brown on top, for 3 to 4 minutes. Transfer to a rack to cool slightly.

4 Lightly spray a 9-inch, deep-dish pie plate or an 8-inch square baking dish with oil spray and spread ½ cup of the salsa on the bottom of the dish. Tear two tortillas in half and position the four halves in the pan so they cover as much of the bottom as possible (it is fine if they overlap). Spread one third of the zucchini-corn mixture evenly over the tortillas, then spread one-third of the chicken mixture, then ½ cup of the salsa, and ⅓ cup of the cheese. Make another layer of the tortillas, this time using 2½ tortillas to cover the

Recipe continues

area, and follow with the zucchini-corn mixture, then the chicken, salsa, and cheese. Repeat the layers once more, starting again with 2½ tortillas. Top with the remaining 4 tortillas (leave them whole and overlap as necessary) and ⅓ cup cheese. Cover tightly with foil. The dish may be refrigerated or frozen at this stage.

5   To continue, preheat the oven to 375°F. Bake in the middle of the oven until heated through, about 40 minutes. Uncover and bake until the cheese is melted and the top is golden brown, about 5 minutes. Let cool for 10 to 15 minutes before slicing. Cut into 6 wedges and serve with a dollop of the yogurt.

Before baking:

TO REFRIGERATE AND SERVE
Cover the unbaked dish tightly and refrigerate for up to 4 days. When ready to cook, allow to sit at room temperature as the oven preheats to 375°F, then bake, covered, for 50 minutes, then uncover and continue to bake until warmed through and the cheese is melted, about 10 minutes more.

TO FREEZE AND SERVE
Cover the unbaked dish tightly with plastic wrap and then with foil and freeze for up to 3 months. Thaw in the refrigerator for 24 hours, then remove the plastic wrap, re-cover with foil and reheat as above.

Alternatively, remove the plastic wrap, re-cover with foil, and place the frozen dish in a cold oven set for 350°F. Once the oven reaches temperature, cook for 30 minutes. Then increase the temperature to 375°F and cook, covered, for 50 minutes, then uncover and cook for 15 minutes more.

Once baked:

TO REFRIGERATE AND REHEAT
Cover tightly with foil and refrigerate for up to 3 days. To reheat, place, covered, into a 350°F oven for 20 to 40 minutes, depending on the amount in the dish. Alternatively, place the amount to be warmed on a microwave-safe plate, cover with a splatter guard, and microwave on high 1 minute for a single portion.

＊ **Serving size:** ⅙ of pie; **Per serving:** Calories 390; Total Fat 18g (Mono Fat 4.5g, Poly Fat 2.6g, Sat Fat 6g); Protein 26g; Carb 33g; Fiber 5g; Cholesterol 75mg; Sodium 880mg; **Excellent source of:** Calcium, Niacin, Phosphorus, Protein, Vitamin B6, Vitamin C; **Good source of:** Fiber, Folate, Magnesium, Manganese, Pantothenic Acid, Potassium, Riboflavin, Selenium, Thiamin, Vitamin A, Vitamin K, Zinc

Chicken with Olives, Oranges, and Fennel in Foil Packets

• MAKES 8 SERVINGS •

SEALING CHICKEN, VEGETABLES, AND SEASONINGS together in individual foil packets means you have parcels of delicious food in your freezer or fridge ready for you to cook as you need them. The flavors in these are Mediterranean inspired: the chicken breast is rubbed with a garlic-herb mixture and piled on top of sliced fresh fennel and green olives, then topped with orange and onion slices and a dash of white wine. As the packets cook, the ingredients release their liquid and create a lovely sauce for the food to steep in and be plated with. Serve over whole-grain orzo, brown rice, or with a hunk of crusty whole-grain bread.

3 MEDIUM ORANGES (1¼ POUNDS)

6 TABLESPOONS OLIVE OIL, DIVIDED

2 CLOVES GARLIC, FINELY MINCED

½ TABLESPOON FINELY CHOPPED FRESH ROSEMARY

1½ TEASPOONS SALT

½ TEASPOON FRESHLY GROUND BLACK PEPPER

¼ TEASPOON CRUSHED RED PEPPER FLAKES

EIGHT 6-OUNCE SKINLESS, BONELESS CHICKEN BREASTS, POUNDED TO AN EVEN ½-INCH THICKNESS

1 VERY LARGE OR 2 MEDIUM FENNEL BULBS, CORED AND THINLY SLICED

½ CUP PITTED GREEN OLIVES, SLICED

¼ SMALL RED ONION, THINLY SLICED INTO HALF-MOONS

½ CUP CHOPPED FRESH ITALIAN PARSLEY LEAVES

½ CUP DRY WHITE WINE, SUCH AS PINOT GRIGIO

1 Finely zest one of the oranges until you have 1 teaspoon of zest, then juice the zested orange. You should wind up with about ½ cup orange juice. Use a knife to cut the top and bottom off of the remaining 2 oranges, then, standing the fruit on a cut end, remove the peel and white pith by cutting downward, following the shape of the fruit. Slice the peeled oranges crosswise into ½-inch rounds.

2 In a small bowl, combine 2 tablespoons of the oil with the garlic, rosemary, salt, orange zest, black pepper, and red pepper flakes. Rub the chicken breasts with the herb mixture and set aside.

3 Place eight large (10 × 18-inch) pieces of heavy-duty aluminum foil on a flat surface.

4 Layer one-eighth of the fennel and the olives in the center of each foil square and top each with one piece of chicken. Place 2 orange rounds, a few slices of onion, and 1 tablespoon of the parsley on top of each piece of chicken. Drizzle each with 1 tablespoon of the wine, 1 tablespoon of the orange juice, and ½ tablespoon of the remaining oil. Tightly seal the packets, leaving some space inside the packet for steam to accumulate. The packets may be refrigerated or frozen at this stage.

Recipe continues

5 To continue, preheat the oven to 400°F. Place the foil packets onto a baking sheet and bake until the chicken is cooked through and vegetables are tender, about 14 minutes. Open the foil pouches slowly, being careful of the hot steam. Transfer the chicken, vegetables, and any accumulated juices to shallow serving bowls or rimmed plates.

TO REFRIGERATE AND HEAT

Place uncooked packets in the refrigerator where they will keep for up to 2 days. When ready to cook, follow the "to continue" instructions above, adding about 5 minutes to the cook time for a total of about 19 minutes.

TO FREEZE AND HEAT

Place uncooked packets into sealable plastic bags, keeping them level and upright. (Two packets fit well into a gallon-sized bag.) Freeze for up to 3 months.

There is no need to thaw before cooking. Remove the frozen packets from the bags and place them on a baking tray in a cold oven set to 400°F. Once the oven comes to temperature, continue to cook for 25 to 30 minutes.

∗ **Serving size:** One packet; **Per serving:** Calories 360; Total Fat 16g (Mono Fat 8.6g, Poly Fat 1.9g, Sat Fat 2.4g); Protein 40g; Carb 12g; Fiber 3g; Cholesterol 125mg; Sodium 610mg; **Excellent source of:** Niacin, Pantothenic Acid, Phosphorus, Potassium, Protein, Riboflavin, Selenium, Vitamin A, Vitamin B6, Vitamin C, Vitamin K; **Good source of:** Folate, Fiber, Magnesium, Thiamin, Vitamin E

Chicken Phyllo Pies
with Green Herb Sauce • MAKES 8 SERVINGS •

FRAGRANTLY SPICED, MOIST GROUND CHICKEN mixed with a nutty crunch of chopped almonds inside, and multiple layers of flaky phyllo outside, these filling, savory pies are a meal that is easy enough to eat with one hand as you dash out the door (though you'll likely leave a trail of crumbs), but they are so delectable, you will want to take a moment to stop and relish one, especially if it is drizzled with Green Herb Sauce. These large pies are a perfect main course, but you can also halve their size and make twice as many to serve as finger food at a cocktail party.

½ CUP WHOLE, NATURAL ALMONDS

8 TABLESPOONS OLIVE OIL, DIVIDED

1 POUND GROUND WHITE-MEAT CHICKEN OR TURKEY

½ POUND GROUND DARK-MEAT CHICKEN OR TURKEY

1 LARGE ONION, FINELY DICED

4 CLOVES GARLIC, MINCED

2 TEASPOONS GROUND CINNAMON

1 TEASPOON GROUND CUMIN

1 TEASPOON SALT

½ TEASPOON FRESHLY GROUND BLACK PEPPER

⅛ TEASPOON GROUND CARDAMOM

⅛ TEASPOON CAYENNE PEPPER

2 TABLESPOONS HONEY

½ CUP FINELY CHOPPED FRESH CILANTRO LEAVES

2 LARGE EGG WHITES, LIGHTLY BEATEN

1 LARGE EGG, LIGHTLY BEATEN

8 SHEETS PHYLLO DOUGH

FOR SERVING:

½ CUP GREEN HERB SAUCE (RECIPE FOLLOWS), OPTIONAL

1 Toast the almonds in a dry skillet over medium-high heat, stirring frequently, until fragrant, about 5 minutes. Allow to cool, then chop very finely.

2 Heat 1 tablespoon of the oil in a large skillet over medium heat. Add the chicken and cook, stirring and breaking up with a spoon, until the meat is no longer pink, about 5 minutes. Transfer the chicken to a plate.

3 Heat another tablespoon of oil in the same skillet, add the onion, and cook, stirring, until lightly golden, 7 to 8 minutes. Add the garlic and cook, stirring, 1 minute more. Add the cinnamon, cumin, salt, black pepper, cardamom, and cayenne pepper and cook, stirring, 1 additional minute. Return the chicken to the pan, add the honey, and stir to incorporate. Remove from the heat and allow to cool for 10 minutes. Then stir in the almonds, cilantro, egg whites, and egg.

4 Preheat the oven to 350°F. Place the remaining 6 tablespoons oil in a small dish. Place one sheet of the phyllo dough on a clean, dry work surface and brush lightly with the oil. Top with another sheet of the phyllo and brush with oil. (Cover the remaining stack of phyllo with a damp paper towel so it doesn't dry out as you

Recipe continues

make the pies.) Using a pizza cutter or sharp knife, gently cut the oiled phyllo in half lengthwise so you have two equal-sized double-layer strips.

5 Spoon about ½ cup of the chicken filling onto one of the double-layer strips about 2 inches from the top. Working from the corner, fold both layers of the strip together over the filling to form a triangle. Continue folding, following the shape of the triangle, three more times. Repeat with other double-layer half of phyllo, then brush the outside of each triangle with more oil. Repeat with the remaining phyllo and filling to yield 8 turnovers.

6 Place the pies on a large parchment-lined baking sheet. Make a couple of small slits in the top of each with a sharp knife, then bake until browned, about 30 minutes. Serve drizzled with Green Herb Sauce, if desired.

TO REFRIGERATE AND HEAT

The pies may be refrigerated before or after baking.

Wrap unbaked pies in foil and refrigerate for up to 1 day, then bake, uncovered, according to the recipe instructions, adding about 10 minutes to the cooking time.

Once baked, allow the pie to cool at room temperature for 30 minutes, then wrap tightly and store in the refrigerator for up to 4 days. Reheat in a 350°F oven, uncovered, for 20 to 30 minutes.

TO FREEZE AND HEAT

The pie may be frozen before or after baking.

Wrap chilled baked or unbaked pies in foil, then place in sealable plastic bags and freeze for up to 3 months.

There is no need to thaw. When ready to cook, uncover the pies completely and place in a cold oven set to 375°F for the unbaked pie or 350°F for the baked pie. Once the oven reaches temperature, bake until warmed through and the crust is flaky and golden brown, about 30 minutes.

---

* **Serving size:** 1 pie; **Per serving:** Calories 380; Total Fat 24g (Mono Fat 14.8g, Poly Fat 3.8g, Sat Fat 3.7g); Protein 24g; Carb 19g; Fiber 2g; Cholesterol 70mg; Sodium 450mg; **Excellent source of:** Protein, Selenium, Vitamin E; **Good source of:** Iron, Manganese, Niacin, Phosphorus, Riboflavin, Thiamin, Vitamin B6, Vitamin K

GREEN HERB SAUCE

• MAKES 8 SERVINGS; 1 CUP •

FINELY CHOPPING TENDER HERBS AND mixing them with some good olive oil and simple seasonings is an ideal way to preserve them, and a delicious, versatile way to enjoy them. Drizzle this herb sauce on the Chicken Phyllo Pies, above, or use it to transform your eggs in the morning, elevate a dish of hummus, or punch up grilled vegetables and meats.

⅓ CUP EXTRA-VIRGIN OLIVE OIL

¼ CUP FINELY CHOPPED FRESH CILANTRO LEAVES

¼ CUP FINELY CHOPPED FRESH ITALIAN PARSLEY LEAVES

¼ CUP FINELY MINCED SHALLOT

2 TABLESPOONS CHAMPAGNE OR WHITE WINE VINEGAR

½ TEASPOON SALT

¼ TEASPOON FRESHLY GROUND BLACK PEPPER

¼ TEASPOON CRUSHED RED PEPPER FLAKES

Mix all the ingredients in a medium bowl with 2 tablespoons of water until well combined.

✳ **Serving size:** 2 tablespoons; **Per serving:** Calories 80; Total Fat 9g (Mono Fat 6.5g, Poly Fat 0.9g, Sat Fat 1.2g); Protein 0g; Carb 1g; Fiber 0g; Cholesterol 0mg; Sodium 150mg; **Excellent source of:** Vitamin K

TO REFRIGERATE
Place in an airtight container in the refrigerator for up to 4 days. Allow to come to room temperature before serving.

TO FREEZE AND THAW
Place the sauce into a sealable plastic bag or pour into ice cube trays and freeze. Once frozen, transfer the cubes of sauce to a sealable plastic freezer bag where they will keep for up to 3 months.

Thaw in the refrigerator for 18 to 24 hours. Allow to come to room temperature before serving. Alternatively, run the bag under hot water to release the sauce from the bag, then place into a small saucepan. Cover and heat over low heat, stirring occasionally until just thawed, 5 to 15 minutes. Or, place in a microwave-safe dish, cover with a splatter guard, and microwave on high for about 15 seconds for a single portion.

Mexican Chicken and Hominy Stew (Posole)

• MAKES 6 SERVINGS •

THIS FULL-FLAVORED BELLY-WARMING TOMATO-BASED STEW is laced with the flavor of chili and lime and loaded with chunks of hominy (a type of corn) and big pieces of roasted chicken. The garnishes make the dish, so don't forget the cooling green contrast of fresh cilantro and avocado.

2 TABLESPOONS OLIVE OIL

1 LARGE ONION, COARSELY CHOPPED

1 MEDIUM JALAPEÑO PEPPER, SEEDED AND FINELY CHOPPED

3 CLOVES GARLIC, MINCED

2 TABLESPOONS CHILI POWDER

½ TEASPOON SALT

3 CUPS LOW-SODIUM CHICKEN BROTH

ONE 28-OUNCE CAN NO-SALT-ADDED DICED TOMATOES

ONE 29-OUNCE CAN HOMINY, DRAINED AND RINSED

3 CUPS TORN ROASTED CHICKEN

2 TABLESPOONS FRESH LIME JUICE

2 TEASPOONS FINELY CHOPPED FRESH OREGANO, OR ¾ TEASPOON DRIED

FOR SERVING:

¾ CUP PACKED FRESH CILANTRO LEAVES

1½ CUPS DICED AVOCADO

HOT SAUCE, TO TASTE, OPTIONAL

1 Heat the oil in a large pot or Dutch oven over medium heat. Add the onion and jalapeño and cook, stirring occasionally, until the onion is golden brown, 8 to 10 minutes. Stir in the garlic, chili powder, and salt and cook, stirring, for 1 minute. Pour in the broth and tomatoes with their juice, and bring to a boil. Add the hominy, chicken, lime juice, and oregano and return to a boil, then lower heat to medium-low and simmer until heated through, about 10 minutes. The stew may be refrigerated or frozen at this stage.

2 Serve each bowl topped with 2 tablespoons of the cilantro, ¼ cup of the diced avocado, and hot sauce, if desired.

TO REFRIGERATE AND REHEAT

Place in an airtight container in the refrigerator for up to 4 days. To reheat, ladle the amount to be warmed into a saucepan, cover, and heat over medium heat for 6 to 20 minutes, depending on the amount. Or place in a microwave-safe bowl, cover with a splatter guard, and microwave on high for 90 seconds to 2 minutes for one portion.

TO FREEZE AND REHEAT

Chill in the refrigerator for 30 minutes, then divide into sealable freezer bags in the portions desired and freeze for up to 3 months.

When ready to heat, run the bag under hot water for 30 seconds to release the frozen stew from the bag. Then place it in a saucepan, cover, and heat over medium heat, breaking it up occasionally with a spoon, until thawed and warmed through, 15 to 45 minutes, depending on the amount.

Alternatively, after releasing the stew from the bag, transfer it to a microwave-safe bowl, cover with a splatter guard, and microwave on the defrost setting for about 10 minutes, then continue to microwave on high for about 90 seconds for one portion.

∗ **Serving size:** About 1½ cups; **Per serving:** Calories 330; Total Fat 13g (Mono Fat 7.9g, Poly Fat 2.1g, Sat Fat 2.2g); Protein 22g; Carb 32g; Fiber 8g; Cholesterol 60mg; Sodium 562mg; **Excellent source of:** Fiber, Niacin, Phosphorus, Protein, Selenium, Vitamin A, Vitamin B6, Vitamin C, Vitamin K; **Good source of:** Iron, Magnesium, Manganese, Pantothenic Acid, Potassium, Riboflavin, Zinc

Chicken Puttanesca Pasta Bake

• MAKES 8 SERVINGS •

PASTA PUTTANESCA, WHICH IS KNOWN for its bold flavor and creative use of cupboard staples—canned tomatoes, olives, capers, and herbs—is a family favorite in my home. Here I turn it into a satisfying make-ahead casserole, with juicy chunks of chicken, ribbons of escarole, and melted mozzarella cheese, that can be made as one big crowd-pleasing dish, or in convenient individual dishes. Escarole is common in Italian cooking and you have most likely been walking past it in your market for years, but if you can't find it, feel free to substitute another green leafy vegetable like spinach, kale, or Swiss chard.

1 POUND WHOLE-GRAIN SPAGHETTI, BROKEN IN HALF

2 POUNDS SKINLESS, BONELESS CHICKEN BREASTS, CUT INTO ½-INCH CHUNKS

2 TABLESPOONS WHOLE-WHEAT PASTRY FLOUR OR ALL-PURPOSE FLOUR

3 TABLESPOONS OLIVE OIL

1 LARGE ONION, CHOPPED

6 CLOVES GARLIC, THINLY SLICED

ONE 28-OUNCE CAN NO-SALT-ADDED DICED TOMATOES

½ CUP PITTED KALAMATA OLIVES, CHOPPED

½ CUP CHOPPED FRESH BASIL OR 1 TABLESPOON DRIED

3 TABLESPOONS CAPERS, DRAINED AND RINSED

2 TABLESPOONS CHOPPED FRESH OREGANO, OR 1 TABLESPOON DRIED

½ TEASPOON CRUSHED RED PEPPER FLAKES

½ TEASPOON SALT

¼ TEASPOON FRESHLY GROUND BLACK PEPPER

1 Bring a large pot of water to boil. Add the spaghetti and cook for 2 minutes fewer than it says on the package directions, drain, then return to the pasta pot. In a medium bowl, toss the chicken with the flour to coat.

2 Heat the oil in a large, deep skillet over medium-high heat. Add the onion, and cook, stirring, until translucent about 5 minutes. Add the garlic and cook, stirring, 30 seconds more. Add the chicken and cook, stirring, until the chicken is just cooked through, 4 to 5 minutes. Add the tomatoes with their juices, olives, basil, capers, oregano, crushed red pepper flakes, salt, and black pepper and cook, stirring, until the mixture thickens slightly, 4 to 5 minutes. Add the escarole and cook, stirring, until it is wilted, 2 minutes. Add the mixture to the pot with the pasta along with 1 cup of the cheese and stir to combine.

3 Use either one 9 × 13-inch baking dish, two 8-inch square baking dishes, or 8 individual 2-cup ovenproof dishes. Fill with the pasta mixture. Top with the remaining cheese. The dish may be made ahead and refrigerated or frozen at this stage.

1 POUND HEAD OF ESCAROLE, CORED
AND THINLY SLICED

2 CUPS SHREDDED PART-SKIM
MOZZARELLA CHEESE (8 OUNCES),
DIVIDED

COOKING SPRAY

4 To continue, preheat the oven to 375°F. Loosely cover the dish(es) with foil and bake for 20 minutes, then uncover and continue to bake until bubbling and the cheese is melted, an additional 15 to 30 minutes, depending on the size of the pan. Allow to rest for 10 minutes before serving.

TO REFRIGERATE AND SERVE

Wrap the unbaked dish(es) tightly in foil and refrigerate for up to 4 days.

When ready to serve, allow to sit at room temperature while the oven heats to 375°F. Loosen the foil and bake for 30 minutes, then uncover and bake for 20 to 40 minutes more, depending on the size of the pan.

TO FREEZE AND SERVE

Wrap the unbaked dish(es) tightly in plastic wrap and then in foil. Freeze for up to 3 months.

Thaw in the refrigerator for 36 to 48 hours, then remove the plastic wrap and heat as in the "to refrigerate" instructions. Or, to reheat without thawing, remove the plastic wrap and re-cover loosely with foil. Place in a cold oven and set the oven to 375°F. Once the oven comes to temperature, allow to cook for 50 to 60 minutes, then remove the foil and cook for another 30 to 40 minutes, depending on the size of the dish.

✻ **Serving size:** 2 cups; **Per serving:** Calories 520; Total Fat 10g (Mono Fat 7.4g, Poly Fat 2.5g, Sat Fat 4.3g); Protein 45g; Carb 52g; Fiber 8g; Cholesterol 100mg; Sodium 704mg; **Excellent source of:** Calcium, Fiber, Iron, Niacin, Pantothenic Acid, Phosphorus, Protein, Selenium, Vitamin A, Vitamin B6, Vitamin C, Vitamin K; **Good source of:** Magnesium, Manganese, Potassium, Riboflavin, Thiamin

Chicken Scarpariello with Cauliflower and Artichokes

• MAKES 8 SERVINGS •

THERE ARE A LOT OF great mom-and-pop Italian-American restaurants, which I still frequent, in the Queens neighborhood where I grew up. These are places where you feel at home and Nonna is really in the kitchen cooking for you. This is a riff on a dish I often order there—bone-in chicken breast simmered with Italian sausage and sweet and hot peppers in a garlicky white wine sauce. I keep mine healthy by using poultry sausage and adding cauliflower and artichokes. Nonna officially approves.

- 4 BONE-IN CHICKEN BREAST HALVES (ABOUT 5 POUNDS), SKIN REMOVED, HALVED CROSSWISE (HAVE YOUR BUTCHER DO THIS)
- 1½ TEASPOONS SALT
- ¼ TEASPOON FRESHLY GROUND BLACK PEPPER
- ¼ CUP OLIVE OIL, DIVIDED
- 2 FULLY COOKED ITALIAN CHICKEN OR TURKEY SAUSAGE LINKS (6 OUNCES TOTAL), SLICED THINLY ON THE BIAS
- ½ HEAD CAULIFLOWER, CUT INTO 1½-INCH FLORETS (4 CUPS)
- 1 MEDIUM RED BELL PEPPER, SLICED THINLY
- 1 MEDIUM ONION, SLICED INTO HALF-MOONS
- 4 CLOVES GARLIC, SMASHED
- 1 9-OUNCE PACKAGE FROZEN ARTICHOKE HEARTS
- 2 JARRED HOT CHERRY PEPPERS, CORED, SEEDED, AND SLICED (¼ CUP)
- ½ CUP DRY WHITE WINE, SUCH AS PINOT GRIGIO
- 1 LARGE SPRIG FRESH ROSEMARY
- 2 CUPS LOW-SODIUM CHICKEN BROTH

1 Season the chicken all over with the salt and pepper. Heat 1 tablespoon of the oil in a large (5- to 6-quart) pot, such as a Dutch oven, over medium heat. Add the sausage and cook, stirring, until it is browned, 2 to 3 minutes. Transfer the sausage to a plate.

2 Raise the heat to medium-high. Add 2 tablespoons of the oil and brown the chicken on both sides, in two batches, about 4 to 6 minutes per batch, and transfer to a plate.

3 Add the remaining 1 tablespoon oil to the pot, then add the cauliflower, bell pepper, onion, and garlic and cook, stirring, until the onion is translucent and beginning to brown at the edges, 5 to 7 minutes. Add the frozen artichokes, cherry peppers, and white wine to pan. Allow the wine to reduce by about half then return the chicken and sausage to the pan and add the rosemary. Add the chicken broth and just enough water, if needed, to cover the chicken. Bring to a boil, lower the heat to medium-low, cover, and simmer until the chicken is cooked through, about 25 to 30 minutes.

4 Using a large slotted spoon, transfer the chicken and vegetables to a large bowl. Bring the liquid to a boil over high heat and continue to boil, uncovered, until it is reduced by about two-thirds and is slightly thickened, 15 to 20 minutes. Pour the sauce over the chicken and serve.

Recipe continues

TO REFRIGERATE AND REHEAT

Place in an airtight container and refrigerate for up to 4 days.

Reheat in a saucepan, covered, over low heat, stirring occasionally, until warmed though, 8 to 30 minutes, depending on the amount. Alternatively, place in a microwave-safe bowl, cover with a splatter guard, and microwave on high 60 to 90 seconds for one portion.

TO FREEZE AND REHEAT

Chill in the refrigerator for 30 minutes, then transfer to sealable freezer bags in the portions desired and freeze for up to 3 months.

Thaw in the refrigerator for 24 to 36 hours, and then reheat following the "to refrigerate" instructions. Alternatively, to thaw and reheat quickly, run hot water over the bag for 30 seconds to release the food. Transfer to a microwave-safe bowl, cover with a splatter guard, and microwave on the defrost setting for 10 minutes, then on high for 1 to 2 minutes for a single portion.

∗ **Serving size:** 1 piece of chicken and 1 cup of sauce and vegetables; **Per serving:** Calories 420; Total Fat 15g (Mono Fat 6.5g, Poly Fat 1.7g, Sat Fat 2.7g); Protein 58g; Carb 9g; Fiber 4g; Cholesterol 180mg; Sodium 800mg; **Excellent source of:** Niacin, Pantothenic Acid, Phosphorus, Potassium, Protein, Riboflavin, Selenium, Vitamin B6, Vitamin C; **Good source of:** Fiber, Folate, Magnesium, Thiamin, Vitamin A, Vitamin E, Vitamin K, Zinc

Chicken and Shrimp Brown Rice Jambalaya

• MAKES 6 SERVINGS •

THIS CLASSIC CREOLE RICE DISH is big on flavor, including the holy trinity of onion, peppers, and celery; bold spices; and smoky Andouille sausage. It also really fills you up, with two kinds of protein—juicy chicken and succulent shrimp—plus whole-grain rice. The dish comes together quickly and easily in one big pot, making it the ultimate make-ahead Southern comfort food.

2 TABLESPOONS CANOLA OIL, OR OTHER NEUTRAL TASTING OIL

1 MEDIUM ONION, CHOPPED

2 MEDIUM GREEN BELL PEPPERS, SEEDED AND DICED

2 STALKS CELERY, CHOPPED

3 OUNCES ANDOUILLE SAUSAGE, VERY THINLY SLICED

5 CLOVES GARLIC, MINCED

4 CUPS LOW-SODIUM CHICKEN BROTH

ONE 28-OUNCE CAN NO-SALT-ADDED DICED TOMATOES

1 CUP INSTANT (PARBOILED) BROWN RICE

1 BAY LEAF

2 TEASPOONS SALT-FREE CREOLE SEASONING

1 TEASPOON SALT

¼ TEASPOON FRESHLY GROUND BLACK PEPPER

¾ POUND SKINLESS, BONELESS CHICKEN THIGHS, CUT INTO 1-INCH CHUNKS

1 POUND MEDIUM SHRIMP, CLEANED, TAILS REMOVED

HOT SAUCE, TO TASTE

1 Heat the oil in a large pot or Dutch oven over medium-high heat. Add the onion, bell peppers, celery, and sausage and cook, uncovered, stirring, until the vegetables begin to soften, 5 minutes. Add the garlic and cook, stirring, 1 minute more. Add the broth, tomatoes with their juices, rice, bay leaf, Creole seasoning, salt, and black pepper and bring to a boil. Lower the heat to medium-low and cook until the rice absorbs some liquid, 10 minutes.

2 Add the chicken and cook, uncovered, for 10 minutes more, then add the shrimp and cook an additional 10 minutes, until the chicken and shrimp are cooked through. Season with hot sauce to taste.

Recipe continues

TO REFRIGERATE AND REHEAT

Place in an airtight container in the refrigerator for up to 4 days.

To reheat, place in a pot over medium-low heat, cover, and cook, stirring occasionally, until warmed through, 5 to 25 minutes, depending on the amount. Alternatively, place in a microwave-safe bowl, cover with a splatter guard, and microwave on full power for about 90 seconds to 2 minutes for one portion.

TO FREEZE AND REHEAT

Chill in the refrigerator for 30 minutes, then transfer into freezer bags in the portions desired and freeze for up to 4 months.

Thaw in the refrigerator for 24 to 36 hours and reheat following the "to refrigerate" directions. Or, to thaw quickly, run the bag under hot water for 30 seconds to release the food, then transfer it to a pot along with 1 to 2 tablespoons of water. Cover and cook over medium-low heat, stirring occasionally, until warmed through, 12 to 45 minutes, depending on the amount. Add a bit more water to the pot if the bottom is getting dry.

Alternatively, after running the bag under hot water, transfer to a microwave-safe bowl, cover with a splatter guard, and microwave on the defrost setting for about 10 minutes per portion, then heat through on full power for 90 seconds to 2 minutes for one portion.

＊**Serving size:** 2 cups; **Per serving:** Calories 300; Total Fat 10g (Mono Fat 3.9g, Poly Fat 2.2g, Sat Fat 1.9g); Protein 33g; Carb 20g; Fiber 3g; Cholesterol 175mg; Sodium 750mg; **Excellent source of:** Copper, Manganese, Niacin, Phosphorus, Protein, Vitamin A, Vitamin B6, Vitamin C; **Good source of:** Fiber, Iron, Magnesium, Potassium, Selenium, Vitamin K, Zinc

Chipotle Chicken Chili with Orange Essence

• MAKES 6 SERVINGS •

THIS BOUNTIFUL CHILI HAS CHUNKS of tender chicken, hearty black beans, sweet red peppers, and tomatoes, simmered with fragrant spices and smoky chipotle chiles, and brightened with a fresh hint of orange. It has all the homey appeal you expect from a chili, but with a fun, unexpected twist.

1¼ POUNDS SKINLESS, BONELESS CHICKEN BREASTS, CUT INTO ½-INCH CHUNKS

2 TABLESPOONS MASA HARINA OR ALL-PURPOSE FLOUR

¾ TEASPOON SALT, DIVIDED

3 TABLESPOONS CANOLA OIL OR OTHER NEUTRAL TASTING OIL, DIVIDED

1 MEDIUM ONION, DICED

1 MEDIUM RED BELL PEPPER, DICED

3 CLOVES GARLIC, MINCED

1 TABLESPOON CHILI POWDER

1 TEASPOON GROUND CUMIN

½ TEASPOON GROUND CORIANDER

½ TEASPOON DRIED OREGANO

TWO 14.5-OUNCE CANS NO-SALT-ADDED BLACK BEANS, DRAINED AND RINSED

ONE 28-OUNCE CAN NO-SALT-ADDED CRUSHED TOMATOES

1 CANNED CHIPOTLE PEPPER IN ADOBO, SEEDED AND MINCED, PLUS 2 TEASPOONS OF THE SAUCE

THREE 3 × ½-INCH STRIPS ORANGE ZEST

⅓ CUP ORANGE JUICE

FOR SERVING:

½ CUP LOW-FAT PLAIN GREEK YOGURT

¼ CUP FRESH CILANTRO LEAVES

1 Toss the chicken with the masa harina or flour and ¼ teaspoon of the salt until evenly coated.

2 Heat 1 tablespoon of the oil in a large pot or Dutch oven over medium-high heat. Add half of the chicken and cook, stirring once or twice until browned, 2 to 3 minutes total, then transfer it to a plate. Add 1 tablespoon of the oil to the pot and repeat with the remaining chicken.

3 Heat the remaining 1 tablespoon oil in the same pot. Lower the heat to medium. Add the onion and bell pepper and cook, stirring occasionally and scraping any brown bits from the bottom of the pot, until the vegetables soften, 3 minutes. Add the garlic, chili powder, cumin, coriander, and oregano and cook, stirring, for 30 seconds more.

4 Add the beans, tomatoes with their juices, 1 cup of water, the chipotle and adobo sauce, orange zest, and orange juice and bring to a boil. Lower the heat to medium-low and partially cover the pot. Simmer, stirring occasionally, until thickened slightly and the ingredients have melded, 20 to 30 minutes. Return the chicken to the pot and cook until it is cooked through, 5 minutes more. Pluck out the pieces of orange zest before serving. The chili may be refrigerated or frozen at this stage.

5 Serve topped with a dollop of the Greek yogurt and a sprinkle of the cilantro.

Recipe continues

TO REFRIGERATE AND REHEAT

Place in an airtight container in the refrigerator for up to 4 days.

To reheat, place in a pot over medium-low heat, cover, and cook, stirring occasionally, until warmed through, 5 to 25 minutes, depending on the amount. Alternatively, place in a microwave-safe bowl, cover with a splatter guard, and microwave on full power for about 90 seconds to 2 minutes for a single portion.

TO FREEZE AND REHEAT

Chill in the refrigerator for 30 minutes then transfer into freezer bags in the portions desired and freeze for up to 4 months.

Thaw in the refrigerator for 36 to 48 hours and reheat following the "to refrigerate" directions. Or, to thaw quickly, run the bag under hot water for 30 seconds to release the food, then transfer it to a pot along with 1 to 2 tablespoons of water. Cover and cook over medium-low heat, stirring occasionally, until warmed through, 15 to 50 minutes, depending on the amount. Add a bit more water to the pot if the bottom is getting dry.

Alternatively, after running the bag under hot water, transfer to a microwave-safe bowl, cover with a splatter guard, and microwave on the defrost setting for about 10 minutes per portion, then heat through on full power for 90 seconds to 2 minutes for one serving.

＊ **Serving size:** 1⅓ cups; **Per serving:** Calories 330; Total Fat 10g (Mono Fat 5.6g, Poly Fat 1.2g, Sat Fat 1.7g); Protein 30g; Carb 33g; Fiber 9g; Cholesterol 70mg; Sodium 690mg; **Excellent source of:** Fiber, Niacin, Phosphorus, Potassium, Protein, Selenium, Vitamin A, Vitamin B6, Vitamin C; **Good source of:** Iron, Pantothenic Acid, Riboflavin

Chicken Braised in Red Wine (Coq au Vin) • MAKES 6 SERVINGS •

IT'S A MYTH THAT CLASSIC French food is always loaded with butter and cream. Coq au vin is case in point, a sumptuous, old-world French dish that is also quite healthy. In it, chicken and vegetables are simmered in red wine (but of course!), along with garlic, smoky bacon (I use the lean Canadian variety), and fresh herbs. Once the chicken is cooked, the liquid is reduced so it is thickened and its flavor is concentrated. Serve it with a whole-grain baguette to sop up every drop.

½ CUP ALL-PURPOSE FLOUR

1 TEASPOON SALT, PLUS MORE TO TASTE

½ TEASPOON FRESHLY GROUND BLACK PEPPER

12 MEDIUM BONE-IN CHICKEN THIGHS (4 POUNDS), SKIN REMOVED AND TRIMMED

4 TABLESPOONS OLIVE OIL, DIVIDED

ONE 14-OUNCE PACKAGE FROZEN PEELED PEARL ONIONS, THAWED AND PATTED DRY

8 OUNCES WHITE BUTTON MUSHROOMS, QUARTERED (ABOUT 4 CUPS)

2 SLICES CANADIAN BACON (3 OUNCES), CHOPPED

3 CLOVES GARLIC, CRUSHED

2 CUPS DRY RED WINE, SUCH AS PINOT NOIR OR BURGUNDY

2 CUPS LOW-SODIUM CHICKEN BROTH

3 MEDIUM CARROTS, SLICED INTO ¼-INCH-THICK ROUNDS

2 MEDIUM PARSNIPS, SLICED INTO ¼-INCH-THICK ROUNDS

2 TABLESPOONS TOMATO PASTE

1 TABLESPOON CHOPPED FRESH THYME

1 BAY LEAF

1 Combine the flour, salt, and pepper in a gallon-sized sealable plastic bag. Toss the chicken in the flour mixture to coat evenly.

2 Heat 3 tablespoons of the oil in a large, heavy pot such as a Dutch oven, over medium-high heat, and brown the chicken in 3 batches, shaking off any excess flour before you add the chicken to the pot. Cook until golden on both sides, about 3 minutes total per batch. Transfer with tongs to a plate as browned.

3 Add the remaining 1 tablespoon oil, then add the onions and cook, stirring, until browned, about 4 minutes. Stir in the mushrooms, bacon, and garlic and cook, stirring, 3 minutes. Add the wine, broth, carrots, parsnips, tomato paste, thyme, and bay leaf and bring to a simmer.

4 Return the chicken to the pot. Lower the heat to medium-low, cover, and simmer until the chicken is cooked through and the vegetables are tender, about 25 minutes. Use tongs to transfer the chicken to a plate, then turn the heat to medium and cook until the sauce is reduced and thickened, 5 to 10 minutes more. Season with additional salt, if desired. Discard the bay leaf and serve.

Recipe continues

TO REFRIGERATE AND REHEAT

Store in an airtight container in the refrigerator for up to 4 days.

To reheat, place in a saucepan with 1 to 2 tablespoons of water per portion, cover, and warm over medium-low heat, stirring occasionally, until warmed through, 8 to 25 minutes, depending on the amount. Alternatively, place in a microwave-safe dish, cover with a splatter guard, and microwave on high for 2 minutes for a single serving.

TO FREEZE AND REHEAT

Chill in the refrigerator for 30 minutes, then place portion sizes desired in sealable freezer bags and freeze for up to 3 months.

Thaw in the refrigerator for 24 to 36 hours and reheat following the "to refrigerate" directions. Or, to thaw a single serving quickly, run the bag under hot water for 30 seconds to release the food, then transfer it to a microwave-safe dish, cover with a splatter guard, and microwave on the defrost setting for 10 minutes, then 2 minutes on high to warm through.

✳ **Serving size:** 2 chicken thighs and 1 cup sauce; **Per serving:** Calories 440; Total Fat 16g (Mono Fat 9g, Poly Fat 2.6g, Sat Fat 3.1g); Protein 36g; Carb 24g; Fiber 4g; Cholesterol 150mg; Sodium 720mg; **Excellent source of:** Copper, Manganese, Niacin, Pantothenic Acid, Phosphorus, Potassium, Protein, Riboflavin, Selenium, Thiamin, Vitamin A, Vitamin B6, Vitamin K, Zinc; **Good source of:** Fiber, Folate, Iron, Magnesium, Vitamin B12, Vitamin C

Green "Tandoori" Grilled Chicken

• MAKES 6 SERVINGS •

THE MARINADE FOR THIS CHICKEN is more like a rub made with the aromatic Indian spices typically used in tandoori seasoning, with a generous handful of cilantro added for fresh green color and flavor. Call it what you will, this seasoning mix is bold and delicious, taking basic chicken breast far from the realm of the ho-hum. Also out of the ordinary, the chicken can be frozen in the "marinade," so you can enjoy its incredible flavor at your convenience.

½ SMALL BUNCH FRESH CILANTRO (ABOUT 1½ OUNCES), THICK STEMS TRIMMED OFF

3 TABLESPOONS CANOLA OIL, OR OTHER NEUTRAL TASTING OIL

5 CLOVES GARLIC, COARSELY CHOPPED

1 INCH PIECE PEELED GINGER, GRATED

1 TEASPOON CRUSHED RED PEPPER FLAKES

1 TEASPOON GROUND CARDAMOM

1 TEASPOON GROUND CORIANDER

1 TEASPOON GROUND CUMIN

1 TEASPOON GROUND TURMERIC

1 TEASPOON SALT

½ TEASPOON FRESHLY GROUND BLACK PEPPER

½ TEASPOON PAPRIKA

SIX 6-OUNCE PIECES SKINLESS, BONELESS CHICKEN BREASTS, POUNDED TO ½-INCH THICKNESS

COOKING SPRAY

1 In the small bowl of a food processor, add the cilantro, ¼ cup of water, the oil, garlic, ginger, red pepper flakes, cardamom, coriander, cumin, turmeric, salt, pepper, and paprika and puree until smooth, about 30 seconds.

2 Arrange the chicken in sealable plastic bags, in the batch size desired. Divide the marinade among the bags, toss to coat, and seal, removing as much air as possible from the bag. Marinate in the refrigerator for at least 4 hours or up to 1 day, or freeze in the marinade for up to 2 months, then thaw in the refrigerator for 24 to 36 hours to be ready to serve.

3 To continue, spray a grill or grill pan with cooking spray and heat it over medium-high heat. Cook the chicken until cooked through and grill marks form, about 3 to 4 minutes per side.

Recipe continues

TO REFRIGERATE AND REHEAT

Place the cooked chicken in an airtight container in the refrigerator for up to 3 days. To reheat, cover with foil and place in a preheated 350°F oven for 10 to 12 minutes, or place on a microwave-safe plate and microwave on high for about 1 minute for one portion.

TO FREEZE AND REHEAT

If the chicken has been marinated in the freezer, refreezing is not recommended.

To freeze the cooked chicken, wrap each piece in plastic wrap or foil and place in a sealable plastic bag for up to 3 months.

Thaw in the refrigerator for about 24 hours, then heat following the "to refrigerate" directions. Or, to thaw more quickly, unwrap the quantity desired and wrap in foil. Place in a cold oven set to 350°F. Once the oven has reached temperature, continue to cook for 25 minutes, until warmed through. Alternatively, unwrap, place on a microwave-safe plate, cover with a splatter guard, and microwave on defrost for 3 minutes per portion, then continue to heat through on high for 1 minute for a single portion.

∗ **Serving size:** 1 piece; **Per serving:** Calories 270; Total Fat 12g (Mono Fat 5.6g, Poly Fat 2.7g, Sat Fat 1.5g); Protein 39g; Carb 1g; Fiber 0g; Cholesterol 125mg; Sodium 470mg; **Excellent source of:** Niacin, Pantothenic Acid, Phosphorus, Protein, Selenium, Vitamin B6, Vitamin K; **Good source of:** Magnesium, Potassium, Riboflavin, Thiamin, Vitamin A, Vitamin E

Grilled Chicken and Vegetable Parmesan
with Simple Marinara Sauce   • MAKES 6 SERVINGS •

THIS DISH HAS ALL THE saucy, melted-cheesy appeal of a classic chicken Parmesan recipe, but with the bonus of a layer of char-grilled vegetables--zucchini, eggplant and peppers--boosting flavor, color and nutrition. Because the chicken is grilled too, there really is no downside, only pleasure.

COOKING SPRAY

¼ CUP EXTRA VIRGIN OLIVE OIL

1 SMALL EGGPLANT (ABOUT ½ POUND), SLICED INTO ⅓-INCH-THICK ROUNDS

1 MEDIUM ZUCCHINI (ABOUT ½ POUND), SLICED INTO ½-INCH-THICK ROUNDS

1 MEDIUM RED BELL PEPPER, CORED AND SLICED INTO ½-INCH-THICK RINGS

SIX 5-OUNCE SKINLESS, BONELESS CHICKEN BREASTS, POUNDED TO ½-INCH THICKNESS

¼ TEASPOON SALT

½ TEASPOON FRESHLY GROUND BLACK PEPPER, TO TASTE

1 TEASPOON DRIED OREGANO

1¼ CUPS SIMPLE MARINARA SAUCE (RECIPE FOLLOWS) OR STORE-BOUGHT MARINARA

1 CUP GRATED PART-SKIM MOZZARELLA CHEESE

3 TABLESPOONS FRESHLY GRATED PARMESAN CHEESE

1 Spray a grill or grill pan with cooking spray and preheat it over medium-high heat. Brush all of the sliced vegetables with oil. Then brush the chicken on both sides with the remaining oil. Season the vegetables and the chicken with the salt and black pepper. Sprinkle the oregano over the zucchini and eggplant.

2 Grill the chicken, in batches if necessary, until just cooked through, 3 minutes per side. Transfer the cooked chicken to a plate.

3 Grill the vegetables, in batches if necessary, turning once or twice, until they have grill marks and are softened, about 9 minutes total for the eggplant, 7 minutes total for the zucchini and bell pepper.

4 Spread a heaping tablespoon of the marinara sauce on the bottom of each of 6 oven-, microwave-, and freezer-safe dishes. Place a chicken breast into each and then top each with 2 slices of eggplant, 2 slices of zucchini, and 1 slice of bell pepper. Drizzle the remaining marinara on top, then sprinkle with the cheeses. (To make in one large pan, spread ½ cup of the sauce on the bottom of a 9 × 13-inch baking pan; add the chicken in one layer, then top with the vegetables, sauce, and cheese.) The dish(es) may be refrigerated or frozen at this stage.

5 To continue, preheat the oven to 400°F. Place the dish(es) in the oven and bake until the cheese is melted and bubbling, about 10 minutes.

Recipe continues

TO REFRIGERATE AND REHEAT

Cover tightly with plastic wrap or foil and refrigerate for up to 3 days.

To reheat, uncover and allow to sit at room temperature as the oven preheats to 350°F, then bake for about 25 minutes. Alternatively, unwrap, cover with a splatter guard, and microwave on high for 2 minutes for one portion.

TO FREEZE AND REHEAT

Wrap well in plastic wrap and then foil. Allow to chill in the refrigerator for 30 minutes, then freeze for up to 3 months.

Thaw in the refrigerator for 18 to 24 hours and reheat following the "to refrigerate" directions. Or, to thaw quickly, uncover completely, and place the frozen dish in a cold oven set to 350°F. Once the oven reaches temperature, cook for an additional 25 to 30 minutes. Alternatively, uncover completely, place a splatter guard over the dish, and thaw in the microwave on the defrost setting for 8 minutes per portion, then microwave on high for 1 to 2 more minutes to warm though.

✳ **Serving size:** 1 piece; **Per serving:** Calories 360; Total Fat 18g (Mono Fat 9.3g, Poly Fat 1.9g, Sat Fat 4.6g); Protein 40g; Carb 10g; Fiber 3g; Cholesterol 115mg; Sodium 640mg; **Excellent source of:** Niacin, Pantothenic Acid, Phosphorus, Potassium, Protein, Riboflavin, Selenium, Vitamin A, Vitamin B6, Vitamin C; **Good source of:** Calcium, Fiber, Folate, Magnesium, Manganese, Thiamin, Vitamin E, Vitamin K, Zinc

SIMPLE MARINARA SAUCE
• MAKES 6 CUPS; 12 SERVINGS •

IT DOESN'T TAKE MUCH TIME, effort, or more than a handful of ingredients to make a good marinara sauce. And when you make your own you save money and get the very best quality. So why wouldn't you, especially since you can make it ahead to have on hand when you need it?

- 2 TABLESPOONS OLIVE OIL
- 1 MEDIUM ONION, FINELY CHOPPED
- 4 CLOVES GARLIC, THINLY SLICED
- TWO 28-OUNCE CANS CRUSHED TOMATOES
- GENEROUS PINCH CRUSHED RED PEPPER FLAKES
- ½ TEASPOON FRESHLY GROUND BLACK PEPPER
- ¼ TEASPOON SALT

Heat the oil in a heavy pot or Dutch oven over medium heat. Add the onion and cook, stirring occasionally, until softened, 3 to 5 minutes. Add the garlic and cook, stirring, until it is softened and golden but not browned, about 2 minutes more. Add the crushed tomatoes with their juices, red pepper flakes, black pepper, and salt and bring to a boil. Lower the heat to medium-low and simmer, uncovered, for 15 minutes.

TO REFRIGERATE AND RE-HEAT

Place the sauce in an airtight container and refrigerate for up to 1 week.

To reheat, place in a covered saucepan over medium-low heat for 4 to 15 minutes, depending on the amount being warmed.

TO FREEZE AND THAW

Chill in the refrigerator for 30 minutes, then transfer to sealable plastic freezer bags in the portions desired and freeze for up to 3 months.

Thaw in the refrigerator for 24 to 36 hours then reheat according to the "to refrigerate" directions above, or to thaw quickly, run the bag under hot water for 30 seconds to release the sauce, then transfer it to a saucepan, cover, and cook over medium-low heat until thawed, 8 to 30 minutes, depending on the amount. Alternatively, once released from the bag, transfer to a microwave-safe bowl, cover with a splatter guard, and microwave on the defrost setting for 6 minutes and then on high for 1 minute for one cup of the sauce.

✳ **Serving size:** ½ cup; **Per serving:** Calories 70; Total Fat 2.5g (Mono Fat 1.6g, Poly Fat 0.2g, Sat Fat 0.3g); Protein 2g; Carb 10g; Fiber 2g; Cholesterol 0mg; Sodium 370mg; **Excellent source of:** Vitamin C

Grandma's Roast Chicken with Pan Juices · MAKES 6 SERVINGS ·

A SIMPLE ROASTED CHICKEN HAS got to be one of the original make-ahead meals, since it can be eaten hot or chilled, and leftovers can be used for any number of dishes, like the Mexican Chicken and Hominy Stew, page 196, for example, or the Turkey Tetrazzini Casserole, page 233 (which of course would then be Chicken Tetrazzini).

This moist, crispy-skinned chicken is seasoned just like my Grandma used to do it, with paprika, lemon, and garlic. Sure, you can buy a rotisserie chicken just about anywhere these days, and they are fine. But they don't come close to being as deliciously fresh-tasting as when you do it yourself.

ONE 4- TO 5-POUND WHOLE CHICKEN

3 TABLESPOONS OLIVE OIL

2 TEASPOONS PAPRIKA

1 TEASPOON GARLIC POWDER

1 TEASPOON SALT

¾ TEASPOON FRESHLY GROUND BLACK PEPPER

3 LEMONS, QUARTERED

8 CLOVES GARLIC, SMASHED

3 CUPS LOW-SODIUM CHICKEN BROTH

1 Preheat the oven to 425°F.

2 Remove the giblets and neck from the cavity of the chicken if provided and discard or reserve for another use. Pat the chicken dry and transfer it to a rack set in a roasting pan.

3 In a small bowl, stir together the oil, paprika, garlic powder, salt, and pepper. Rub the chicken all over with the spice mixture inside and out. Stuff the cavity of the bird with the lemons and garlic and tie the legs together with cooking twine. Pour 2½ cups of the chicken broth into the bottom of the pan.

4 Roast the chicken in middle of the oven for 20 minutes, then lower the oven temperature to 375°F and continue to roast, adding some water to the bottom if necessary to keep at least about ¼ inch of liquid in the pan, until an instant-read thermometer inserted into a meaty part of the thigh (not touching the bone) registers at least 165°F, and up to 175°F, if you like it more well done, 1¼ to 1½ hours more. Transfer the chicken to a cutting board and let rest, loosely covered with foil for 20 minutes.

Recipe continues

5 While the chicken rests, pour the pan juices into a cup, let it sit for a few minutes, then skim off and discard the fat that accumulates on top. Transfer the pan juices to a small saucepan along with the remaining ½ cup broth. Bring to a boil, then lower the heat to medium and simmer until reduced to about 1 cup.

6 Carve the chicken and serve with the pan juices.

TO REFRIGERATE AND SERVE

Pack the chicken and pan juices in separate airtight containers for up to 4 days.

Serve the chicken at room temperature, or to heat, wrap chicken in foil and place in a 350°F oven for about 20 minutes. Warm the sauce in a saucepan, uncovered, over medium-low heat for 6 to 8 minutes.

To heat a single portion of chicken and sauce in the microwave, place on a microwave-safe plate, cover with a splatter guard, and microwave for about 1 minute.

TO FREEZE AND SERVE

Freezing the cooked chicken is not recommended.

The juices may be frozen in a sealable plastic freezer bag and frozen for up to 3 months. Thaw in the refrigerator for 24 hours then reheat following the "to refrigerate" directions. To thaw the pan juices quickly, run the bag under hot water for 30 seconds, then transfer the sauce to a saucepan, cover, and heat over medium heat for 6 to 12 minutes, or place in a microwave-safe bowl and microwave on the defrost setting for about 8 minutes, then on high for 90 seconds for the full 2-cup batch.

✳ **Serving size:** ⅙ chicken and ⅓ cup pan juices; **Per serving (eaten without the skin):** Calories 460; Total Fat 16g (Mono Fat 7.7g, Poly Fat 3.4g, Sat Fat 3g); Protein 70g; Carb 4g; Fiber 1g; Cholesterol 220mg; Sodium 680mg; **Excellent source of:** Iron, Niacin, Pantothenic Acid, Phosphorus, Protein, Riboflavin, Selenium, Vitamin B6, Vitamin C, Zinc

Mini Turkey Meatloaves • MAKES 6 SERVINGS •

A SIMPLE MUFFIN TIN MAKES for adorable, perfectly portioned meatloaves that are easy to freeze individually so you can pull out as many, or as few, as you need for an effortless, family-friendly main course on a busy night.

These taste like a classic turkey meatloaf, but they are extra moist and much better for you thanks to an entire zucchini that's grated into the mix, as well the use of whole-grain quick-cooking oats instead of bread crumbs. The oats lock in juices and meld seamlessly into the mix so you can't tell they are there. Feel free to reveal the secret ingredients to any picky eaters after they have gobbled it up!

COOKING SPRAY

1 TABLESPOON OLIVE OIL

1 SMALL ONION, FINELY CHOPPED

¼ MEDIUM RED BELL PEPPER, FINELY CHOPPED

2 CLOVES GARLIC, MINCED

1½ POUNDS LEAN GROUND TURKEY

1 SMALL ZUCCHINI (6 OUNCES) SHREDDED (1¼ CUPS)

2 LARGE EGGS, LIGHTLY BEATEN

¾ CUP QUICK-COOKING OATS

ONE 8-OUNCE CAN NO-SALT-ADDED TOMATO SAUCE

1 TABLESPOON WORCESTERSHIRE SAUCE

1 TABLESPOON YELLOW MUSTARD

1 TEASPOON SALT

1 Preheat the oven to 350°F. Spray a muffin tin with cooking spray.

2 Heat the oil in a medium nonstick skillet over medium-high heat. Add the onion and cook, stirring occasionally, until it softens slightly, 2 minutes. Add the bell pepper and cook, stirring, for 1 minute more. Stir in the garlic and cook for 30 seconds. Set aside to cool slightly.

3 In a large bowl, combine the turkey, onion-pepper mixture, zucchini, egg, oats, ¼ cup of the tomato sauce, the Worcestershire sauce, mustard, and salt. Mix with your hands until just combined. Using an ice-cream scoop, transfer the mixture into the muffin tin, then top each meatloaf with 1 tablespoon of the remaining tomato sauce. Bake until an instant-read thermometer registers 165°F, about 25 minutes. Allow to rest for 5 minutes, then remove from the tin by running a butter knife or offset spatula around each loaf.

Recipe continues

TO REFRIGERATE AND REHEAT

Chill in the refrigerator, uncovered for 30 minutes, then place in an airtight container in the refrigerator for up to 4 days.

To reheat, place loaves, uncovered, on a baking tray or piece of foil and bake in a 350°F oven until warmed through, about 15 minutes. Alternatively, place on a microwave-safe plate, cover with a splatter guard, and microwave on full power for 60 to 90 seconds for a single 2-loaf portion.

TO FREEZE AND REHEAT

Chill in the refrigerator, uncovered, for 30 minutes, then wrap each loaf individually in plastic wrap or foil and place in an airtight freezer-safe container or sealable plastic freezer bag. Freeze for up to 3 months.

There is no need to thaw. To reheat, unwrap frozen loaves and place them on a baking tray or on foil, uncovered, in a cold oven set to 350°F. Once the oven reaches temperature, continue cooking for 45 minutes. Alternatively, unwrap frozen loaves, place on a microwave-safe plate, cover with a splatter guard, and microwave on high for 2½ minutes for a single 2-loaf portion.

＊ **Serving size:** 2 loaves; **Per serving:** Calories 240; Total Fat 7g (Mono Fat 2.4g, Poly Fat 0.6g, Sat Fat 0.9g); Protein 33g; Carb 14g; Fiber 3g; Cholesterol 115mg; Sodium 540mg; **Excellent source of:** Protein, Vitamin C; **Good source of:** Fiber, Iron, Potassium

Polenta Casserole with Broccoli Rabe, White Beans, and Sausage

• MAKES 6 SERVINGS •

THE INGREDIENTS IN THIS DISH are a tried-and-true combination of creamy yellow cornmeal (polenta), peppery broccoli rabe, hearty white beans, and savory sausage found on many Italian menus for good reason. They really work together, each excellent on its own, but somehow elevated when paired with the others. Here they come together as a casserole, for a stunning and satisfying make-ahead dinner. If you can't find, or don't care for, broccoli rabe, regular broccoli will work too.

- 1 POUND BROCCOLI RABE, TRIMMED OF THICKER COARSE BOTTOMS (ABOUT ½ OF A LARGE BUNCH), OR ONE 16-OUNCE BAG FROZEN CHOPPED BROCCOLI RABE, THAWED AND DRAINED
- 12 OUNCES UNCOOKED ITALIAN POULTRY SAUSAGE, HOT OR SWEET, CASINGS REMOVED
- 2 TABLESPOONS OLIVE OIL, DIVIDED
- ONE 15-OUNCE CAN LOW-SODIUM CANNELLINI BEANS, DRAINED AND RINSED
- 2 CLOVES GARLIC, SLICED
- 3 CUPS LOW-SODIUM CHICKEN BROTH
- ¼ CUP CHOPPED SUN-DRIED TOMATOES, NOT OIL-PACKED
- ½ TEASPOON SALT
- ¼ TEASPOON CRUSHED RED PEPPER FLAKES, OPTIONAL
- 1½ CUPS YELLOW CORNMEAL (POLENTA)
- ½ CUP FINELY GRATED PARMESAN CHEESE
- 1 TABLESPOON UNSALTED BUTTER, OPTIONAL

1 If using fresh broccoli rabe, place the broccoli rabe in a steamer basket set over a pot of boiling water. Cover, and steam until just tender, 4 to 5 minutes. Once cool enough to handle, chop into bite-size pieces.

2 Heat a large nonstick skillet over medium-high heat. Add the sausage and cook, stirring and breaking it up with a spoon, until it is browned and cooked through, about 4 minutes. Transfer to a plate.

3 Heat 1 tablespoon of the oil in the same skillet. Add the broccoli rabe, beans, and garlic and cook, stirring, until everything is warmed through and the garlic has softened, 2 to 3 minutes.

4 Place the broth, 3 cups of water, the sundried tomatoes, salt, and red pepper flakes, if using, into a large pot and bring to a boil. Add the cornmeal in a stream, whisking constantly, until no lumps remain and it returns to a simmer. Lower the heat to low and cook, whisking frequently, until thick and creamy, 8 to 10 minutes. Whisk in the remaining 1 tablespoon oil, the Parmesan, and butter, if using.

5   Immediately spoon the polenta into one 9 × 13-inch baking dish or divide among two 8-inch baking dishes or 6 individual microwave and ovenproof dishes. Spread the broccoli rabe mixture and cooked sausage over the polenta. The dish may be refrigerated or frozen at this stage.

6   To continue, preheat the oven to 350°F. Bake until heated through, about 20 minutes.

TO REFRIGERATE AND SERVE

Chill in the refrigerator, uncovered, for 30 minutes, then cover tightly and refrigerate for up to 4 days.

To heat, allow to sit at room temperature as you preheat the oven to 350°F. Bake, covered, for 35 minutes. Alternatively, place a single serving in the microwave, uncover, then cover with a splatter guard and microwave on high for about 2 minutes.

TO FREEZE AND SERVE

Chill in the refrigerator, uncovered, for 30 minutes, then cover tightly with an airtight lid or both plastic wrap and then aluminum foil and freeze for up to 3 months.

Thaw in the refrigerator for 18 to 24 hours and then heat following the "to refrigerate" directions. Or, to heat without thawing, remove the lid or plastic wrap, and re-cover with foil. Place in a cold oven set for 350°F. When the oven reaches temperature, continue to cook for about 50 minutes, until warmed through. Alternatively, place a single serving in the microwave, cover with a splatter guard, and microwave on the defrost setting for about 7 minutes, and then on high for 2 minutes more.

∗ **Serving size:** About 1¾ cups; **Per serving:** Calories 360; Total Fat 15g (Mono Fat 4.4g, Poly Fat 0.7g, Sat Fat 4.3g); Protein 21g; Carb 36g; Fiber 9g; Cholesterol 55mg; Sodium 690mg; **Excellent source of:** Fiber, Protein, Thiamin, Vitamin C, Vitamin K; **Good source of:** Calcium, Folate, Iron, Magnesium, Manganese, Phosphorus, Potassium, Riboflavin, Vitamin A

Turkey Sausage–Stuffed Pizza Pockets

• MAKES 4 SERVINGS •

THIS FUN MEAL YOU CAN eat with your hands is like having a slice of pizza with all the best toppings—sauce, cheese, and sausage—wrapped up into the crust. It's even more fun when you dip it in some extra marinara sauce. Two pockets make for a filling meal, but one is a perfect afternoon snack that is easy for an older child like my husband (kidding, Thom) to reheat on his own. These also make for great game-day party food. Also check out the vegetarian Portobello Pizza Pockets on page 295.

1 TABLESPOON OLIVE OIL

8 OUNCES UNCOOKED ITALIAN POULTRY SAUSAGE, CASINGS REMOVED

⅓ CUP SIMPLE MARINARA SAUCE (PAGE 214), OR STORE-BOUGHT MARINARA

4 CUPS LIGHTLY PACKED CHOPPED FRESH ARUGULA OR SPINACH LEAVES

1 TABLESPOON CORNMEAL OR FLOUR

1 POUND WHOLE WHEAT PIZZA DOUGH, THAWED IF FROZEN

1 CUP SHREDDED PART-SKIM MOZZARELLA CHEESE

1 EGG, BEATEN

2 TABLESPOONS FRESHLY GRATED PARMESAN CHEESE

FOR SERVING:

1 CUP SIMPLE MARINARA SAUCE (PAGE 214), OR STORE-BOUGHT MARINARA, OPTIONAL

1 Preheat the oven to 400°F. Line a baking sheet with parchment paper.

2 Heat the oil in a medium skillet over medium-high heat. Add the sausage to the pan and cook, breaking it up with a spoon, until it is browned and crumbled, about 4 minutes. Add the marinara sauce and cook, stirring, until the liquid is nearly all absorbed or evaporated, 1 to 2 minutes. Stir in the arugula or spinach and cook until just wilted, 1 minute more. Set aside to cool slightly.

3 Meanwhile, sprinkle the cornmeal or flour onto a clean work surface and use a rolling pin and/or your hands to stretch out the dough into a large rectangle about 12 × 18 inches. (Helpful hint: if the dough keeps springing back, let it rest for a few minutes before you begin to stretch it again.) Using a sharp knife or pizza cutter, cut the dough into eight equal-sized rectangles.

4 Stir the mozzarella cheese into the cooled sausage mixture. Place about ¼ cup of the filling on one side of each rectangle.

Recipe continues

5 Brush the border of each rectangle with some of the egg, then close the dough over the topping and use a fork to crimp the edges and seal each one closed. Brush the tops with the egg and sprinkle with the Parmesan cheese. Place the pockets on the prepared baking tray and bake until golden brown, 15 to 18 minutes.

6 Serve with warmed marinara sauce, if desired.

TO REFRIGERATE AND REHEAT

Allow to cool at room temperature 30 minutes, then wrap each pizza pocket in plastic wrap or foil and refrigerate for up to 4 days. To reheat, unwrap, place on a foil sheet or baking tray, and warm in a preheated 350°F oven for 20 to 25 minutes. Alternatively, unwrap, then rewrap in a paper towel, place on a microwave-safe plate, and microwave on high for 1 minute for one pocket.

TO FREEZE AND REHEAT

Allow to cool at room temperature for 30 minutes, then wrap each pizza pocket in plastic wrap or foil and place in a sealable freezer bag for up to 3 months. There is no need to thaw. To reheat, unwrap, then place on a foil sheet or baking tray in a cold oven set to 350°F. Once the oven reaches temperature, continue to cook for 30 to 35 minutes until warmed through. Alternatively, unwrap, then rewrap in a paper towel, place on a microwave-safe plate, and microwave on high for 2 minutes for one pocket.

✴ **Serving size:** 2 pockets and ¼ cup sauce; **Per serving:** Calories 480; Total Fat 19g (Mono Fat 4.8g, Poly Fat .9g, Sat Fat 5.6g); Protein 28g; Carb 54g; Fiber 6.5g; Cholesterol 110mg; Sodium 970mg; **Excellent source of:** Calcium, Folate, Iron, Protein, Vitamin A, Vitamin C, Vitamin K; **Good source of:** Fiber, Manganese, Phosphorus, Riboflavin, Selenium

Sicilian Braised Chicken • MAKES 6 SERVINGS •

IN ITALIAN "AGRODOLCE" MEANS SWEET and sour, but the classic sauce also has savory and salty elements that make it sing. In this Sicilian-inspired dish the sweet comes from plump raisins and honey, and the sour from a splash of red wine vinegar. Then there are lots of savory vegetables and a salty punch from briny capers. The ingredients come together easily for a truly special one-pot meal that tastes even better after some time in the fridge or freezer. I use chicken thighs here because they stay very moist, but you can substitute bone-in chicken breasts if you prefer.

3 TABLESPOONS PINE NUTS

¼ CUP WHOLE-WHEAT PASTRY FLOUR, OR ALL-PURPOSE FLOUR

1 TEASPOON SALT, DIVIDED

¼ TEASPOON FRESHLY GROUND BLACK PEPPER

6 LARGE BONE-IN CHICKEN THIGHS (ABOUT 2¼ POUNDS), SKIN REMOVED

3 TABLESPOONS OLIVE OIL, DIVIDED

1 LARGE ONION, DICED

5 CLOVES GARLIC, MINCED

1 TEASPOON DRIED OREGANO

2 LARGE CARROTS, CHOPPED

5 STALKS CELERY, DICED

½ CUP DRY WHITE WINE, SUCH AS PINOT GRIGIO

1 CUP LOW-SODIUM CHICKEN BROTH

2 TABLESPOONS RED WINE VINEGAR

1 TABLESPOON HONEY

¼ CUP CHOPPED FRESH ITALIAN PARSLEY LEAVES

3 TABLESPOONS RAISINS

3 TABLESPOONS CAPERS, DRAINED AND RINSED

1 Toast the pine nuts in a dry skillet over medium-high heat, stirring frequently, until lightly browned, 3 to 5 minutes.

2 In a sealable plastic bag, combine the flour with ¼ teaspoon of the salt and the pepper. Add the chicken and toss to coat.

3 In a large, deep skillet heat 1 tablespoon of the oil over medium-high heat. Working in two batches, brown the chicken until golden, 3 to 4 minutes per side, adding another 1 tablespoon of oil between batches. Transfer the chicken to a plate after browning.

4 Lower the heat to medium, add the remaining 1 tablespoon of oil, then add the onion and cook, stirring, until softened and lightly golden, 6 to 7 minutes. Add the garlic and oregano and cook, stirring, 30 seconds more. Add the carrots and celery and cook, stirring, until the vegetables begin to soften, 4 to 5 minutes.

5 Return the heat to medium-high, add the wine, and cook, stirring, until the liquid is mostly evaporated, 3 to 4 minutes. Stir in the broth, vinegar, and honey, then add the parsley, raisins, capers, and pine nuts and return the chicken to the pan. Bring to a boil, then lower the heat to low, cover and cook until the chicken is cooked through and the sauce has melded, 10 to 12 minutes.

Recipe continues

TO REFRIGERATE AND REHEAT

Store in an airtight container in the refrigerator for up to 4 days.

To reheat, place in a saucepan with 1 to 2 tablespoons of water per portion, cover, and warm over medium-low heat, stirring occasionally, until warmed through, 8 to 30 minutes, depending on the amount. Alternatively, place a single serving in a microwave-safe dish, cover with a splatter guard, and microwave on high for 2 minutes. Add a splash of red wine vinegar, if needed, before serving, as the acidity tends to fade over time.

TO FREEZE AND REHEAT

Allow to chill in the refrigerator for 30 minutes, then place portion sizes desired in sealable freezer bags and freeze for up to 3 months.

Thaw in the refrigerator for 24 to 36 hours and reheat following the "to refrigerate" directions. Or, to thaw a single serving quickly, run the bag under hot water for 30 seconds to release the food, then transfer it to a microwave-safe dish, cover with a splatter guard, and microwave on the defrost setting for 12 minutes and then 90 seconds on high to warm through. Add a splash of red wine vinegar, if needed, before serving, as the acidity tends to fade over time.

✳ **Serving size:** 1 chicken thigh and ⅔ cup sauce; **Per serving:** Calories 300; Total Fat 15g (Mono Fat 6.9g, Poly Fat 3.2g, Sat Fat 2.2g); Protein 22g; Carb 17g; Fiber 3g; Cholesterol 75mg; Sodium 350mg; **Excellent source of:** Manganese, Niacin, Phosphorus, Protein, Selenium, Vitamin A, Vitamin B6, Vitamin K; **Good source of:** Fiber, Iron, Magnesium, Pantothenic Acid, Potassium, Riboflavin, Vitamin C, Zinc

Southwest Chicken Stew

• MAKES 6 SERVINGS •

HERE, JUICY BONE-IN CHICKEN BREASTS are simmered in a broth kicked-up with aromatic, Southwest spices, and brimming with colorful vegetables—corn, tomatoes, sweet red peppers, and poblano peppers. It is one of those dishes that is easy to transform into two or three totally different meals: after serving the stew, you can shred leftover chicken and scoop the vegetables out of the broth to use as filling for tacos or quesadillas, then you can add some more chicken broth, onion, and garlic to whatever is left in the pot, and top with crushed tortilla chips to turn it into a tasty tortilla soup. With all its delicious utility, think of it as the Swiss Army knife of home cooking, something you definitely want in your back pocket.

6 BONE-IN CHICKEN BREAST HALVES, SKIN REMOVED (ABOUT 3½ POUNDS TOTAL)

1½ TEASPOONS SALT, DIVIDED

½ TEASPOON FRESHLY GROUND BLACK PEPPER, DIVIDED

2 TABLESPOONS CANOLA OIL OR OTHER NEUTRAL TASTING OIL, DIVIDED

2 MEDIUM ONIONS, FINELY CHOPPED

4 POBLANO PEPPERS (1 POUND), SEEDED AND CHOPPED

6 CLOVES GARLIC, MINCED

4 TEASPOONS CHILI POWDER

2 TEASPOONS GROUND CUMIN

½ TEASPOON GROUND CORIANDER

½ TEASPOON CRUSHED RED PEPPER FLAKES

TWO 28-OUNCE CANS LOW-SODIUM DICED TOMATOES (FIRE-ROASTED OR REGULAR)

3 CUPS LOW-SODIUM CHICKEN BROTH

2 CUPS CORN KERNELS, FRESH OR FROZEN

4 RED BELL PEPPERS (2 POUNDS), SEEDED AND CHOPPED

1 Season the chicken with ½ teaspoon of the salt and ¼ teaspoon of the black pepper. Heat 1 tablespoon of the oil in a large (8-quart) Dutch oven over medium high heat. Add half the chicken and brown until lightly golden, about 2 minutes per side. Transfer the browned chicken to a plate and repeat with the remaining chicken.

2 Heat the remaining 1 tablespoon of oil to the pot. Add the onions and poblano peppers and cook, stirring occasionally, until the onions are translucent and the peppers are softened, 5 to 6 minutes. Add the garlic and cook, stirring, for 30 seconds more. Add the chili powder, cumin, remaining 1 teaspoon of salt, the coriander, red pepper flakes, and the remaining ¼ teaspoon of black pepper and cook, stirring, until fragrant, 30 seconds.

3 Return the chicken, with any accumulated juices, to the pot, piling the chicken pieces on top of one another. Add the tomatoes with their juices, chicken broth, corn, and bell peppers and bring to a boil. Lower the heat to medium-low, cover, and cook until the chicken is just cooked through, about 30 minutes. Serve the chicken, vegetables, and sauce in bowls.

Recipe continues

TO REFRIGERATE AND REHEAT

Transfer to an airtight container and refrigerate for up to 4 days.

To reheat, place the desired amount in a pot, cover, and heat over low heat, stirring occasionally, until warmed through, 8 to 30 minutes, depending on the amount. Alternatively, place in a microwave-safe dish, cover with a splatter guard, and microwave on high for about 4 minutes for a single serving.

TO FREEZE AND REHEAT

Allow to chill in the refrigerator for 30 minutes, then transfer to sealable freezer bags and freeze for up to 3 months.

Allow to thaw in the refrigerator for 36 to 48 hours, then reheat following the "to refrigerate" directions. Or, to thaw a single serving quickly, run the bag under hot water for 30 seconds to release the food, place in a microwave-safe dish, cover with a splatter guard, and microwave on the defrost setting for about 12 minutes then on high for 1 to 2 minutes.

∗ **Serving size:** 1 piece of chicken and 1¼ cups vegetables and sauce; **Per serving:** Calories 490; Total Fat 11g (Mono Fat 2.7g, Poly Fat 4.6g, Sat Fat 1.5g); Protein 56g; Carb 41g; Fiber 7g; Cholesterol 155mg; Sodium 830mg; **Excellent source of:** Fiber, Iron, Magnesium, Niacin, Pantothenic Acid, Phosphorus, Potassium, Protein, Riboflavin, Selenium, Thiamin, Vitamin A, Vitamin B6, Vitamin C; **Good source of:** Folate, Copper, Manganese, Vitamin E, Vitamin K, Zinc

Hero-Food-Stuffed Peppers · MAKES 4 SERVINGS ·

THESE TASTY AND SATISFYING STUFFED peppers are brimming with ingredients that are like health-protecting superheroes, including the full spectrum of colorful vegetables—dark green spinach, bright red bell peppers, and orange carrots—plus lean, protein-packed turkey and whole-grain quinoa. And they are seasoned generously with dried oregano, one of the most antioxidant-rich herbs out there. But don't make them just because they are so good for you; that is really just a bonus. Make them because they are absolutely delicious, enticingly beautiful, and sure to please the whole family.

8 MEDIUM RED BELL PEPPERS (4 POUNDS)

1 POUND LEAN GROUND TURKEY

ONE 14.5-OUNCE CAN NO-SALT-ADDED DICED TOMATOES, STRAINED, JUICE RESERVED

ONE 10-OUNCE PACKAGE FROZEN CHOPPED SPINACH, THAWED, SQUEEZED OF ALL EXCESS LIQUID

1 CUP COOKED QUINOA (FROM ⅓ CUP UNCOOKED)

½ MEDIUM ZUCCHINI, FINELY DICED

1 SMALL CARROT, FINELY DICED

2 TABLESPOONS CHOPPED FRESH ITALIAN PARSLEY LEAVES

1½ TEASPOONS DRIED OREGANO, DIVIDED

1 TEASPOON SALT, DIVIDED

¼ TEASPOON FRESHLY GROUND BLACK PEPPER

¼ TEASPOON CRUSHED RED PEPPER FLAKES

ONE 15-OUNCE CAN NO-SALT-ADDED TOMATO SAUCE

1 Preheat the oven to 375°F. Cut the tops off of the peppers and remove the core, ribs, and seeds.

2 Place the turkey, tomatoes, spinach, quinoa, zucchini, carrot, parsley, 1 teaspoon of the oregano, ¾ teaspoon of the salt, the black pepper, and red pepper flakes into a large bowl and mix with your hands until just combined.

3 Pack the turkey mixture into the peppers, then place them, standing upright, into a large, ovenproof pot with a lid, such as a Dutch oven.

4 In a small bowl, combine the reserved tomato liquid with the tomato sauce, remaining ½ teaspoon oregano, and remaining ¼ teaspoon salt. Pour the tomato sauce over the top and sides of the peppers, cover, and bake until the peppers are tender but retain their shape, about 90 minutes. Serve the peppers with their sauce in small bowls.

Recipe continues

TO REFRIGERATE AND REHEAT

Place in an airtight container and refrigerate up to 4 days. To reheat, allow to sit at room temperature as you preheat the oven to 350°F, loosely cover with foil, and cook for about 50 minutes, until warmed through. (Note: if you want to warm a single serving in the oven, two peppers fit nicely into an 8 × 4-inch loaf pan.) Alternatively, place in a microwave-safe bowl, cover with a splatter guard, and microwave on high for about 5 minutes for one serving.

TO FREEZE AND REHEAT

Allow the peppers to chill in the refrigerator for 30 minutes, then place the peppers with their sauce in an oven-safe baking dish and cover tightly with a lid or with a layer of plastic wrap and then a layer of foil. Freeze for up to 3 months. (Note: two peppers fit nicely into an 8 × 4-inch loaf pan.)

There is no need to thaw. Remove any lid or plastic wrap, cover loosely with foil, and place in a cold oven set to 350°F. Once the oven comes to temperature, continue to cook for 90 minutes, until warmed through. Alternatively, place the frozen peppers in a microwave-safe dish, cover with a splatter guard, and microwave on the defrost setting for 25 minutes, then on high for 6 minutes for one two-pepper portion.

∗ **Serving size:** 2 peppers and ½ cup sauce; **Per serving:** Calories 330; Total Fat 4g (Mono Fat 0.3g, Poly Fat 0.9g, Sat Fat 0.3g); Protein 37g; Carb 41g; Fiber 11g; Cholesterol 45mg; Sodium 750mg; **Excellent source of:** Fiber, Folate, Iron, Magnesium, Manganese, Molybdenum, Niacin, Phosphorus, Potassium, Protein, Riboflavin, Vitamin A, Vitamin B6, Vitamin C, Vitamin E, Vitamin K; **Good source of:** Calcium, Copper, Thiamin, Pantothenic Acid, Zinc

Turkey Tetrazzini Casserole • MAKES 8 SERVINGS •

THE NAME OF THIS DISH might sound Italian, but it's about as American as you can get, and I mean that in the best possible comfort-food way. It is a mix of turkey, mushrooms, and vegetables in a mild creamy sauce, usually served over noodles. Here I baked it all together in a cozy casserole, and made it healthier by making it creamy and flavorful using fresh herb and thickened milk, instead of loads of butter and cream.

2 TABLESPOONS OLIVE OIL, DIVIDED

12 OUNCES WHITE BUTTON MUSHROOMS, SLICED (5 CUPS)

1 TABLESPOON UNSALTED BUTTER

1 LARGE ONION, CHOPPED

1 LARGE STALK CELERY, CHOPPED

1 LARGE CARROT, CHOPPED

¾ TEASPOON SALT

½ TEASPOON FRESHLY GROUND BLACK PEPPER

2 CLOVES GARLIC, MINCED

1¼ TABLESPOONS CHOPPED FRESH THYME

5 TABLESPOONS ALL-PURPOSE FLOUR

2 CUPS LOW-SODIUM CHICKEN BROTH

2 CUPS 1% MILK

½ CUP DRY WHITE WINE, SUCH AS PINOT GRIGIO

2 CUPS FROZEN PEAS

¾ POUND COOKED TURKEY OR CHICKEN BREAST, CUT INTO BITE-SIZE PIECES (1½ CUPS)

8 OUNCES WHOLE-WHEAT WIDE EGG NOODLES, COOKED 2 MINUTES FEWER THAN THE INSTRUCTIONS ON THE PACKAGE

½ CUP WHOLE-WHEAT PANKO BREAD CRUMBS

⅓ CUP FINELY GRATED PARMESAN CHEESE

1 Heat 1 tablespoon of the oil in a large (5-quart) pot over medium-high heat. Add the mushrooms and cook, turning once, until golden brown, about 6 minutes. Transfer the mushrooms to a plate.

2 Let the pan cool slightly, then add the butter and melt it over medium heat. Add the onion, celery, carrot, salt, and pepper, and cook, stirring, until softened, about 4 minutes. Stir in the garlic and thyme and cook for 1 minute more. Add the flour and cook, stirring constantly, 2 minutes more. Whisking, slowly pour in the broth, milk, and wine until combined well. Bring the mixture just to a boil and then lower the heat to medium-low and simmer, stirring occasionally, until thickened, about 7 minutes. Stir in the peas, turkey, noodles, and mushrooms, tossing until coated well.

3 Spray one 9 × 13-inch baking dish or two 8-inch square baking dishes with cooking spray and transfer mixture to prepared dish(es). In a small bowl, toss together the panko, Parmesan, and the remaining 1 tablespoon of oil. Sprinkle over the top. The casserole(s) may be refrigerated or frozen at this stage.

4 To continue, preheat the oven to 400°F. Bake in the middle of the oven until bubbly and the top is golden, about 12 minutes.

Recipe continues

TO REFRIGERATE AND REHEAT

Chill in the refrigerator, uncovered, for 30 minutes, then cover tightly and refrigerate for up to 4 days.

To reheat, allow the dish to sit at room temperature while the oven heats to 350°F. Place the casserole dish in the oven, cover with foil, and cook until warmed through, about 30 to 40 minutes, then uncover and cook for 10 to 15 minutes more. Alternatively, scoop the amount desired onto a microwave-safe plate, cover with a splatter guard, and microwave on high, about 2 minutes for one serving.

TO FREEZE

Allow to chill in the refrigerator, uncovered, for 1 hour then cover tightly with plastic wrap and then foil and freeze for up to 3 months.

Thaw in the refrigerator for 24 to 36 hours then reheat following the "to refrigerate" directions. Or, to reheat directly from the freezer to the oven, remove the plastic wrap and re-cover with foil, then place in a cold oven set to 350°F. Once the oven comes to temperature, continue to cook until warmed through, about 60 to 75 minutes, depending on the size of the dish, then cook uncovered for 10 to 15 minutes more.

＊ **Serving size:** 1½ cups; **Per serving:** Calories 360; Total Fat 9g (Mono Fat 4.2g, Poly Fat 1.3g, Sat Fat 3.1g); Protein 25g; Carb 41g; Fiber 4g; Cholesterol 80mg; Sodium 390mg; **Excellent source of:** Folate, Manganese, Niacin, Pantothenic Acid, Phosphorus, Protein, Riboflavin, Selenium, Thiamin, Vitamin A, Vitamin B6; **Good source of:** Calcium, Copper, Iron, Magnesium, Potassium, Vitamin C, Vitamin K, Zinc

Turkey Burgers Stuffed with Spinach and Feta with Herbed Yogurt and Cucumber Dip (Tzatziki) • MAKES 4 SERVINGS •

BY STUFFING FLAVORFUL "TOPPINGS" INSIDE a burger you turn it into a big, juicy, protein-packed pocket that can easily be made ahead. Here lean ground turkey gets the Greek treatment, filled with spinach, feta, and dill, then served in a pita with a spread of creamy tzatziki yogurt sauce, for a richly satisfying Mediterranean burger experience.

- 2 TEASPOONS OLIVE OIL
- 2 SCALLIONS, THINLY SLICED, GREEN AND WHITE PARTS ONLY
- 2 CUPS LIGHTLY PACKED BABY SPINACH LEAVES, COARSELY CHOPPED
- ¼ CUP CRUMBLED FETA CHEESE
- 1 TABLESPOON CHOPPED FRESH DILL, OR 1 TEASPOON DRIED
- ¼ TEASPOON FRESHLY GROUND BLACK PEPPER, DIVIDED
- 1¼ POUNDS LEAN GROUND TURKEY
- ¼ TEASPOON OF SALT

FOR SERVING:
- COOKING SPRAY
- 4 WHOLE-WHEAT PITA POCKET BREADS
- ½ CUP HERBED YOGURT AND CUCUMBER DIP (RECIPE FOLLOWS)
- 1 CUP SHREDDED ROMAINE LETTUCE
- 1 MEDIUM TOMATO, CHOPPED

1 Heat the oil in a medium skillet over medium-high heat. Add the scallions and cook, stirring, until softened, about 2 minutes. Add the spinach and cook, stirring, until wilted, about 1 minute. Remove the pan from the heat. Stir in the feta cheese, dill, and ⅛ teaspoon of the pepper. If planning to freeze or refrigerate the burgers, allow the mixture to cool completely before making the patties.

2 To make the patties, divide the turkey into 4 equal-size rounds. Make 2 equal-size patties out of each round so you have 8 patties total. Put 2 tablespoons of the spinach-feta mixture onto half of the patties. Top with the remaining patties, working the turkey around the edges to seal the burgers closed. Season the burgers on both sides with the salt and remaining ⅛ teaspoon pepper. The burgers may be refrigerated or frozen at this stage.

3 To continue, spray a nonstick grill pan with cooking spray and heat over medium-high heat, or prepare the grill. Grill until cooked through, about 5 minutes per side. Transfer the burgers to a plate.

4 Place the pitas, in batches if necessary, on the grill or grill pan to toast, about 30 seconds per side. Slice the top ¼ off of each pita and open to form a pocket. Spread about 2 tablespoons of the dip inside a pita, then place a burger into the pita along with about ¼ cup of the lettuce and about 2 tablespoons of the tomato.

Recipe continues

TO REFRIGERATE AND SERVE
Place the uncooked burgers in an airtight container in the refrigerator for up to 2 days. Allow to come to room temperature for 20 to 30 minutes, then follow with the "to continue" directions in the recipe.

TO FREEZE AND SERVE
Wrap the uncooked burgers individually in plastic wrap or foil and place in a sealable plastic freezer bag. Freeze for up to 3 months.

Thaw in the refrigerator for 24 hours, then allow to come to room temperature for 20 to 30 minutes. Or, to thaw quickly, unwrap and place on a microwave-safe plate, cover with a splatter guard, and thaw in the microwave on the defrost setting for about 6 minutes for one burger, turning once. One thawed, pat dry, then follow with the "to continue" directions in the recipe.

❋ **Serving size:** 1 burger; **Per serving:** Calories 410; Total Fat 10g (Mono Fat 3.5g, Poly Fat 1.2g, Sat Fat 2.5g); Protein 46g; Carb 40g; Fiber 6g; Cholesterol 65mg; Sodium 690mg; **Excellent source of:** Fiber, Folate, Iron, Manganese, Protein, Selenium, Vitamin A, Vitamin K; **Good source of:** Calcium, Copper, Phosphorus, Magnesium, Niacin, Riboflavin, Thiamin, Vitamin B6, Vitamin C

HERBED YOGURT AND CUCUMBER DIP (TZATZIKI) • MAKES 8 SERVINGS •

THIS FRESH-TASTING, CREAMY, HERBAL CONDIMENT can be used as a sauce, dip, or spread to add a luxurious flavor dimension to all kinds of foods. Spread it on sandwiches and burgers, serve it as dip for vegetables and pita chips, or use it as sauce for fish or chicken.

1 MEDIUM ENGLISH CUCUMBER, TRIMMED, UNPEELED

1½ CUPS LOW-FAT PLAIN GREEK YOGURT

2 TABLESPOONS EXTRA-VIRGIN OLIVE OIL

2 TABLESPOONS CHOPPED FRESH ITALIAN PARSLEY LEAVES

1½ TABLESPOONS FRESH LEMON JUICE

2 SMALL CLOVES OF GARLIC, FINELY MINCED

1 TEASPOON FINELY GRATED LEMON ZEST

½ TEASPOON SALT

⅛ TEASPOON FRESHLY GROUND BLACK PEPPER

1 Coarsely grate the cucumber on a box grater. Place it in a fine-mesh strainer and strain for a minute or two, pressing out the liquid.

2 In a medium bowl, stir together the grated cucumber, yogurt, oil, parsley, lemon juice, garlic, lemon zest, salt, and pepper.

TO REFRIGERATE
The dip will keep in an airtight container in the refrigerator for up to 5 days. Give it a stir before serving.

Freezing is not recommended.

❋ **Serving size:** About ¼ cup; **Per serving:** Calories 60; Total Fat 4.2g (Mono Fat 2.5g, Poly Fat 0.4g, Sat Fat 1g); Protein 4g; Carb 3g; Fiber 0g; Cholesterol 5mg; Sodium 160mg; **Excellent source of:** Vitamin K

Seafood

Cajun Shrimp in Foil Packets

• MAKES 8 SERVINGS •

OPENING ONE OF THESE FOIL packets is like unwrapping a celebration of aroma, color, and flavor. Tucked inside are plump shrimp that have been tossed with Cajun spices and a rainbow of vegetables: zucchini, red bell peppers, and corn, along with slices of Andouille sausage and fresh herbs. They all simmer together in the pouch and contribute to a mouthwatering sauce that accumulates. The packets go straight from freezer to oven, so when you get home from your busy day, you can pop them in the oven and relax until dinner. I like to serve this over rice.

2 TABLESPOONS SALT-FREE CAJUN OR CREOLE SEASONING

½ TEASPOON SALT

¼ TEASPOON FRESHLY GROUND BLACK PEPPER

2¼ POUNDS CLEANED LARGE SHRIMP

2 FULLY COOKED ANDOUILLE SAUSAGE LINKS (6 OUNCES TOTAL), VERY THINLY SLICED

2 MEDIUM ZUCCHINI (8 OUNCES EACH), SLICED INTO ¼-INCH-THICK ROUNDS

2 LARGE RED BELL PEPPERS, SEEDED AND CUT INTO THIN STRIPS

3 CUPS CORN KERNELS (ONE 1-POUND BAG FROZEN CORN)

½ CUP CHOPPED FRESH ITALIAN PARSLEY LEAVES

½ CUP CHOPPED FRESH BASIL LEAVES

1 CUP DRY WHITE WINE, SUCH AS PINOT GRIGIO

⅓ CUP OLIVE OIL

1 In a medium bowl, combine the Cajun seasoning, salt, and pepper. Add the shrimp and toss to coat.

2 Place eight large (10 × 18-inch) pieces of heavy-duty aluminum foil on a flat surface.

3 Divide the sausage, zucchini, bell peppers, and corn among the foil pieces, placing the vegetables in the center of each. Top each with shrimp (about 5 or 6), and sprinkle each with 1 tablespoon of the parsley and 1 tablespoon of the basil. Drizzle each with 2 tablespoons of the wine and about 2 teaspoons of the oil. Fold each piece of the foil to form a packet, sealing tightly and leaving a little room inside for air to circulate in the packet. The packets may be refrigerated or frozen at this stage.

4 To continue, preheat the oven to 425°F. Arrange the packets on a baking sheet and cook until the shrimp is cooked through and the vegetables are crisp-tender, 13 minutes. Open the packets slowly, being careful of the hot steam. Transfer the shrimp, vegetables, and sauce that has accumulated to individual bowls or rimmed plates.

Recipe continues

TO REFRIGERATE AND HEAT
Place uncooked packets in the refrigerator where they will keep for up to 1 day. When ready to cook, follow the "to continue" instructions in the recipe, adding about 5 minutes to the cook time for a total of about 18 minutes.

TO FREEZE AND HEAT
Place uncooked packets into sealable plastic bags, keeping them level and upright. (Two packets fit well into a gallon-sized bag.) Freeze for up to 2 months. There is no need to thaw before cooking. Remove the frozen packets from the bags, and place them on a baking tray in a cold oven set to 425°F. Once the oven comes to temperature, continue to cook for 35 to 40 minutes.

✳ **Serving size:** 1 packet; **Per serving:** Calories 350; Total Fat 16g (Mono Fat 9.5g, Poly Fat 1.5g, Sat Fat 3.8g); Protein 32g; Carb 17g; Fiber 2g; Cholesterol 225mg; Sodium 440mg; **Excellent source of:** Copper, Phosphorus, Protein, Vitamin A, Vitamin C, Vitamin K, Zinc; **Good source of:** Folate, Iron, Magnesium, Manganese, Niacin, Potassium, Vitamin B6

Cod and Potato Cakes
with Smoky Roasted Red Pepper Sauce

• MAKES 2 SERVINGS •

THESE CROQUETTES ARE PURE NEW England to me, a straightforward, gratifying mix of mashed potatoes and flaky cod fish, held together with some egg and seasoned with mustard, scallion, parsley, and capers. The potatoes and fish are steamed together, making preparation super simple.

Serving them with the brilliantly colorful Smoky Roasted Red Pepper Sauce lifts them out of the traditional in just the right way.

- 2 MEDIUM RUSSET POTATOES (¾ POUND), SKINS ON, SCRUBBED AND CUT INTO 1-INCH CUBES
- 1½ POUNDS FRESH SKINLESS COD FILLET, CUT INTO 1-INCH CUBES
- 1 LARGE EGG, BEATEN
- ½ TABLESPOON DIJON MUSTARD
- 1 LARGE SCALLION, SLICED
- 2 TABLESPOONS CHOPPED FRESH ITALIAN PARSLEY LEAVES
- ½ TABLESPOON CAPERS, DRAINED AND RINSED
- ½ TEASPOON SALT
- ¼ TEASPOON FRESHLY GROUND BLACK PEPPER
- 3 TABLESPOONS OLIVE OIL, DIVIDED

FOR SERVING:

- ½ CUP SMOKY ROASTED RED PEPPER SAUCE (RECIPE FOLLOWS)

1 Place the potatoes in a steamer basket set over a pot of boiling water. Cover and steam for 10 minutes. Add the cod to the potatoes and steam them together, covered, until the potatoes are tender and the cod is flaky and opaque, 6 minutes more. Transfer the potatoes and cod to a large bowl and allow to cool slightly, 10 minutes.

2 Add the egg and mustard and mash, using a potato masher, until it has the texture of mashed potatoes with some chunks in it. Stir in the scallions, parsley, capers, salt, and pepper, mixing well to incorporate. Form the mixture into 8 patties.

3 Heat 1 tablespoon of the oil in a large skillet, over medium-high heat. Place 4 of the cod cakes in the pan and lower the heat to medium. Cook for 5 minutes, then add another ½ tablespoon oil to the pan, flip, and cook another 5 minutes, until browned on both sides and heated through. Repeat with the remaining cakes and oil. Cod cakes may be refrigerated or frozen at this stage.

4 Serve each cod cake with 1 tablespoon of the Smoky Roasted Red Pepper Sauce.

Recipe continues

TO REFRIGERATE AND REHEAT

Place the cod cakes in an airtight container in the refrigerator for up to 2 days.

To reheat, place on a baking tray and heat, uncovered, in a 350ºF oven for 15 minutes.

Microwave reheating is not recommended.

TO FREEZE AND REHEAT

Allow the cod cakes to chill in the refrigerator for 30 minutes, then wrap individually in plastic wrap or foil and place in a sealable plastic freezer bag in the freezer for up to 3 months.

There is no need to thaw. To reheat, place the unwrapped frozen cakes on a baking sheet in a cold oven set to 350ºF. Once the oven reaches temperature, continue to cook for 20 minutes, until heated through.

Microwave thawing/reheating is not recommended.

∗ **Serving size:** 2 cod cakes and 2 tablespoons sauce; **Per serving:** Calories 330; Total Fat 13g (Mono Fat 8.2g, Poly Fat 1.8g, Sat Fat 2g); Protein 34g; Carb 20g; Fiber 2g; Cholesterol 120mg; Sodium 500mg; **Excellent source of:** Magnesium, Niacin, Phosphorus, Potassium, Protein, Selenium, Vitamin B6, Vitamin B12, Vitamin C, Vitamin K; **Good source of:** Folate, Iron, Manganese, Riboflavin, Thiamin, Vitamin D

SMOKY ROASTED RED PEPPER SAUCE   • MAKES 8 SERVINGS •

THIS SAUCE IS DOUBLE-SMOKED THANKS to the charred flavor of the roasted peppers and the aromatic smoked paprika used to season it. It has so much flavor intensity it is hard to believe it takes just minutes to make and is good for you too. Not only is it delicious with the Cod and Potato Cakes, it is a perfect sauce for the Grilled Eggplant Roll-ups, page 288 and it's wonderful to drizzle on roasted or grilled chicken.

5 MEDIUM ROASTED RED PEPPERS, ABOUT 1 CUP, RINSED AND DRAINED IF JARRED

1 TABLESPOON EXTRA-VIRGIN OLIVE OIL

1 TABLESPOON BALSAMIC VINEGAR

1 TEASPOON HONEY

1 CLOVE GARLIC, COARSELY CHOPPED

¼ TEASPOON SMOKED PAPRIKA

¼ TEASPOON SALT

PINCH FRESHLY GROUND BLACK PEPPER

Place all the ingredients in a blender and blend until smooth.

* **Serving size:** About 2 tablespoons; **Per serving:** Calories 35; Total Fat 1.5g (Mono Fat 1.23g, Poly Fat 0.18g, Sat Fat 0.23g); Protein 0g; Carb 4g; Fiber 1g; Cholesterol 0mg; Sodium 75mg; **Good source of:** Vitamin C

TO REFRIGERATE
Place in an airtight container in the refrigerator for up to 2 weeks. Allow to come to room temperature before serving.

TO FREEZE AND THAW
Place the sauce into a sealable plastic bag or pour into ice cube trays and freeze. Once frozen, transfer the cubes of sauce to a sealable plastic freezer bag where it will keep for up to 3 months.

Thaw in the refrigerator for 18 to 24 hours. Allow to come to room temperature before serving. Alternatively, place in a microwave-safe dish, cover, and microwave on high for about 15 seconds for one portion.

Easy Bouillabaisse

• MAKES 8 SERVINGS •

IF YOU'RE LOOKING FOR A deeply flavorful, elegant, yet homey meal that's a breeze to prepare, and perfect to serve company, bookmark this recipe. It is one of my personal go-tos for dinner guests, and it has never failed to impress. You make the herb-and-saffron-infused tomato-y base ahead of time and, if you'd like, refrigerate or freeze it, then just get it bubbling again and add a bounty of fresh seafood a few minutes before serving. Dish it up into big bowls with some crusty bread and a simple green salad to start.

4 SPRIGS FRESH ITALIAN PARSLEY, PLUS ¼ CUP COARSELY CHOPPED FRESH ITALIAN PARSLEY LEAVES FOR GARNISH

3 SPRIGS FRESH THYME

1 BAY LEAF

ONE 1 × 3-INCH STRIP LEMON ZEST

2 TABLESPOONS OLIVE OIL

1 LARGE ONION, THINLY SLICED

4 LARGE CLOVES GARLIC, MINCED

4 CUPS FISH STOCK

1 LARGE FENNEL BULB (ABOUT 1 POUND), CORED AND THINLY SLICED

ONE 28-OUNCE CAN PLUS ONE 14-OUNCE CAN LOW-SODIUM DICED TOMATOES

1 TEASPOON SALT, PLUS MORE TO TASTE

¼ TEASPOON FRESHLY GROUND BLACK PEPPER

1 GENEROUS PINCH SAFFRON

½ POUND BAY SCALLOPS

½ POUND LARGE CLEANED SHRIMP

½ POUND SKINLESS COD FILLETS, CUT INTO 1-INCH CHUNKS

1 Tie together the parsley sprigs, thyme, bay leaf, and lemon zest with a piece of kitchen twine.

2 In a 6-quart Dutch oven or stockpot, heat the oil over medium-high heat. Add the onion and cook, stirring, until translucent, about 6 minutes. Add the garlic and cook, stirring, for 1 minute more.

3 Add the fish stock, fennel, tomatoes with their juices, 2½ cups of water, the herb bundle, salt, pepper, and saffron and bring to a boil. Lower the heat to medium-low and simmer, covered, until the fennel is tender, 45 to 60 minutes. Remove the herb bundle and discard. Add more salt to taste, depending on the saltiness of the fish stock. The bouillabaisse may be made ahead up to this stage and refrigerated or frozen.

4 To continue, add the scallops, shrimp, and cod and cook until the seafood is just cooked through, 5 to 6 minutes. Garnish with the remaining chopped parsley.

Recipe continues

To make the base ahead:

TO REFRIGERATE AND SERVE

Before adding the seafood, transfer to an airtight container and place in the refrigerator where it will keep for up to 4 days. When ready to serve, return either a half or full batch to the pot, bring the mixture to a boil, then lower the heat to medium-low and follow the "to continue" directions in the recipe, using half the seafood if making a half batch.

TO FREEZE AND SERVE

Before adding the seafood, chill in the refrigerator for 30 minutes, then freeze in two batches in gallon-sized, sealable plastic freezer bags.

Thaw in the refrigerator for about 24 hours or, to thaw quickly, run the plastic bag(s) under hot water for 30 seconds until the mixture releases. Then transfer the frozen mixture to a large pot, cover, and heat over medium heat, stirring occasionally and breaking it up with a spoon, 30 to 45 minutes. Once thawed, bring to a boil, then lower the heat to medium-low and follow the "to continue" directions in the recipe, using half the seafood if making a half batch.

---

* **Serving size:** 1¾ cups; **Per serving:** Calories 170; Total Fat 5g (Mono Fat 2.8g, Poly Fat 0.7g, Sat Fat 0.8g); Protein 19g; Carb 12g; Fiber 3g; Cholesterol 65mg; Sodium 670mg; **Excellent source of:** Phosphorus, Protein, Selenium, Vitamin A, Vitamin B12, Vitamin C, Vitamin K; **Good source of:** Copper, Fiber, Magnesium, Niacin, Potassium

Halibut with Carrot Ginger Sauce

• MAKES 6 SERVINGS •

THIS DISH TURNS THE HARD-WORKING, everyday "Cinderella" carrot into a stunningly beautiful, elegant sauce that could grace the most regal table. The vegetable is simmered with shallots and broth, and then pureed with Asian seasonings that highlight and contrast its earthy sweetness: soy sauce, ginger, rice vinegar, honey, and sesame oil. It is then strained to yield a silken, jewel-toned, flavorful sauce that is used to simmer the halibut fillet. Cod or monkfish would also work well here.

1 TABLESPOON CANOLA OR PEANUT OIL

3 TABLESPOONS DICED SHALLOT

2½ CUPS FISH STOCK OR VEGETABLE BROTH

2 POUNDS CARROTS, PEELED AND CUT INTO COINS (ABOUT 3 CUPS)

3 TABLESPOONS REDUCED-SODIUM SOY SAUCE

2 TABLESPOONS UNSEASONED RICE VINEGAR

1 TABLESPOON HONEY

1 TABLESPOON FINELY GRATED FRESH GINGER

1 TEASPOON TOASTED SESAME OIL

FOR SERVING

SIX 6-OUNCE SKINLESS HALIBUT FILLETS

¼ TEASPOON SALT

FRESH CILANTRO LEAVES, OPTIONAL

1 Heat the oil in a medium saucepan over medium-low heat. Add the shallot and cook, stirring, until tender but not brown, about 2 minutes. Add the stock or broth and bring to a boil over high heat. Stir in the carrots, return to a boil, then lower the heat to medium low and simmer, uncovered, until the carrots are just tender, 12 to 15 minutes.

2 Allow to cool for 15 minutes, then ladle the carrot mixture into a blender and add the soy sauce, rice vinegar, honey, ginger, and sesame oil. Puree until smooth. Pour the mixture into a fine-mesh strainer set over a bowl. Press the mixture through the strainer with a spatula or wooden spoon, straining out most of the solids, until you have about 2½ cups of sauce. Discard the solids. The sauce may be refrigerated or frozen at this stage.

3 To continue, warm the sauce in a saucepan or deep skillet over medium heat until simmering. Season the halibut with the salt and arrange it in the pan. Spoon some of the sauce over the top of the fish. (It is okay that the fish is not completely covered with the sauce.) Lower the heat to medium-low, then cover and cook until the fish flakes easily with a fork, about 10 minutes per inch thickness. To serve, transfer each piece of fish to a shallow bowl. Ladle the sauce over it and garnish with cilantro leaves, if desired.

Recipe continues

To make the sauce ahead:

TO REFRIGERATE AND REHEAT

Place the sauce an airtight container in the refrigerator where it will keep for 3 days. To reheat, place in a saucepan or deep skillet, cover, and heat over medium-low heat until simmering, 5 to 10 minutes, depending on the amount, then follow the "to continue" directions in the recipe, using 2 pieces of fish and a scant cup of sauce for each two servings. Use a smaller pan if not making the entire batch.

TO FREEZE AND REHEAT

Place the sauce into sealable freezer bag(s) as one full batch, or divide it into two or three batches, and freeze for up to 3 months. To thaw and reheat, run the bag under hot water for 30 seconds to release it, and then transfer to a saucepan or deep skillet. Cover and cook until thawed and heated through, 15 to 30 minutes, depending on the amount, adding 1 to 2 tablespoons of water if the pan appears dry, then follow the "to continue" directions in the recipe, using 2 pieces of fish and a scant cup of sauce for each two servings. Use a smaller pan if not making the entire batch.

✳ **Serving size:** 1 piece of fish and a scant ½ cup of sauce; **Per serving:** Calories 270; Total Fat 7g (Mono Fat 3.1g, Poly Fat 2.3g, Sat Fat 0.9g); Protein 37g; Carb 13g; Fiber 2g; Cholesterol 55mg; Sodium 510mg; **Excellent source of:** Magnesium, Niacin, Phosphorus, Potassium, Protein, Selenium, Vitamin A, Vitamin B6, Vitamin B12, Vitamin D; **Good source of:** Calcium, Iron, Riboflavin, Vitamin K

Herbed Salmon and Orzo Casserole with Feta

• MAKES 6 SERVINGS •

I HATE TO PLAY FAVORITES with my recipes because each one genuinely comes from my heart, but I have a special soft spot for this dish. It is a one skillet meal that is both light and filling, with fresh chunks of salmon, spinach, and tomatoes, all cooked along with the orzo they are nestled in. It's lemony and herbaceous and made dreamy topped with a salty sprinkle of feta that melts in the oven. I know that, like I did, once you try it you will put it into regular rotation.

2 TABLESPOONS OLIVE OIL

2 LARGE SCALLIONS, CHOPPED

1½ CUPS WHOLE-GRAIN ORZO PASTA

2 CUPS FISH STOCK OR WATER

1 PINT CHERRY TOMATOES, HALVED

2 CUPS LIGHTLY PACKED, CHOPPED FRESH SPINACH LEAVES

¼ CUP FINELY CHOPPED FRESH ITALIAN PARSLEY LEAVES

2 TABLESPOONS CHOPPED FRESH DILL

2 TABLESPOONS FRESH LEMON JUICE

½ TEASPOON SALT

¼ TEASPOON FRESHLY GROUND BLACK PEPPER

2 POUNDS SKINLESS SALMON FILLET, CUT INTO 1-INCH CHUNKS

1 CUP CRUMBLED FETA CHEESE

1 Heat the oil in a large, deep ovenproof skillet over medium heat, add the scallions, and cook, stirring, until they are softened, 2 minutes. Add the orzo and cook, stirring, for 2 minutes more. Add the stock and bring to a boil, then reduce the heat to medium-low, cover, and simmer until the orzo is about halfway cooked, 5 minutes.

2 Stir in the tomatoes, spinach, parsley, dill, lemon juice, salt, and pepper and cook until the spinach is wilted, 1 to 2 minutes. Gently stir in the fish, cover, and cook, stirring once or twice, until the fish is cooked on the outside but still a bit translucent inside, 4 to 5 minutes. The mixture may be refrigerated or frozen at this stage.

3 To continue, preheat the oven to 450°F. Sprinkle the feta over the top of the skillet, then place in the oven until the feta is lightly browned and melted, 8 to 10 minutes.

Recipe continues

TO REFRIGERATE AND SERVE

Transfer the mixture to one 9 × 13-inch, two 8-inch square, or 6 individual oven- and microwave-safe baking dishes. Sprinkle the feta on top, then cover tightly and refrigerate for up to 2 days.

When ready to serve, allow to sit at room temperature while the oven preheats to 375°F. Bake, covered with foil, for 20 minutes, then uncover and bake 10 to 15 minutes more. Alternatively, to heat a single serving in the microwave, uncover, then re-cover with a splatter guard, and microwave on high for 60 to 90 seconds.

TO FREEZE AND SERVE

Transfer the mixture to one 9 × 13-inch, two 8-inch square, or 6 individual freezer, oven- and microwave-safe baking dishes and chill in the refrigerator, uncovered, for 30 minutes. Then sprinkle the feta on top, cover with an airtight lid or with plastic wrap and then foil, and freeze for up to 3 months.

Thaw in the refrigerator for 18 to 24 hours then heat according to the "to refrigerate" directions. Or, to thaw quickly, uncover, then re-cover with just foil and place in a cold oven set for 375°F. Once the oven reaches temperature, continue to cook for 35 minutes, then remove the foil and cook for 15 to 20 minutes more, until heated through. Alternatively, to microwave a single serving, uncover, then re-cover with a splatter guard and microwave on the defrost setting for about 7 minutes, and then on high for 1 minute.

＊ **Serving size:** About 1½ cups; **Per serving:** Calories 460; Total Fat 17g (Mono Fat 7.1g, Poly Fat 3.4g, Sat Fat 6.1g); Protein 40g; Carb 30g; Fiber 4g; Cholesterol 95mg; Sodium 550mg; **Excellent source of:** Calcium, Magnesium, Manganese, Niacin, Pantothenic Acid, Phosphorus, Potassium, Protein, Riboflavin, Selenium, Thiamin, Vitamin A, Vitamin B6, Vitamin B12, Vitamin C, Vitamin D, Vitamin K; **Good source of:** Chloride, Copper, Fiber, Folate, Iron, Zinc

Asian Shrimp Cakes
with Avocado-Wasabi Sauce • MAKES 4 SERVINGS •

THESE SHRIMP CAKES ARE AMBROSIAL! Each bite starts with a crispy panko crunch that's contrasted with the creamy, citrusy, subtly tingly avocado wasabi sauce, and leads you to chunks of succulent shrimp seasoned with toasted sesame oil and ginger. They can be served as a main course, perhaps along with the Asian Slaw, page 65, or served as a pass-around dish at a party. Be sure not to make them any larger than indicated here, to insure that they cook through properly.

- 2 TABLESPOONS SESAME SEEDS, TOASTED
- 1 POUND SHRIMP, PEELED, DEVEINED, AND FINELY CHOPPED
- 1 CUP WHOLE-WHEAT PANKO BREAD CRUMBS, DIVIDED
- ¼ CUP FINELY CHOPPED RED BELL PEPPER
- 3 TABLESPOONS CHOPPED SCALLION GREENS
- 1 LARGE EGG, LIGHTLY BEATEN
- 1 TABLESPOON CHOPPED FRESH CILANTRO
- 2 TEASPOONS TOASTED SESAME OIL
- 1 TEASPOON FINELY GRATED FRESH GINGER
- ½ TABLESPOON FRESH LIME JUICE
- ½ TEASPOON SALT
- ½ TEASPOON FRESHLY GROUND BLACK PEPPER
- ¼ CUP CANOLA OIL, OR OTHER NEUTRAL TASTING OIL

FOR SERVING:
- 1 RECIPE AVOCADO-WASABI SAUCE (RECIPE FOLLOWS)

1 Toast the sesame seeds in a small dry skillet over medium-high heat, stirring constantly, until they are fragrant and begin to pop, 1 minute. Set aside to cool.

2 In a large bowl, stir together the shrimp, ½ cup of the panko, the bell pepper, scallion, toasted sesame seeds, egg, cilantro, sesame oil, ginger, lime juice, salt, and black pepper until just combined. Place the remaining ½ cup panko in a shallow bowl or rimmed plate.

3 Divide the shrimp mixture into 12 mounds. Shape each mound into a round patty about 2½ inches in diameter. If the mixture seems overly moist, stir in more panko a tablespoon at a time. Coat each patty well with the remaining panko. Place the cakes in the refrigerator for 20 to 30 minutes to firm up.

4 Heat the canola oil in a very large nonstick skillet over medium heat. Cook the shrimp cakes over medium-low heat, until golden brown on both sides and cooked through, about 5 to 6 minutes per side. The shrimp cakes may be refrigerated or frozen at this stage.

5 To serve, dollop each with 1 tablespoon of the Avocado-Wasabi Sauce.

Recipe continues

TO REFRIGERATE AND REHEAT
Place the shrimp cakes in an airtight container in the refrigerator for up to 2 days.

To reheat, place uncovered on a baking tray and heat in a 350°F oven for 15 minutes.

Microwave reheating is not recommended.

TO FREEZE AND REHEAT
Allow the shrimp cakes to chill in the refrigerator for 30 minutes, then wrap two or three together in plastic wrap or foil and place in a sealable plastic freezer bag in the freezer for up to 3 months.

There is no need to thaw. To reheat, place the frozen unwrapped cakes on a baking sheet in a cold oven set for 350°F. Once the oven reaches temperature, continue to cook for 20 minutes, until heated through.

Microwave thawing and reheating is not recommended.

＊ **Serving size:** 3 cakes and 3 tablespoons sauce; **Per serving:** Calories 440; Total Fat 28g (Mono Fat 15.3g, Poly Fat 6.3g, Sat Fat 2.9g); Protein 30g; Carb 21g; Fiber 6g; Cholesterol 230mg; Sodium 640mg; **Excellent source of:** Copper, Fiber, Phosphorus, Protein, Vitamin C, Vitamin E, Vitamin K; **Good source of:** Calcium, Iron, Folate, Magnesium, Potassium, Zinc

AVOCADO-WASABI SAUCE   • MAKES ¾ CUP; 4 SERVINGS •

WASABI AND AVOCADO WORK IN a California Roll, so why not use the combo to top Asian-style shrimp cakes? This sauce is perfect for the above recipe, as suspected. But it also makes a tasty dip for shrimp cocktail or rice crackers, or spread for a grilled fish sandwich.

1 RIPE AVOCADO

1 TABLESPOON FRESH LIME JUICE

½ TEASPOON PREPARED WASABI PASTE, PLUS MORE TO TASTE

¼ TEASPOON SALT

Halve, pit, and peel the avocado. Mash together the avocado, lime juice, wasabi paste, and salt with a fork until smooth. Taste, and mix in more wasabi paste if needed. If not using immediately, refrigerate as quickly as possible.

TO REFRIGERATE
Place the sauce in an airtight container, placing a layer of plastic wrap directly over the top of the sauce before putting the lid on. Refrigerate for up to 2 days.

Freezing is not recommended.

＊ **Serving size:** 3 tablespoons; **Per serving:** Calories 80; Total Fat 7g (Mono Fat 4.9g, Poly Fat 0.9g, Sat Fat 1.1g); Protein 1g; Carb 5g; Fiber 3g; Cholesterol 0mg; Sodium 160mg; **Good source of:** Fiber, Folate, Vitamin C, Vitamin K

Crab and Artichoke Dip Casserole

• MAKES 8 SERVINGS •

THIS DISH HAS THE ESSENCE of an indulgently creamy, warm artichoke dip in the body of a noodle casserole that's loaded with succulent crabmeat. It manages to be both down-home and luxurious at the same time, so it shines for any occasion, from an everyday dinner to party buffet.

8 OUNCES WHOLE-WHEAT WIDE EGG NOODLES

2 TABLESPOONS OLIVE OIL

2 MEDIUM STALKS CELERY RIBS, FINELY CHOPPED

¼ CUP FINELY CHOPPED SHALLOT

½ TEASPOON SALT

½ TEASPOON FRESHLY GROUND BLACK PEPPER

3 CLOVES GARLIC, MINCED

3 CUPS 1% MILK

½ CUP LOW-FAT PLAIN YOGURT

ONE 8-OUNCE PACKAGE NEUFCHÂTEL CHEESE (REDUCED-FAT CREAM CHEESE)

1 POUND LUMP CRABMEAT, PICKED OVER FOR CARTILAGE

ONE 12-OUNCE BAG FROZEN ARTICHOKE HEARTS, THAWED AND COARSELY CHOPPED (2 CUPS)

5 CUPS LIGHTLY PACKED BABY SPINACH (5 OUNCES), CHOPPED

3 TABLESPOONS FRESH LEMON JUICE

COOKING SPRAY

1 CUP FINELY GRATED PARMESAN

1 Bring a large pot of water to a boil and cook the noodles 2 minutes fewer than it says on the package directions; drain.

2 Heat the oil in a large pot over medium heat. Add the celery, shallot, salt, and pepper, and cook, stirring occasionally, until softened, about 4 minutes. Add the garlic and cook, stirring, 1 minute more. Whisk in the milk, yogurt, and Neufchâtel, and cook until the cheese is melted. Add the crabmeat, artichokes, cooked pasta, spinach, and lemon juice and stir until well combined.

 Spray one 9 × 13-inch baking dish or two 8-inch square baking dishes with cooking spray. Transfer the crab-artichoke mixture to the dish(es) and sprinkle evenly with the Parmesan. The casserole may be refrigerated or frozen at this stage.

4 To continue, preheat the oven to 400°F and bake until bubbling and the top is golden, 25 to 30 minutes.

Recipe continues

TO REFRIGERATE AND REHEAT

Chill in the refrigerator, uncovered, for 30 minutes, then cover tightly and refrigerate for up to 4 days.

To reheat, allow the dish to sit at room temperature while the oven heats to 400°F. Place the casserole dish in the oven, uncovered, and cook until warmed through, about 40 to 50 minutes. Alternatively, scoop the amount desired onto a microwave-safe plate, cover with a splatter guard, and microwave on high, about 2 minutes for one serving.

TO FREEZE AND REHEAT

Allow to chill in the refrigerator, uncovered, for 1 hour, then cover tightly with plastic wrap and then foil and freeze for up to 3 months.

Thaw in the refrigerator for 24 to 36 hours then reheat following the "to refrigerate" directions. Or, to reheat directly from freezer to oven, remove the plastic wrap and cover with foil, then place the frozen dish in a cold oven set for 350°F. Once the oven reaches temperature, continue to cook until warmed through, about 60 to 75 minutes, depending on the size of the dish, then cook uncovered for 15 to 20 minutes more.

---

* **Serving size:** 1½ cups; **Per serving:** Calories 390; Total Fat 16g (Mono Fat 5.7g, Poly Fat 1.4g, Sat Fat 7.1g); Protein 26g; Carb 34g; Fiber 5g; Cholesterol 105mg; Sodium 680mg; **Excellent source of:** Calcium, Copper, Folate, Manganese, Phosphorus, Protein, Riboflavin, Selenium, Thiamin, Vitamin A, Vitamin B12, Vitamin K, Zinc; **Good source of:** Chloride, Fiber, Iron, Magnesium, Niacin, Pantothenic Acid, Potassium, Vitamin B6, Vitamin C

Roasted Salmon and Fennel with Lemon and Thyme • MAKES 6 SERVINGS •

A HONEY-SWEETENED, LEMON-THYME VINAIGRETTE AND a little time in the oven bring fresh salmon fillets and sliced fennel together in this Mediterranean-inspired dish. The dressing is tossed with the fennel as well as brushed on the fish fillets, and then they are both roasted until the salmon is cooked to perfection and the fennel has softened, caramelized, and its flavor is concentrated. They are wonderful together served hot, or at room temperature.

3 TABLESPOONS FRESH LEMON JUICE

3 TABLESPOONS OLIVE OIL

1 TABLESPOON HONEY

1 TABLESPOON CHOPPED FRESH THYME

1½ TEASPOONS FINELY GRATED FRESH LEMON ZEST

¾ TEASPOON SALT

½ TEASPOON FRESHLY GROUND BLACK PEPPER

3 MEDIUM FENNEL BULBS

COOKING SPRAY

SIX 6-OUNCE CENTER-CUT SKINLESS SALMON FILLETS

FOR SERVING:
LEMON WEDGES

1 Preheat the oven to 400°F.

2 In a small bowl, whisk together the lemon juice, olive oil, honey, thyme, lemon zest, salt, and pepper.

3 Trim any stems and fronds from the fennel and remove the outermost layer of the bulb and discard. Cut the bulb in half so that each half retains part of the stem end. Cut each half into 8 thin wedges so each wedge is held together by a little piece of stem. Transfer the fennel to a bowl and toss with ¼ cup of the dressing.

4 Spray two sheet pans with cooking spray. Arrange the fennel on one of the sheet pans in one layer. Arrange the salmon on the other sheet pan and brush the tops with the remaining dressing.

5 Place the fennel in the oven on the lower rack and roast for 12 minutes. Then turn each piece of fennel over and return to the oven. Place the salmon in the upper third of the oven and continue to cook the salmon and fennel until the salmon is cooked to your liking, and the fennel is tender, 10 to 15 minutes more. Serve the salmon with the fennel alongside, garnished with lemon wedges.

TO REFRIGERATE AND REHEAT

The fennel and salmon may be stored, together or separately, in airtight containers in the refrigerator for up to 3 days. Serve at room temperature, or reheat.

To reheat, wrap the desired amount in foil and place on a baking sheet in a 350°F oven for 12 to 15 minutes. Alternatively, place on a microwave-safe plate, cover with a splatter guard, and microwave on high for 2 minutes for a single portion.

TO FREEZE AND REHEAT

Wrap individual portions of the salmon and fennel together into foil pouches, then place in sealable plastic freezer bags.

To reheat, place the foil pouch(es) on a baking tray in a cold oven set to 350°F. Once the oven comes to temperature, continue cooking for 20 minutes, until warmed through. Or, remove the food from the foil, place on a microwave-safe plate, cover with a splatter guard, and microwave on the defrost setting for 8 minutes, then on high for 90 seconds for a single portion.

---

* **Serving size:** 1 salmon fillet and 6 pieces of fennel; **Per serving:** Calories 350; Total Fat 18g (Mono Fat 8.6g, Poly Fat 5.2g, Sat Fat 2.7g); Protein 35g; Carb 12g; Fiber 4g; Cholesterol 95mg; Sodium 430mg; **Excellent source of:** Copper, Niacin, Pantothenic Acid, Phosphorus, Potassium, Protein, Riboflavin, Selenium, Thiamin, Vitamin A, Vitamin B6, Vitamin B12, Vitamin C, Vitamin D, Vitamin K; **Good source of:** Fiber, Iron, Magnesium, Manganese

Salmon and Goat Cheese Quesadilla

• MAKES 8 SERVINGS •

THESE TOASTED TORTILLA SANDWICHES ARE above and beyond the typical quesadilla. They are filled with fresh-cooked, Creole-spiced salmon, sautéed baby kale, and a spread of soft goat cheese, which melts luxuriously when warmed as the tortilla is browned and crisped. They are perfect as a dinner with a salad alongside, but you can also eat them with one hand, on the go, if need be. What's more, they are a great make-ahead party food.

2 TABLESPOONS OLIVE OIL, DIVIDED

1 MEDIUM RED ONION, SLICED

½ TEASPOON SALT, DIVIDED

2 CLOVES GARLIC, MINCED

5 OUNCES BABY KALE, COARSELY CHOPPED (5 CUPS LIGHTLY PACKED)

1½ TABLESPOONS CIDER VINEGAR

12 OUNCES SKINLESS SALMON FILLET

2 TEASPOONS SALT-FREE CREOLE OR CAJUN SEASONING

8 OUNCES MILD SOFT GOAT CHEESE (CHÈVRE), AT ROOM TEMPERATURE

8 WHOLE-WHEAT TORTILLAS (8 INCHES IN DIAMETER)

COOKING SPRAY

1 Heat 1 tablespoon of the oil in a large nonstick skillet over medium-high heat. Add the onion and ¼ teaspoon of the salt and cook, stirring frequently, until golden brown, about 5 minutes. Stir in the garlic and cook, 1 minute. Add the kale and cook, stirring, until tender, 2 to 3 minutes. Remove the pan from the heat and stir in the cider vinegar. Transfer the mixture to a bowl and cover to keep warm. Wipe out the skillet and reserve.

2 Season the salmon all over with the Creole seasoning and the remaining ¼ teaspoon salt. Heat the remaining 1 tablespoon oil in the skillet over medium-high heat. Add the salmon, lower the heat to medium, and cook, turning once, until browned on both sides and just cooked through, about 9 minutes per inch thickness. Transfer the salmon to a plate and allow to cool slightly. When cool enough to handle, break the salmon into chunks.

3 Spread the goat cheese evenly among tortillas and top half of each side evenly with the kale mixture and then the salmon. Fold the other half over the filling to create a half-moon.

4   Spray a large skillet with cooking spray and heat over medium-high heat. Brown the quesadillas 2 at a time until they are golden brown on both sides and the cheese is melting, 1 to 2 minutes per side. Repeat with the remaining quesadillas. The quesadillas may be refrigerated or frozen at this stage.

5   To continue, cut warm quesadillas cut into wedges and serve.

TO REFRIGERATE AND REHEAT

Chill in the refrigerator for 15 minutes, then wrap in foil and refrigerate for up to 3 days.

To reheat, open the foil all the way and place the quesadilla in an oven that has been preheated to 350°F. Cook, flipping once, until warmed through, 12 minutes. Alternatively, remove from the foil, wrap in a paper towel, and microwave on high for 90 seconds to 2 minutes, flipping once, for one quesadilla. (Oven reheating is preferred because the edges of the tortilla will recrisp.)

TO FREEZE AND REHEAT

Chill in the refrigerator for 15 minutes, then wrap in foil, and place in a sealable freezer bag in the freezer for up to 3 months.

There is no need to thaw. To reheat, open the foil all the way and place the quesadilla in a cold oven set for 350°F. Once the oven reaches temperature, continue to cook, flipping once, for 15 minutes. Alternatively, remove the quesadilla from the foil, wrap in a paper towel, and microwave on the defrost setting for 3 minutes, then on high for 40 to 60 seconds, for one quesadilla. (Oven reheating is preferred because the edges of the tortilla will recrisp.)

＊ **Serving size:** 1 quesadilla; **Per serving:** Calories 320; Total Fat 18g (Mono Fat 5.3g, Poly Fat 1.7g, Sat Fat 7.7g); Protein 20g; Carb 22g; Fiber 5g; Cholesterol 45mg; Sodium 610mg; **Excellent source of:** Copper, Phosphorus, Protein, Riboflavin, Vitamin A, Vitamin B6, Vitamin B12, Vitamin C, Vitamin D; **Good source of:** Calcium, Fiber, Niacin, Potassium

Sole Florentine with Crispy Bread Crumbs • MAKES 6 SERVINGS •

HERE, A FLAKY, MOIST FILLET of sole is baked on a bed of creamed spinach and topped with a crispy bread crumb topping. It full-on comfort food, the healthy way. If you are planning to make-ahead and freeze the spinach mixture, pick up a package of frozen fish fillets so you have those on hand too. Any flaky white fish will work. The spinach also stands on its own as a fabulous side dish with some grilled meat or poultry.

FOR THE TOPPING:

½ CUP WHOLE-WHEAT PANKO BREAD CRUMBS

1 TABLESPOON OLIVE OIL

¼ TEASPOON SALT

PINCH FRESHLY GROUND BLACK PEPPER

FOR THE SPINACH MIXTURE:

3 TABLESPOONS WHOLE-WHEAT PASTRY FLOUR, OR ALL-PURPOSE FLOUR

4 CUPS 1% MILK

2 TABLESPOONS OLIVE OIL

1 MEDIUM ONION, FINELY CHOPPED

3 CLOVES GARLIC, MINCED

THREE 10-OUNCE PACKAGES FROZEN SPINACH, THAWED AND SQUEEZED DRY

2 TABLESPOONS DIJON MUSTARD

½ TEASPOON SALT

¼ TEASPOON FRESHLY GROUND PEPPER

FOR SERVING:

COOKING SPRAY

SIX 6-OUNCE SOLE OR FLOUNDER FILLETS

1 LEMON, CUT INTO 6 WEDGES

1 To make the topping: In a small bowl, stir together the bread crumbs, oil, salt, and pepper.

2 To make the spinach mixture: In a medium bowl or pitcher, whisk the flour into the milk until it is completely dissolved. Heat the oil in a very large skillet over medium heat. Add the onion and cook, stirring, until tender, 7 to 8 minutes. Add the garlic and cook, stirring, 1 minute more. Add the spinach and cook, stirring, until warmed through, 2 to 3 minutes. Add the flour-thickened milk, raise the heat up to medium-high, and cook, stirring, until the mixture begins to simmer. Lower the heat to medium-low and cook until the mixture thickens, 4 to 5 minutes. Stir in the mustard, salt, and pepper. The spinach mixture and topping may be refrigerated or frozen at this stage.

3 To continue, preheat the oven to 350°F. Spray one 9 × 13-inch glass baking dish or 6 individual (2-cup capacity) oval baking dishes with cooking spray.

4 Place the spinach in the dish(es), ¾ cup per serving. Arrange the fish on top of the spinach and sprinkle 1½ tablespoons of the bread crumb topping onto each piece of fish. Bake, uncovered, until the fish is cooked through, 13 to 15 minutes. Then broil until the topping is browned and crispy, 1 minute. Serve with the lemon wedges.

TO REFRIGERATE AND SERVE

Place the topping and spinach mixture in separate airtight containers and refrigerate for up to 4 days.

When ready to prepare, follow the "to continue" instructions in the recipe, allowing an extra 5 to 10 minutes baking time, 20 to 25 minutes total.

TO FREEZE AND SERVE

Allow the spinach mixture to cool in the refrigerator for 30 minutes, then transfer to sealable plastic freezer bags in the portions desired and freeze for up to 3 months. The topping may also be frozen for up to three months in a separate freezer bag.

Thaw the spinach mixture in the refrigerator for 12 to 18 hours. Or, to thaw quickly, run the bag under hot water for 30 seconds to release, then transfer the spinach to a saucepan, add 2 tablespoons water per portion, and cook, covered, over medium-low heat, breaking up occasionally with a spoon, until warmed through, 8 to 25 minutes, depending on the amount.

Or, after releasing the spinach from the bag, place it in a microwave-safe bowl or baking dish, cover with a splatter guard, and microwave on the defrost setting for 8 minutes for one portion.

The bread crumb topping does not need to be thawed. Once the spinach mixture is thawed, follow the "to continue" instructions in the recipe, allowing an extra 5 to 10 minutes baking time, 20 to 25 minutes total.

✳ **Serving size:** ¾ cup spinach and 1 fish fillet; **Per serving:** Calories 370; Total Fat 11g (Mono Fat 5.8g, Poly Fat 1.5g, Sat Fat 2.5g); Protein 44g; Carb 25g; Fiber 5g; Cholesterol 90mg; Sodium 740mg; **Excellent source of:** Calcium, Folate, Magnesium, Manganese, Niacin, Phosphorus, Potassium, Protein, Riboflavin, Selenium, Thiamin, Vitamin A, Vitamin B6, Vitamin B12, Vitamin C, Vitamin E, Vitamin K; **Good source of:** Copper, Fiber, Iron, Pantothenic Acid, Vitamin D, Zinc

Shrimp with Thai Coconut Curry Sauce · MAKES 6 SERVINGS ·

THIS RICH, LIGHTLY SPICED SAUCE is made decadent and aromatic with coconut milk and virgin coconut oil, and has a colorful touch of sweet-savory flavor from a rainbow array of bell peppers. It's a perfect simmer for succulent shrimp. I like to serve it over jasmine rice.

FOR THE SAUCE:

- 2 TEASPOONS VIRGIN COCONUT OIL, OR CANOLA OIL
- 1 LARGE SWEET ONION, SUCH AS VIDALIA, SLICED INTO HALF-MOONS
- 3 MEDIUM RED, ORANGE, AND/OR YELLOW BELL PEPPERS, SLICED (ABOUT 5 CUPS)
- ¾ TEASPOON SALT, OR TO TASTE
- 1 TABLESPOON PLUS 2 TEASPOONS THAI GREEN CURRY PASTE
- 3 CUPS FISH STOCK
- 1 CUP UNSWEETENED LIGHT COCONUT MILK

FOR SERVING:

- 2 TABLESPOONS VIRGIN COCONUT OIL OR CANOLA OIL
- 2 POUNDS LARGE SHRIMP, PEELED AND DEVEINED
- 1 TABLESPOON FRESH LIME JUICE
- ½ CUP COARSELY CHOPPED FRESH CILANTRO

1 Heat the 2 teaspoons oil in a large, deep skillet over medium-high heat. Add the onion and cook, stirring, until softened, 4 minutes. Add the peppers and ½ teaspoon of the salt and cook, stirring, until the onion is golden brown and the peppers have begun to soften, about 4 minutes more. Lower the heat to medium-low, add the curry paste, and cook, stirring, until fragrant, about 30 seconds. Add the stock and coconut milk. Bring to a simmer over medium-high heat, then lower the heat to medium-low and simmer until reduced and thickened slightly, to about 5½ cups, 12 minutes. Season with the remaining ¼ teaspoon of salt, if needed, depending on the saltiness of your fish stock. The sauce may be refrigerated or frozen at this stage.

2 To continue, heat the 2 tablespoons oil in another large, deep skillet over medium heat. Add the shrimp and cook, stirring occasionally, until they are pink on the outside but not quite cooked through, about 4 minutes. Add the sauce to the skillet with the shrimp and bring it to a simmer over medium heat, then continue to cook, stirring, until the shrimp is cooked through, 1 to 2 minutes. Stir in the lime juice. Serve in bowls and garnish with the fresh cilantro.

Make the sauce ahead:

TO REFRIGERATE AND REHEAT

Place the sauce in an airtight container in the refrigerator for up to 2 days. When ready to cook, follow the "to continue" directions in the recipe, using half of the "for serving" ingredients if making a half-batch.

TO FREEZE AND REHEAT

Chill the sauce in the refrigerator for 30 minutes, then place the full batch or separate half-batches of sauce into sealable freezer bags and freeze for up to 3 months.

Thaw in the refrigerator for 24 to 36 hours, or, to thaw quickly, run the bag(s) under hot water for 30 seconds to release, then place in a saucepan, cover, and cook over medium-low heat for 15 to 30 minutes, depending on the amount.

Alternatively, once released from the bag, place the sauce in a microwave-safe bowl, cover with a splatter guard, and microwave on the defrost setting for 7 to 10 minutes, depending on the amount. Once thawed, continue to cook, following the "to continue" directions in the recipe, using half the "for serving" ingredients for a half batch of the sauce.

⚹ **Serving size:** About 8 shrimp and a scant cup of sauce; **Per serving:** Calories 210; Total Fat 7g (Mono Fat 0.4g, Poly Fat 0.6g, Sat Fat 5g); Protein 29g; Carb 8g; Fiber 2g; Cholesterol 210mg; Sodium 660mg; **Excellent source of:** Copper, Phosphorus, Protein, Vitamin A, Vitamin C; **Good source of:** Calcium, Magnesium, Niacin, Potassium, Vitamin B6, Zinc

Vegetarian

African Peanut Stew

THIS DEEPLY FLAVORFUL STEW, BRIMMING with a rainbow of hearty vegetables—sweet potato, eggplant, red peppers, tomatoes, and collard greens—is made rich, creamy, and totally irresistible with a generous scoop of peanut butter melted into the mix. The crunch of peanuts on top echoes the flavor in the stew and add a delightfully crunchy contrast.

- 1 MEDIUM EGGPLANT (1 POUND), PEELED AND CUT INTO 1-INCH CUBES (ABOUT 6 CUPS)
- 3 TABLESPOONS PEANUT OIL, DIVIDED
- 1 TEASPOON SALT, DIVIDED
- 2 LARGE ONIONS, CHOPPED
- 2 CLOVES GARLIC, MINCED
- 2 TABLESPOONS FINELY GRATED FRESH GINGER
- 1 TEASPOON GROUND CORIANDER
- ½ TEASPOON GROUND CUMIN
- ¼ TEASPOON GROUND CINNAMON
- ¼ TEASPOON GROUND TURMERIC
- 3 CUPS LOW-SODIUM VEGETABLE BROTH
- ONE 14-OUNCE CAN NO-SALT-ADDED DICED TOMATOES
- ½ POUND COLLARD GREENS, TOUGH RIB REMOVED AND DISCARDED, LEAVES CHOPPED (ABOUT 3 CUPS)
- ½ POUND SWEET POTATO, PEELED, CUT INTO 1-INCH CUBES (ABOUT 1¾ CUPS)
- 2 MEDIUM RED BELL PEPPERS, CHOPPED
- ¼ CUP NATURAL-STYLE PEANUT BUTTER

FOR SERVING:
- 6 TABLESPOONS CHOPPED PEANUTS

1 Preheat the broiler on high.

2 On a sheet pan, toss the eggplant with 1 tablespoon of the oil and ½ teaspoon of the salt. Broil about 6 inches from the heat, stirring occasionally, until golden brown, 10 to 12 minutes.

3 Heat the remaining 2 tablespoons oil in a large, heavy pot, such as a Dutch oven, over medium heat. Add the onions and cook, stirring, until softened, about 5 minutes. Add the garlic, ginger, coriander, cumin, the remaining ½ teaspoon salt, the cinnamon, and turmeric, and cook, stirring, for 1 minute.

4 Stir in the broth, tomatoes with their juices, collard greens, sweet potatoes, bell peppers, and broiled eggplant and bring to a boil. Lower the heat to medium-low and simmer, covered, until the vegetables are tender, about 25 minutes.

5 Stir in the peanut butter and simmer until it is incorporated, 3 minutes. The stew may be refrigerated or frozen at this stage. Serve garnished with the chopped peanuts.

Recipe continues

TO REFRIGERATE AND REHEAT

The stew will keep in the refrigerator in an airtight container for up to 4 days.

To reheat, place in a pot over medium-low heat, cover, and cook, stirring occasionally, until warmed through, 8 to 20 minutes, depending on the amount. Alternatively, place a single serving in a microwave-safe bowl, cover with a splatter guard, and microwave on full power for about 90 seconds to 2 minutes.

TO FREEZE AND REHEAT

Chill in the refrigerator for 30 minutes, then transfer into freezer bags in the portions desired and freeze for up to 3 months.

Thaw in the refrigerator for 24 to 36 hours and reheat following the "to refrigerate" directions. Or, to thaw quickly, run the bag under hot water for 30 seconds to release the stew from the bag, then transfer it to a pot along with 1 to 2 tablespoons of water. Cover and cook over medium-low heat, stirring occasionally, until warmed though, 15 to 40 minutes, depending on the amount. Add more water to the pot if the bottom is getting dry.

Alternatively, after running the bag under hot water, transfer the stew to a microwave-safe bowl, cover with a splatter guard, and microwave on the defrost setting for about 10 minutes, then heat through on full power for 90 seconds to 2 minutes for one serving.

✳ **Serving size:** 1½ cups plus 1 tablespoon chopped peanuts; **Per serving:** Calories 290; Total Fat 18g (Mono Fat 5.6g, Poly Fat 3.8g, Sat Fat 2.7g); Protein 9g; Carb 29g; Fiber 8g; Cholesterol 0mg; Sodium 500mg; **Excellent source of:** Fiber, Folate, Manganese, Vitamin A, Vitamin B6, Vitamin C, Vitamin K; **Good source of:** Calcium, Copper, Magnesium, Molybdenum, Niacin, Phosphorus, Potassium, Protein, Vitamin E

Black Bean Veggie Burger • MAKES 8 SERVINGS •

I LIKE MY VEGGIE BURGERS to taste like what they are made of rather than mimic meat. This burger is true to that, a supremely delicious combination of the beans, vegetables, and whole grains, enhanced with deeply flavorful seasonings like cumin, paprika, onions, and garlic.

But the fun thing about these is that the color of the grated beets, mixed with the black beans and mushrooms, makes them look very much like red meat. They are no impostors though. They satisfy completely on their own tasty terms.

2 TABLESPOONS OLIVE OIL, DIVIDED

1 MEDIUM ONION, DICED

4 OUNCES BABY BELLA OR WHITE BUTTON MUSHROOMS, DICED (ABOUT 6 MUSHROOMS)

1 SMALL RED BEET, PEELED AND SHREDDED (¾ CUP)

1 MEDIUM CARROT, SHREDDED (½ CUP)

3 CLOVES GARLIC, MINCED

1 TEASPOON GROUND CUMIN

1 TEASPOON PAPRIKA

⅛ TEASPOON CAYENNE PEPPER

TWO 15-OUNCE CANS LOW-SODIUM BLACK BEANS, DRAINED AND RINSED, DIVIDED

½ CUP COOKED BROWN RICE

¼ CUP CHOPPED CHIVES

¼ CUP UNSEASONED, WHOLE-GRAIN, DRIED BREAD CRUMBS

1 TABLESPOON WORCESTERSHIRE SAUCE

1 LARGE EGG WHITE

1 TEASPOON SALT

¼ TEASPOON FRESHLY GROUND BLACK PEPPER

Ingredients continue

1 Heat 1 tablespoon of the olive oil in a nonstick skillet over medium heat. Add the onion and cook, stirring occasionally, until softened and lightly browned at the edges, about 3 to 4 minutes. Add the mushrooms, beet, and carrot and continue to cook, stirring, until the vegetables are softened, 4 to 5 minutes more. Add the garlic, cumin, paprika, and cayenne pepper and continue to cook, stirring, until fragrant, 30 seconds. Transfer to a large bowl.

2 Pulse half of the black beans, the rice, and remaining 1 tablespoon oil in a food processor about 8 to 10 times until finely chopped but not mushy. Add the pulsed mixture along with the other can of black beans and the chives to the bowl with the cooked vegetables. Add the bread crumbs, Worcestershire sauce, egg white, salt, and black pepper and stir to combine. Use your hands to make 8 round patties. The burgers may be refrigerated or frozen at this stage.

3 To continue, spray a nonstick skillet with cooking spray and heat over medium-high heat. Cook the patties until browned on one side, about 3 minutes, then spray the top of the patties with cooking spray, turn gently, and cook until the other side is browned, another 3 minutes.

Recipe continues

FOR SERVING:

OLIVE OIL COOKING SPRAY

16 BUTTER OR BIBB LETTUCE LEAVES

2 MEDIUM RIPE AVOCADOS, SLICED

½ MEDIUM RED ONION, CUT THINLY INTO RINGS

1 LIME, CUT INTO WEDGES

4 Serve the black bean burgers on the lettuce, topped with a couple of avocado slices and a couple of the onion rings, with one of the lime wedges alongside.

TO REFRIGERATE AND SERVE

Place in an airtight container and refrigerate for up to 4 days.

To heat and serve, follow the "to continue" directions in the recipe. After browning on both sides, lower heat to low, cover, and cook until warmed through, 2 minutes more..

TO FREEZE AND SERVE

Chill the burgers in the refrigerator for 30 minutes, then wrap individually in plastic wrap and place in a sealable plastic freezer bag in the freezer for up to 3 months.

There is no need to thaw. To heat and serve, unwrap the burgers and cook following the "to continue" directions in the recipe. After browning on both sides, lower the heat to low, cover, and cook until warmed through, 5 to 6 minutes more.

---

* **Serving size:** 1 burger; **Per serving:** Calories 220; Total Fat 11g (Mono Fat 2.5g, Poly Fat 0.4g, Sat Fat 0.5g); Protein 7g; Carb 30g; Fiber 10g; Cholesterol 0mg; Sodium 343mg; **Excellent source of:** Fiber, Potassium, Vitamin A, Vitamin C, Vitamin K; **Good source of:** Copper, Folate, Iron, Manganese, Pantothenic Acid, Protein, Riboflavin, Vitamin B6

Broccoli and Sun-Dried Tomato Flatbread Pizzas • MAKES 4 SERVINGS •

THESE EASY PIZZAS ARE A complete meal in themselves, with a tasty topping of sautéed broccoli and onions with sun-dried tomatoes, and two cheeses, all piled on whole-grain flatbread. You can make the broccoli topping ahead and have it handy for a quick pizza pull-together, or you can premake the pizzas themselves and stash them in the freezer so they are ready to pop in the oven for an effortless meal whenever you need one. You can also slice these into wedges and serve as party finger-food.

1 TABLESPOON PLUS 2 TEASPOONS OLIVE OIL, DIVIDED

½ SMALL RED ONION, SLICED THINLY INTO HALF-MOONS

2 CLOVES GARLIC, SLICED

4 CUPS BROCCOLI FLORETS, CHOPPED (7 OUNCES)

⅛ TEASPOON SALT

4 WHOLE-GRAIN FLATBREADS, PITA OR NAAN BREADS (ABOUT 2 OUNCES EACH)

1½ CUPS (6 OUNCES) SHREDDED PART-SKIM MOZZARELLA CHEESE

¼ CUP SUNDRIED TOMATOES (ABOUT 6), REHYDRATED IN BOILING WATER FOR 10 MINUTES IF VERY DRY, COARSELY CHOPPED

2 TABLESPOONS GRATED PARMESAN CHEESE

1 Heat 1 tablespoon of the oil in a medium skillet over medium heat. Add the onion and garlic and cook, stirring, until slightly softened, 1 minute. Add the broccoli and cook, stirring frequently, until it is crisp-tender, 2 minutes. Season with the salt.

2 If you are planning to freeze the pizzas, allow the broccoli mixture to cool completely before continuing. The broccoli mixture may be made ahead and refrigerated.

3 Brush the top of each flatbread with the remaining 2 teaspoons oil. Top each with 3 tablespoons of the mozzarella, then scatter the broccoli mixture and some of the sundried tomatoes on top. Sprinkle with the remaining mozzarella and the Parmesan. The pizzas may be frozen at this stage.

4 To continue, place a baking sheet in the oven and preheat the oven and the baking sheet together to 450°F. Place the flatbread pizzas on the preheated tray and bake for 8 to 9 minutes, until the bread is toasted and the cheese is melted.

Recipe continues

TO REFRIGERATE AND SERVE

The broccoli mixture may be made up to 3 days ahead and stored separately in the refrigerator in an airtight container.

Refrigerating the prepared pizzas is not recommended.

TO FREEZE AND SERVE

Wrap each pizza individually in foil and place, level, in a sealable plastic freezer bag. Freeze for up to 3 months.

To heat, there is no need to thaw. Open the foil and follow the "to continue" directions in the recipe, adding about 5 minutes to the cooking time for a total of 13 to 14 minutes.

∗ **Serving size:** 1 pizza; **Per serving:** Calories 370; Total Fat 14g (Mono Fat 4.5g, Poly Fat 1.3g, Sat Fat 5.2g); Protein 22g; Carb 44g; Fiber 7g; Cholesterol 25mg; Sodium 700mg; **Excellent source of:** Fiber, Calcium, Manganese, Protein, Selenium, Vitamin A, Vitamin C, Vitamin K; **Good source of:** Copper, Folate, Iron, Magnesium, Niacin, Pantothenic Acid, Phosphorus, Potassium, Thiamin, Vitamin B6

Cumin-Spiced Lentils with Sautéed Onions

• MAKES 6 SERVINGS •

HERE, PILES OF ONIONS ARE caramelized with fragrant cumin seeds, then simmered with tomatoes and tossed with tender lentils for a true comfort-food stew, Egyptian style. Crushing the canned whole tomatoes by hand as you drop them into the pan give them a rustic, home-style texture. Besides, it's fun to do. Serve over whole-grain rice, macaroni, or even a mixture of the two.

2 CUPS LOW-SODIUM VEGETABLE BROTH

1¼ CUPS BROWN OR GREEN LENTILS (8 OUNCES)

2 TABLESPOONS OLIVE OIL

2 LARGE ONIONS, SLICED THINLY INTO HALF-MOONS

2 TEASPOONS WHOLE CUMIN SEEDS

3 CLOVES GARLIC, MINCED

¾ TEASPOON SALT, DIVIDED

ONE 28-OUNCE CAN WHOLE PEELED TOMATOES

2 TABLESPOONS FRESH ITALIAN PARSLEY LEAVES, COARSELY CHOPPED

½ TEASPOON CRUSHED RED PEPPER FLAKES

½ TEASPOON GROUND CORIANDER

¼ TEASPOON HONEY

⅛ TEASPOON FRESHLY GROUND BLACK PEPPER

FOR SERVING:

CHOPPED FRESH ITALIAN PARSLEY LEAVES, OPTIONAL

1 Place the broth, lentils, and 1 cup of water into a medium pot and bring to a boil. Lower the heat to medium-low and simmer, partially covered, for 25 to 30 minutes, until just tender. Drain any remaining liquid and set aside.

2 Heat the oil in a large, deep skillet over medium heat. Add the onions and cook, stirring, until they are softened and lightly golden, 10 to 12 minutes. Add the cumin seeds and cook, stirring occasionally, until they are fragrant and the onions are a shade darker, 3-4 minutes. Add the garlic and ¼ teaspoon of the salt and continue to cook, stirring, for 30 seconds more.

3 Add the tomatoes to the skillet, one at a time, crushing them with your hands over the pan as you put them in. Add any juice remaining in the can. Stir in the parsley, red pepper flakes, coriander, honey, the remaining ½ teaspoon of salt, and the black pepper. Scrape the bottom of pan with a wooden spoon to loosen any browned bits. Bring to a boil, then lower the heat to medium-low and simmer until slightly thickened, about 5 to 7 minutes. Mix the cooked lentils into the tomato-onion mixture. Serve garnished with additional chopped parsley.

TO REFRIGERATE AND REHEAT

Place in an airtight container in the refrigerator for up to 5 days.

To reheat, place in a saucepan, cover, and warm over low heat, stirring occasionally, until warmed through, 3 to 15 minutes, depending on the amount. Add a few tablespoons of water to loosen, if needed. Alternatively, place in a microwave-safe bowl, cover with a splatter guard, and microwave for about 60 seconds for one portion.

TO FREEZE AND REHEAT

Allow to cool in the refrigerator for 30 minutes, then place in sealable freezer bags in the quantities desired.

Thaw in the refrigerator for 18 to 24 hours, then reheat, following the "to refrigerate" directions. Or, to thaw quickly, run hot water over the bag for 30 seconds to release the food, then place in a covered saucepan on the stove with about 1 tablespoon water per portion, and warm over medium-low heat, stirring occasionally and breaking the mixture up with a spoon, 12 to 40 minutes, depending on the amount. Alternatively, after releasing from the bag, place in a microwave-safe dish, and microwave on the defrost setting for 4 minutes and then on high for 2 minutes for one portion.

---

* **Serving size:** 1 cup; **Per serving:** Calories 230; Total Fat 5g (Mono Fat 3.4g, Poly Fat 0.7g, Sat Fat 0.7g); Protein 13g; Carb 35g; Fiber 14g; Cholesterol 0mg; Sodium 600mg; **Excellent source of:** Fiber, Folate, Iron, Manganese, Protein, Thiamin, Vitamin C; **Good source of:** Copper, Magnesium, Phosphorus, Potassium, Vitamin A, Vitamin B6, Zinc

Forbidden Rice Bowl

• MAKES 6 SERVINGS •

RICE BOWLS ARE ON THE menu at all the hip farm-to-table restaurants these days, and for good reason. These meals-in-a-bowl—which involve a mound of warm rice, or other grain topped with an array of vegetables, some kind of protein, and a pour of tasty sauce—are templates for creativity and can easily be built around whatever ingredients are in season, what you are in the mood for, and what you have on hand.

I used black rice (also called forbidden rice) here for its nutty texture and sex appeal, but you could use brown or red rice, or even farro, barley, or quinoa. Any mix of vegetables will work, but I recommend including something leafy, something crunchy, and something pickled. As for the protein, here it is a hardboiled egg, but some marinated tofu (like the one on page 297) or sliced chicken for the carnivores would also be delicious.

FOR THE SAUCE:

- ¼ CUP REDUCED-SODIUM SOY SAUCE
- 2 TABLESPOONS UNSEASONED RICE VINEGAR
- 2 TABLESPOONS PEANUT OIL
- 2 TEASPOONS TOASTED SESAME OIL

FOR THE RICE BOWL:

- 5 OUNCES BABY KALE OR SPINACH LEAVES
- 6 CUPS HOT, COOKED BLACK ("FORBIDDEN") RICE OR BROWN RICE (SEE GRAIN FREEZE, PAGE 149)
- 6 LARGE EGGS, HARDBOILED, HALVED
- 1 CUP PICKLED RED ONIONS (PAGE 166) OR STORE-BOUGHT KIMCHI
- 1½ CUPS BEAN SPROUTS
- 2 MEDIUM CARROTS, SHREDDED (1½ CUPS)
- ½ CUP COARSELY CHOPPED ROASTED PEANUTS
- 1 SCALLION, THINLY SLICED

1 For the sauce, in a small bowl, whisk together the soy sauce, rice vinegar, peanut oil, and sesame oil. The sauce may be made ahead and kept in an airtight container in the refrigerator for at least 2 weeks.

2 For the rice bowl, place the kale or spinach leaves in a steamer basket set over a pot of boiling water. Cover and steam until wilted, 4 minutes. Alternatively, place in a microwave-safe bowl with 1 tablespoon of water, cover tightly, and microwave on high for 4 minutes, then drain. The greens may be made ahead and stored in an airtight container in the refrigerator for up to 4 days.

3 Place 1 cup of the hot rice into each bowl. Arrange ⅓ cup of the greens (still warm or chilled), two of the egg halves, a few of the pickled onions or some kimchi, ¼ cup of the beans sprouts, and ¼ cup of the carrots on top of the rice. Sprinkle 1 heaping tablespoon of the peanuts on top of each and drizzle each with about 1½ tablespoons of the sauce and some of the scallion.

Recipe continues

TO REFRIGERATE

The sauce, hardboiled eggs, pickled onions, chopped peanuts, carrots, greens, and scallion may all be prepared ahead and stored in separate airtight containers in the refrigerator. The sauce, hardboiled eggs (unshelled), onions, and peanuts will keep for 1 week. The shredded carrot, steamed greens, and sliced scallion will keep for 4 days. Allow to come to room temperature before serving.

Refrigerating cooked rice is not recommended for this dish.

TO FREEZE

Cooked rice may be made ahead, frozen, and reheated following the directions in Grain Freeze, page 149.

＊ **Serving size:** 1 rice bowl; **Per serving:** Calories 480; Total Fat 20g (Mono Fat 8.5g, Poly Fat 5.5g, Sat Fat 3.7g); Protein 17g; Carb 60g; Fiber 7g; Cholesterol 185mg; Sodium 390mg; **Excellent source of:** Copper, Fiber, Folate, Magnesium, Manganese, Niacin, Phosphorus, Potassium, Protein, Riboflavin, Selenium, Thiamin, Vitamin A, Vitamin B6, Vitamin C, Vitamin K; **Good source of:** Calcium, Chloride, Iodine, Iron, Molybdenum, Pantothenic Acid, Vitamin D, Vitamin E, Zinc

Garden Penne Bake • MAKES 8 SERVINGS •

BAKED ZITI IS AN ALL-TIME favorite crowd-pleaser, with its saucy noodles and cheese cooked casserole-style until bubbling and the cheese is melted. This recipe is all of that, but better, because it is chock-full of colorful, fresh garden vegetables as well—zucchini, mushrooms, carrots, and tomatoes. I used whole-grain penne (which is similar to ziti in its tube shape) because for some reason it is easier to find in a whole-grain variety, but feel free to use whatever pasta shape you have on hand.

1 POUND WHOLE-WHEAT PENNE PASTA

2 TABLESPOONS OLIVE OIL

6 CLOVES GARLIC, THINLY SLICED

4 MEDIUM ZUCCHINI AND/OR YELLOW SUMMER SQUASH, 8 OUNCES EACH, CUT INTO ½-INCH PIECES

10 MEDIUM WHITE BUTTON MUSHROOMS, (10 OUNCES TOTAL), SLICED

1 PINT CHERRY OR GRAPE TOMATOES, HALVED

1 TEASPOON DRIED BASIL

1 TEASPOON SALT, DIVIDED

¾ TEASPOON FRESHLY GROUND BLACK PEPPER, DIVIDED

4 CUPS SIMPLE MARINARA SAUCE (PAGE 214), OR STORE-BOUGHT MARINARA

2 CUPS PART-SKIM RICOTTA CHEESE

1 LARGE CARROT, GRATED (ABOUT 1 CUP)

COOKING SPRAY

1 CUP SHREDDED PART-SKIM MOZZARELLA (4 OUNCES)

1 Bring a large pot of water to a boil. Add the pasta and cook for 2 minutes fewer than suggested in the package directions. Drain and return the pasta to the pot.

2 Heat the oil in a large nonstick skillet over medium heat. Add the garlic and cook, stirring frequently, for 1 minute. Add the zucchini and/or yellow squash and mushrooms and cook, stirring, until the liquid from the vegetables has evaporated and they begin to brown, about 10 minutes. Add the cherry tomatoes, basil, ½ teaspoon of the salt, and ½ teaspoon of the pepper and cook, stirring, until the tomatoes are soft and broken down, 10 minutes.

3 Add the cooked vegetables to the cooked pasta in the pot along with the marinara, ricotta, carrot, and the remaining ½ teaspoon salt and ¼ teaspoon pepper. Stir to combine well.

4 Spray one 9 × 13-inch baking dish, or two 8-inch square baking dishes, or 8 individual (2- to 3-cup capacity) dishes with cooking spray and fill with the pasta mixture. Top each with the mozzarella. The dish(es) may be made ahead and refrigerated or frozen at this stage.

5 To continue, preheat the oven to 350°F. Cover loosely with foil and bake for 15 minutes, then remove the foil and bake for another 15 to 25 minutes, depending on the size of the dish. Let sit for 5 minutes before serving.

Recipe continues

TO REFRIGERATE AND HEAT

Wrap the dish(es) tightly with foil and refrigerate for up to 4 days.

To heat, let the dish(es) sit at room temperature as the oven preheats to 350°F. Loosen the foil and bake, loosely covered, for 30 minutes, then uncover and bake for 15 to 25 minutes more.

TO FREEZE AND HEAT

Wrap the dish(es) tightly with plastic wrap and then foil, and freeze for up to 3 months.

There is no need to thaw. To heat, uncover completely, then cover loosely with foil. Place in a cold oven set to 350°F. Once the oven comes to temperature, continue cooking for 45 to 60 minutes, until thawed and slightly warm, then uncover and continue to bake for 20 to 30 minutes more, until bubbling and the cheese is melted.

---

* **Serving size:** About 2 cups; **Per serving:** Calories 440; Total Fat 14g (Mono Fat 5.7g, Poly Fat 1.1g, Sat Fat 5.3g); Protein 23g; Carb 61g; Fiber 8g; Cholesterol 25mg; Sodium 840mg; **Excellent source of:** Calcium, Copper, Fiber, Magnesium, Manganese, Phosphorus, Protein, Riboflavin, Selenium, Thiamin, Vitamin A, Vitamin C; **Good source of:** Chloride, Iron, Pantothenic Acid, Potassium, Vitamin B6, Vitamin K, Zinc

Greek Mixed Greens Pie with Phyllo Crust

• MAKES 8 SERVINGS •

ONE OF MY FORMATIVE FOOD memories is of my very first taste of spanakopita (Greek spinach pie) at a church festival in Queens. I was probably around 8 years old and I remember being totally and overwhelmingly transported by the shatteringly flaky layered crust and savory filling. This pie takes me right back there, but has a twist because I use a mix of greens including spinach, kale, and collards, which makes for a more interesting flavor and texture without veering too far from the classic.

If you haven't worked with phyllo dough before, don't be intimidated. It's not difficult, and with this pie, it doesn't matter a lick if the dough happens to tear a bit; it is a very forgiving recipe, so it's great for phyllo beginners.

⅓ CUP OLIVE OIL, DIVIDED

6 SCALLIONS, CHOPPED (½ CUP)

THREE 10-OUNCE PACKAGES FROZEN CHOPPED SPINACH, KALE, AND/OR COLLARD GREENS, THAWED AND SQUEEZED VERY DRY

1¼ CUPS CRUMBLED FETA CHEESE (7 OUNCES)

1 CUP LOW-FAT COTTAGE CHEESE (8 OUNCES)

3 LARGE EGGS, LIGHTLY BEATEN, DIVIDED

½ CUP FINELY CHOPPED FRESH DILL

½ CUP FINELY CHOPPED FRESH ITALIAN PARSLEY LEAVES

½ TEASPOON SALT

¼ TEASPOON FRESHLY GROUND BLACK PEPPER

10 SHEETS PHYLLO DOUGH, THAWED AND AT ROOM TEMPERATURE (½ POUND)

1 Heat 2 teaspoons of the oil in a medium skillet over medium heat. Add the scallions and cook, stirring, until they have softened, about 3 minutes. Transfer the scallions to a large mixing bowl, add the greens, feta, cottage cheese, two of the eggs, the dill, parsley, salt, and pepper and stir until well combined.

2 Brush one 9 × 13-inch casserole dish or two 8-inch square casserole dishes with oil. Cut the stack of phyllo sheets in half to fit the large dish if making one pie and in quarters to fit the small dishes if making two pies. Cover the sheets of phyllo with a damp paper towel and keep them covered as much as possible as you work.

3 Brush the top of one sheet of the dough lightly with some of the remaining oil and place in the pan. Continue to brush and layer until you have 8 sheets in the pan. Top with the mixed greens filling (or half of it if you are making 2 pies), spreading the mixture out evenly. Then brush and layer the top with the remaining 10 or so layers of phyllo. If making two pies, repeat with the second pan.

Recipe continues

4 Brush the top lightly with the remaining egg, then score the top of the pie with a sharp knife (being careful not to cut all the way down to the filling) into 8 sections for the large pie or 4 sections each for the smaller pies. The dish may be frozen at this stage.

5 To continue, preheat the oven to 375°F and bake for 35 to 45 minutes, until the top is flaky and golden brown.

TO REFRIGERATE AND HEAT

The pie may be refrigerated before (in its dish) or after baking (in or out of its dish).

Cover the unbaked pie tightly and refrigerate for up to 1 day, then bake, uncovered, according to the recipe instructions, adding about 10 minutes to the cooking time.

Once baked, allow the pie to cool in the refrigerator, uncovered, for 30 minutes, then wrap tightly and store in the refrigerator for up to 4 days. Reheat in a 350°F oven, uncovered, for 20 to 30 minutes.

TO FREEZE AND HEAT

The pie may be frozen before (in its dish) or after baking (in or out of its dish). Chill the baked pie, uncovered, in the refrigerator for 30 minutes before wrapping and freezing.

Wrap in plastic wrap and then in foil and freeze for up to 3 months. There is no need to thaw. When ready to cook, uncover the pie completely and place it in a cold oven set to 375°F for the unbaked pie or 350°F for the baked pie. Once the oven reaches temperature, cook until warmed through and the crust is flaky and golden brown, about 45 minutes.

---

* **Serving size:** 1 piece; **Per serving:** Calories 310; Total Fat 18g (Mono Fat 9.2g, Poly Fat 1.8g, Sat Fat 6g); Protein 15g; Carb 23g; Fiber 4g; Cholesterol 80mg; Sodium 730mg; **Excellent source of:** Calcium, Chloride, Folate, Iron, Magnesium, Manganese, Phosphorus, Protein, Riboflavin, Selenium, Thiamin, Vitamin A, Vitamin C, Vitamin E, Vitamin K; **Good source of:** Copper, Fiber, Iodine, Niacin, Potassium, Vitamin B6, Vitamin B12, Zinc

Grilled Eggplant Roll-Ups
with Feta and Mint in Smoky Roasted Red Pepper Sauce • MAKES 8 SERVINGS •

HERE, TENDER CHAR-GRILLED EGGPLANT BLANKETS a ricotta and feta filling that melts to creamy lusciousness when baked. That, along with a hint of mint, and the jewel-toned roasted red pepper sauce the roll-ups are baked in, makes for an exciting Eastern Mediterranean flavor twist. Serve as a meatless main, or do half-portions as a side or appetizer with, say, roasted lamb skewers.

1½ CUPS PART-SKIM RICOTTA CHEESE

1¼ CUPS PACKED COARSELY CRUMBLED FETA (7 OUNCES), DIVIDED

3 TABLESPOONS FINELY CHOPPED FRESH MINT

½ TEASPOON FRESHLY GROUND BLACK PEPPER, DIVIDED

OLIVE OIL COOKING SPRAY

5 MEDIUM EGGPLANTS (3½ POUNDS EACH), STEMS TRIMMED AND CUT LENGTHWISE INTO ¼-INCH-THICK SLICES, SKIN ENDS DISCARDED

1 TEASPOON SALT

1 RECIPE SMOKY ROASTED RED PEPPER SAUCE, PAGE 245

1 In a medium bowl, mash together the ricotta, ¾ cup of the feta, the mint, and ¼ teaspoon of the pepper with a fork until almost smooth.

2 Spray a grill pan or grill with olive oil cooking spray and preheat over medium heat. Spray the eggplant slices with olive oil spray on both sides and sprinkle with the salt and remaining ¼ teaspoon pepper. Grill the eggplant slices, in batches if necessary, until golden brown on both sides, for 2 to 3 minutes per side. Transfer to a plate.

3 Coat the bottom of one 9 × 13-inch baking dish or two 8-inch square baking dishes with the roasted red pepper sauce. Working with 1 eggplant slice at a time, put 1 tablespoon of the filling on one end of an eggplant slice and gently roll up eggplant to enclose filling. Place seam side down in the baking dish, nestling it into the sauce. Repeat with the remaining slices and filling. Sprinkle with the remaining ½ cup feta. The dish(es) may be refrigerated or frozen at this stage.

4 To continue, preheat the oven to 375°F. Bake in the middle of the oven, until the sauce is bubbling, the cheese is melted, and the filling is heated through, about 20 minutes.

TO REFRIGERATE AND SERVE

Cover the unbaked dish(es) tightly and refrigerate for up to 4 days. To heat, allow to sit at room temperature as the oven preheats to 350°F, then cook, uncovered, for 30 to 35 minutes. Alternatively, scoop a single serving onto a microwave-safe plate, cover with a splatter guard, and microwave on high for 1 minute. You may also use this method to refrigerate and reheat already baked roll-ups.

TO FREEZE AND SERVE

Cover the uncooked dish(es) tightly and freeze for up to 3 months. There is no need to thaw. Place, covered with foil, in a cold oven set for 350°F. Once the oven comes to temperature, cook for 15 minutes, then uncover and cook for 15 to 20 minutes more, until warmed through.

✽ **Serving size:** 4 roll-ups and about ¼ cup sauce; **Per serving:** Calories 410; Total Fat 12g (Mono Fat 3.6g, Poly Fat 1.2g, Sat Fat 6.4g); Protein 18g; Carb 65g; Fiber 28g; Cholesterol 35mg; Sodium 650mg, **Excellent source of:** Calcium, Chloride, Copper, Folate, Fiber, Magnesium, Manganese, Molybdenum, Niacin, Pantothenic Acid, Phosphorus, Potassium, Protein, Riboflavin, Selenium, Thiamin, Vitamin B6, Vitamin C, Vitamin K; **Good source of:** Iron, Vitamin A, Vitamin E, Zinc

Individual Mac and Cheese Cups

• MAKES 6 SERVINGS •

BAKING MACARONI AND CHEESE IN a muffin tin makes for adorable, individual comfort-food cups that are fun for kids and grown-ups alike. Stirring in pureed butternut squash for extra creaminess and color, and using whole-grain noodles, low-fat milk, and just the right amount of real sharp cheddar means you can have your favorite feel-good food in a healthier way to boot. Having a stash of these in your freezer makes them even more convenient on a busy day than the boxed stuff.

8 OUNCES WHOLE-GRAIN ELBOW MACARONI

⅔ CUP COLD 1% MILK

1 TABLESPOON ALL-PURPOSE FLOUR

1½ CUPS SHREDDED SHARP CHEDDAR CHEESE (5 OUNCES), DIVIDED

2 TABLESPOONS NEUFCHÂTEL CHEESE (REDUCED-FAT CREAM CHEESE)

1 CUP BUTTERNUT OR WINTER SQUASH PUREE

1½ TEASPOONS DIJON MUSTARD

½ TEASPOON PAPRIKA

½ TEASPOON SALT

1 LARGE EGG YOLK

1 Preheat the oven to 400°F. Place paper muffin cups in the wells of a 12-cup muffin tin.

2 Cook the macaroni in a large pot of boiling water for 2 minutes fewer than suggested on the package directions and then drain.

3 In a large saucepan, whisk together the milk and flour until the flour is dissolved. Whisking constantly, bring the mixture to a gentle boil over medium heat. Lower the heat to medium-low and simmer until the mixture is slightly thickened, 1 to 2 minutes. Add 1¼ cups of the cheddar cheese and the Neufchâtel and whisk until melted. Add the squash puree, mustard, paprika, and salt and whisk to incorporate. Remove from the heat and then whisk in the egg yolk. Add in the macaroni and stir until evenly coated.

4 Spoon the mixture into the muffin tin. Sprinkle with the remaining cheddar and then bake until bubbling and the tops are slightly browned, 18 to 20 minutes. Remove from the oven and allow to cool and set for 10 minutes before serving.

Recipe continues

TO REFRIGERATE AND REHEAT

Allow to cool in the refrigerator, uncovered, for 30 minutes, then, keeping them in their paper cups, cover tightly and refrigerate for up to 4 days.

To reheat, allow to sit at room temperature as the oven preheats to 350°F. Keeping them in their paper cups, place in the muffin tin or on a baking tray, cover with foil, and bake for 10 minutes, then uncover and bake 8 to 10 minutes more, until warmed through. Alternatively, place in their paper cups on a microwave-safe plate, cover with a splatter guard, and microwave on high for about 60 seconds for one 2-cup portion.

TO FREEZE AND REHEAT

Allow to cool in the refrigerator, uncovered, for 30 minutes, then, keeping them in their paper cups, wrap each individually in plastic wrap and place in a freezer-safe container or sealable plastic freezer bag and freeze for up to 3 months.

There is no need to thaw. To reheat, remove the plastic wrap, then place them, still in their paper cups in a muffin tin or on a baking sheet, cover with foil, and place in a cold oven set to 350°F. Once the oven reaches temperature, bake for 15 minutes, then uncover and bake 10 minutes more, until warmed through.

Alternatively, remove the plastic wrap, place the frozen cups on a microwave-safe plate, cover with a splatter guard, and microwave for 90 seconds to 2 minutes for one 2-cup portion.

∗ **Serving size:** 2 cups; **Per serving:** Calories 290; Total Fat 11g (Mono Fat 0.8g, Poly Fat 0.4g, Sat Fat 7g); Protein 13g; Carb 35g; Fiber 4g; Cholesterol 60mg; Sodium 410mg; **Excellent source of:** Calcium, Manganese, Protein, Vitamin A; **Good source of:** Fiber, Copper, Magnesium, Niacin, Phosphorus, Thiamin

Moroccan Vegetable Stew (Tagine)

• MAKES 8 SERVINGS •

THIS AROMATICALLY SPICED, HEARTY STEW has a colorful sweet-savory mix of flavors, from sweet chunks of butternut squash and dried fruit, to savory zucchini and chickpeas. Whatever you do, do not forget the final topping of mint leaves and toasted almonds. They add just the right notes of freshness and crunch that make the dish. Serve over whole-grain couscous.

2 TABLESPOONS OLIVE OIL

2 LARGE ONIONS, THINLY SLICED INTO HALF-MOONS (4 CUPS)

4 CLOVES GARLIC, MINCED

2 TEASPOONS GROUND CUMIN

2 TEASPOONS SALT

1 TEASPOON GROUND CINNAMON

1 TEASPOON GROUND CORIANDER

½ TEASPOON CRUSHED RED PEPPER FLAKES

½ TEASPOON GROUND TURMERIC

1 CARDAMOM POD

3½ CUPS LOW-SODIUM VEGETABLE BROTH

8 CUPS 1½-INCH CUBES BUTTERNUT SQUASH (2½ POUNDS)

3 LARGE ZUCCHINI (2 POUNDS), CUT INTO 1-INCH CUBES

TWO 15-OUNCE CANS NO-SALT-ADDED CHICKPEAS, DRAINED AND RINSED

12 DRIED APRICOTS, COARSELY CHOPPED

12 PRUNES, COARSELY CHOPPED

1 TABLESPOON HONEY

FOR SERVING:

½ CUP CHOPPED FRESH MINT LEAVES

½ CUP SLICED ALMONDS, TOASTED IN A DRY SKILLET OVER MEDIUM-HIGH HEAT, STIRRING FREQUENTLY, UNTIL FRAGRANT, 3 TO 5 MINUTES

1 Heat the oil in a large soup pot or Dutch oven over medium heat. Add the onions and cook, stirring, until translucent, 7 to 8 minutes. Add the garlic, cumin, salt, cinnamon, coriander, crushed red pepper, turmeric, and cardamom and cook, stirring, until the spices are fragrant, 30 seconds. Add the broth and cook, stirring, to loosen any bits from the bottom of the pot. Add the butternut squash, zucchini, chickpeas, apricots, prunes, and honey. Bring to a boil, then lower the heat to medium-low, cover, and cook, stirring once or twice, until the squash is tender, and the ingredients have melded, about 1 hour. Refrigerate or freeze at this stage.

2 Serve garnished with 1 tablespoon each of the mint and almonds.

Recipe continues

TO REFRIGERATE AND REHEAT

The stew will keep in the refrigerator in an airtight container for up to 4 days. To reheat, place in a pot over medium-low heat, cover, and cook, stirring occasionally, until warmed through, 8 to 20 minutes, depending on the amount. Alternatively, place in a microwave-safe bowl, cover with a splatter guard, and microwave on full power for about 90 seconds to 2 minutes for a single portion.

TO FREEZE AND REHEAT

Chill in the refrigerator for 30 minutes, then transfer into freezer bags in the portions desired. Freeze for up to 3 months. Thaw in the refrigerator for 24 to 36 hours and reheat following the "to refrigerate" directions.

Or, to thaw quickly, run the bag under hot water for 30 seconds to release the stew from the bag, then transfer it to a pot along with 1 to 2 tablespoons of water. Cover and cook over medium-low heat, stirring occasionally, until warmed though, 20 to 50 minutes, depending on the number of portions being thawed. Add more water to the pot if the bottom is getting dry.

Alternatively, after running the bag under hot water, transfer the stew to a microwave-safe bowl, cover with a splatter guard, and microwave on the defrost setting for about 10 minutes, then heat through on full power for 90 seconds to 2 minutes for a single portion.

∗ **Serving size:** 1½ cups; **Per serving:** Calories 370; Total Fat 9g (Mono Fat 4.6g, Poly Fat 2.8g, Sat Fat 0.8g); Protein 13g; Carb 64g; Fiber 14g; Cholesterol 0mg; Sodium 970mg; **Excellent source of:** Calcium, Copper, Fiber, Folate, Iron, Magnesium, Manganese, Molybdenum, Potassium, Protein, Vitamin A, Vitamin B6, Vitamin C, Vitamin E; **Good source of:** Niacin, Pantothenic Acid, Phosphorus, Thiamin, Vitamin K

Portobello Pizza Pockets • MAKES 4 SERVINGS •

I HAVE BEEN EXPERIMENTING A lot with whole-grain pizza dough, and I am amazed at its fun versatility. This tasty creation involves folding pizza toppings into the crust, calzone style, to make a pocket which is easy to freeze, reheat, and even eat on the fly if necessary. You can use whatever "toppings" you like. Two of my favorite combinations are in this book, the Turkey Sausage–Stuffed Pizza Pockets, page 223, and this vegetarian option, which is packed with meaty portobello mushrooms, pine nuts, sundried tomatoes, marinara, and cheese.

1 TABLESPOON OLIVE OIL

1 POUND PORTOBELLO MUSHROOMS, CHOPPED (ABOUT 5½ CUPS)

⅓ CUP PINE NUTS

2 TABLESPOONS CHOPPED SUNDRIED TOMATOES (REHYDRATED BY SOAKING IN HOT WATER, IF VERY DRY)

¼ TEASPOON SALT

¼ TEASPOON FRESHLY GROUND BLACK PEPPER

PINCH CRUSHED RED PEPPER FLAKES

⅓ CUP SIMPLE MARINARA SAUCE (PAGE 214), OR STORE-BOUGHT MARINARA

4 CUPS LIGHTLY PACKED CHOPPED FRESH ARUGULA OR SPINACH LEAVES

1 TABLESPOON CORNMEAL OR FLOUR

1 POUND WHOLE-WHEAT PIZZA DOUGH, THAWED IF FROZEN

1 CUP SHREDDED PART-SKIM MOZZARELLA CHEESE

1 EGG, BEATEN

2 TABLESPOONS FRESHLY GRATED PARMESAN CHEESE

FOR SERVING:

1 CUP SIMPLE MARINARA SAUCE (PAGE 214), OR STORE-BOUGHT MARINARA, OPTIONAL

1 Preheat the oven to 400°F. Line a baking sheet with parchment paper.

2 Heat the oil in a large skillet over medium-high heat. Add the mushrooms and cook, stirring a few times, until they have released their water and begin to brown, about 7 minutes. Add the pine nuts and cook, stirring, until they are toasted, 3 to 5 minutes more. Stir in the sundried tomatoes, salt, black pepper, and red pepper flakes, then add the marinara sauce and cook until the liquid is nearly all absorbed or evaporated, 1 minute. Stir in the arugula or spinach and cook until just wilted, 1 minute more. Set aside to cool slightly.

3 Meanwhile, sprinkle the cornmeal or flour onto a clean work surface and use a rolling pin and/or your hands to stretch out the dough into a large rectangle about 12 × 18 inches. (Helpful hint: if the dough keeps springing back, let it rest for a few minutes before you begin to stretch it again.) Using a sharp knife or pizza cutter, cut the dough into eight equal-sized rectangles.

4 Stir the mozzarella cheese into the cooled mushroom mixture. Place about ¼ cup of the filling on one side of each rectangle.

Recipe continues

5 Brush the border of each rectangle with the egg, then close the dough over the topping and use a fork to crimp the edges and seal each one closed. Brush the tops with egg and sprinkle with the Parmesan cheese. Place the pockets on the prepared baking tray and bake until golden brown, 15 to 18 minutes.

6 Serve with warmed marinara sauce, if desired.

TO REFRIGERATE AND REHEAT

Allow to cool at room temperature for 30 minutes, then wrap each pizza pocket in plastic wrap or foil and refrigerate for up to 4 days. To reheat, unwrap, place on a foil sheet or baking tray, and warm in a preheated 350°F oven for 20 to 25 minutes. Alternatively, unwrap, then rewrap in a paper towel, place on a microwave-safe plate, and microwave on high for 1 minute for one pocket.

TO FREEZE AND REHEAT

Allow to cool at room temperature for 30 minutes, then wrap each pizza pocket in plastic wrap or foil and place in a sealable freezer bag for up to 3 months. There is no need to thaw. To reheat, unwrap, then place on a foil sheet or baking tray in a cold oven set to 350°F. Once the oven reaches temperature, continue to cook for 30 to 35 minutes until warmed through. Alternatively, unwrap, then rewrap in a paper towel, place on a microwave-safe plate, and microwave on high for 2 minutes for one pocket.

✳ **Serving size:** 2 pockets and ¼ cup sauce; **Per serving:** Calories 500; Total Fat 23g (Mono Fat 6.7g, Poly Fat 4.7g, Sat Fat 4.7g); Protein 22g; Carb 61g; Fiber 8.5g; Cholesterol 40mg; Sodium 800mg; **Excellent source of:** Calcium, Copper, Folate, Iron, Manganese, Niacin, Phosphorus, Protein, Selenium, Vitamin K; **Good source of:** Fiber, Magnesium, Pantothenic Acid, Potassium, Riboflavin, Vitamin A, Vitamin B6, Vitamin C, Zinc

Roasted Marinated Tofu and Broccolini • MAKES 6 SERVINGS •

THE SIMPLE TRICK FOR MAKING really tasty tofu is to squeeze all of the water out of it first, so it can absorb the marinade and, with cooking, develop a firmer texture. Here, the tofu is infused with big Asian flavors: soy, ginger, garlic, and sesame, and then roasted alongside broccolini, which becomes tender and slightly charred in the oven. They are perfect together for a double-hitter on the plate, but you can also make the tofu separately and freeze or refrigerate it to add to salads, sandwiches, or stir-fries.

¼ CUP ORANGE JUICE

¼ CUP REDUCED-SODIUM SOY SAUCE

¼ CUP TOASTED SESAME OIL

¼ CUP UNSEASONED RICE VINEGAR

1 TABLESPOON FINELY GRATED FRESH GINGER

4 CLOVES GARLIC, MINCED, DIVIDED

TWO 14-OUNCE PACKAGES EXTRA-FIRM TOFU

2 TABLESPOONS SESAME SEEDS

3 HEADS BROCCOLINI (1½ POUNDS), TRIMMED

2 TABLESPOONS PEANUT OIL

¼ TEASPOON SALT

1 In a medium bowl or measuring pitcher, whisk together the orange juice, soy sauce, sesame oil, rice vinegar, ginger, and half of the garlic.

2 Drain the tofu, then slice each block of tofu into two ½-inch-thick slabs. Lay the slabs on top of a paper towel. Use more paper towels (you will need about 6 altogether) and firmly pat the tofu, removing as much of the water as possible. Then cut the tofu into ¾-inch cubes and place into a sealable plastic bag. Pour half of the marinade into the bag and shake the bag gently to coat evenly. Place in the refrigerator to marinate for at least 2 hours and up to 24 hours.

3 Preheat the oven to 350°F. Drain the marinade from the tofu, then spread the tofu in a single layer onto a parchment-lined baking sheet and bake it until it is golden brown, about 45 minutes.

4 Meanwhile, put the sesame seeds on another small baking sheet or a piece of foil and place in the oven to toast until golden and fragrant, about 10 minutes.

Recipe continues

5 On another baking sheet, toss the broccolini with the peanut oil, remaining garlic, and salt. Place it in the oven and roast, alongside the tofu, until the stems are firm-tender and the tops and leaves are crisped and slightly charred, 25 to 30 minutes.

6 Place the remaining soy sauce mixture into a small saucepan over medium-high heat. Bring to a boil and continue to cook until it is reduced by about half, about 4 minutes.

7 Serve the tofu and broccolini on a plate, drizzled with the reduced sauce, and sprinkled with the sesame seeds.

TO REFRIGERATE AND REHEAT

Place the broccolini, tofu, sauce, and sesame seeds into separate airtight containers in the refrigerator for up to 4 days.

To reheat, place the broccolini and tofu on a baking tray into a preheated 350°F oven for 15 minutes. Alternatively, place on a microwave-safe plate, cover with a splatter guard, and microwave on high for 1 minute per portion. Top with the sauce and sesame seeds after heating.

TO FREEZE AND REHEAT THE TOFU

Allow to cool at room temperature for 30 minutes, then place in a sealable plastic bag and freeze for up to 3 months.

Do not thaw. To reheat, place the frozen tofu on a baking sheet and place in a cold oven set to 350°F. Once the oven reaches temperature, continue to cook the tofu until it is warmed through, about 20 minutes.

Microwave thawing is not recommended. Freezing the broccolini is not recommended.

✱ **Serving size:** ⅔ cup tofu, 5 stalks broccolini, 1 teaspoon sesame seeds, and 1 tablespoon sauce; **Per serving:** Calories 330; Total Fat 23g (Mono Fat 8g, Poly Fat 9.7g, Sat Fat 3g); Protein 18g; Carb 16g; Fiber 5g; Cholesterol 0mg; Sodium 430mg; **Excellent source of:** Fiber, Protein, Vitamin C, Vitamin K; **Good source of:** Calcium, Folate, Iron, Manganese, Potassium, Vitamin A, Vitamin B6

Spinach and Pesto Lasagna Roll-Ups

• MAKES 6 SERVINGS •

THESE LASAGNA WHEELS ARE CLASSICALLY stuffed with creamy ricotta and doused in zesty marina, but they have an added punch of herbal flavor and color from a spread of basil pesto, and another green hit from spinach that is stirred into the cheese mix. Making lasagna roll-up style makes it easy to bake and store them in individual portions, so they are easy to have on hand to serve as many or as few as you need to, whenever you need to.

12 WHOLE-WHEAT LASAGNA NOODLES (ABOUT ¾ POUND)

ONE 15-OUNCE CONTAINER PART-SKIM RICOTTA CHEESE

ONE 10-OUNCE PACKAGE FROZEN CHOPPED SPINACH, THAWED AND SQUEEZED DRY

1 EGG, LIGHTLY BEATEN

¼ CUP GRATED PARMESAN CHEESE

⅓ CUP BASIL PESTO (PAGE 107), OR STORE-BOUGHT PESTO, DIVIDED

¼ TEASPOON SALT

¼ TEASPOON FRESHLY GROUND BLACK PEPPER

2 CUPS SIMPLE MARINARA SAUCE (PAGE 214), OR STORE-BOUGHT MARINARA, DIVIDED

¾ CUP SHREDDED PART-SKIM MOZZARELLA CHEESE

1 Cook the noodles according to the directions on the package. Drain and lay out on wax paper to cool so they don't stick together.

2 In a medium bowl, combine the ricotta cheese, spinach, egg, Parmesan, 2 tablespoons of the pesto, salt, and pepper.

3 Spread about ¾ cup of the marinara sauce on the bottom of a 9 × 13- inch baking dish, or to make individual portions, spread 2 tablespoons on the bottom of each of 6 oven- and freezer-safe ceramic or glass dishes.

4 Spread 2 heaping tablespoons of the ricotta mixture onto a lasagna noodle, then roll it up and place it in the dish seam side down. Repeat with the remaining noodles, placing two in each individual dish if using. Top with the remaining marinara sauce, remaining pesto, and shredded cheese. The lasagna roll-ups may be refrigerated or frozen at this stage.

5 To continue, preheat the oven to 350°F. Cover the dish(es) loosely with foil and bake for 30 minutes. Uncover and bake for 10 minutes more. Let rest for 5 minutes before serving.

Recipe continues

TO REFRIGERATE AND SERVE

Cover the unbaked dish(es) tightly and refrigerate for up to 4 days. To heat, allow to sit at room temperature as the oven preheats to 350°F, cover loosely with foil, and bake for 45 minutes, then uncover and bake for 10 to 15 minutes more. You may also use this method to reheat leftover, already baked roll-ups.

TO FREEZE AND SERVE

Cover the unbaked dish(es) tightly and freeze for up to 3 months. There is no need to thaw. Cover loosely with foil and place in a cold oven set for 350°F. Once the oven comes to temperature, cook for 60 minutes, until warmed though. Uncover and bake for 10 to 15 minutes more.

＊**Serving size:** 2 lasagna rolls-ups; **Per serving:** Calories 520; Total Fat 22g (Mono Fat 3.3g, Poly Fat 0.6g, Sat Fat 7.5g); Protein 28g; Carb 53g; Fiber 11g; Cholesterol 70mg; Sodium 680mg; **Excellent source of:** Calcium, Folate, Iron, Manganese, Niacin, Phosphorus, Potassium, Thiamin, Riboflavin, Selenium, Vitamin A, Vitamin K; **Good source of:** Chloride, Magnesium, Potassium, Vitamin B6, Vitamin E, Zinc

Fettuccini with Vegetable Bolognese • MAKES 8 SERVINGS •

MY DAUGHTER, ISABELLA, WAS HALFWAY through a plate of this "Bolognese" when I told her there was no meat in it. She was incredulous, but barely skipped a beat before continuing to enjoy it. It's remarkable how much this sauce of finely chopped mushrooms (thank you food processor!), carrots, celery, tomatoes, garlic, onions, herbs, and wine resembles the taste and feel of the classic meat sauce. It's the kind of hearty, comfort-food dish that will please vegetarians and omnivores alike.

2 LARGE ONIONS, PEELED AND QUARTERED

5 LARGE CARROTS

3 LARGE CELERY STALKS

2¼ POUNDS MUSHROOMS, TRIMMED, QUARTERED IF LARGE

4 CLOVES GARLIC, COARSELY CHOPPED

3 TABLESPOONS OLIVE OIL

1 TABLESPOON CHOPPED FRESH THYME

1 TABLESPOON CHOPPED FRESH ROSEMARY

1½ TEASPOONS SALT

1 TEASPOON FRESHLY GROUND BLACK PEPPER

1 CUP DRY RED WINE, SUCH AS PINOT NOIR OR MERLOT

ONE 28-OUNCE CAN WHOLE TOMATOES

3 TABLESPOONS TOMATO PASTE

FOR SERVING:

1½ POUNDS WHOLE-GRAIN FETTUCCINI PASTA

1 CUP FRESHLY GRATED PARMESAN CHEESE

1 Shred the onions, carrots, and celery in a food processor fitted with a shredding disc or by hand using a box grater. Transfer the vegetables to a bowl. Remove the shredding disc from the food processor and insert the blade. Pulse the mushrooms and garlic, in two batches if necessary depending on the size of your processor, until finely chopped. Alternatively, you can chop the mushrooms and garlic by hand.

2 Heat the oil in a large pot over medium-high heat. Add the onions, carrots, celery, thyme, rosemary, salt, and pepper, and cook, stirring occasionally, until softened, about 8 minutes.

3 Add the mushrooms and garlic and cook, stirring occasionally, until the liquid from the mushrooms evaporates, about 10 minutes. Pour in the wine and simmer until it is reduced by half, about 4 minutes. Add the tomatoes one at a time, crushing them over the pot with your hands as you add them. Add the remaining juice from the tomato can and tomato paste and simmer, stirring occasionally, until reduced and thickened, 20 to 25 minutes more. The sauce may be refrigerated or frozen at this stage.

4 To continue, cook the pasta in a large pot of boiling water al dente, following the package directions. Drain and return the pasta to the pasta pot. Add the sauce, and cook the pasta and sauce together, stirring, until integrated, 1 to 2 minutes. Serve topped with the Parmesan cheese.

Make the sauce ahead:

TO REFRIGERATE AND REHEAT

Place the sauce in an airtight container in the refrigerator for up to 4 days. When ready to cook, warm the sauce in a pot on the stove over medium-low heat, 8 to 25 minutes, depending on the amount. Then follow the "to continue" directions in the recipe, using 3 ounces of the pasta, 1¼ cups of the sauce, and 1 tablespoon of the Parmesan cheese per portion.

TO FREEZE AND REHEAT

Allow the sauce to chill in the refrigerator for 30 minutes, then divide, in the portions desired, into sealable freezer bags and freeze for up to 3 months.

To thaw, place in the refrigerator for about 24 to 36 hours. Or, to thaw quickly, run the bag(s) under hot water for 30 seconds to release, then place in a saucepan, cover, and cook over medium-low heat for 10 to 40 minutes, depending on the amount. Alternatively, once released from the bag, place into a microwave-safe bowl, cover with a splatter guard, and microwave on the defrost setting for 8 minutes, stirring once or twice, then on high for 1 minute for a single portion. Then follow the "to continue" directions in the recipe, using 3 ounces of the pasta, 1¼ cups of the sauce, and 1 tablespoon of the Parmesan cheese per portion.

* **Serving size:** 1½ cups pasta and 1¼ cups sauce, **Per serving:** Calories 480; Total Fat 11g (Mono Fat 4.6g, Poly Fat 2.3g, Sat Fat 2.5g); Protein 23g; Carb 80g; Fiber 12g; Cholesterol 10mg; Sodium 880mg; **Excellent source of:** Calcium, Copper, Fiber, Iron, Manganese, Niacin, Pantothenic Acid, Phosphorus, Potassium, Riboflavin, Selenium, Vitamin A, Vitamin C, Vitamin K; **Good source of:** Folate, Thiamin, Vitamin B6, Zinc

White Bean Burrito Verde

• MAKES 6 SERVINGS •

THIS BURRITO IS STUFFED WITH flavorful, satisfying, white and green goodies: white beans, sharp cheddar, poblano and jalapeño peppers, and fresh spinach, sautéed with garlic, onions, earthy spices, and lime. It is topped with more green and white—yogurt and tomatillo salsa for cool and tangy contrast—when serving. It's a bi-colored, multiflavored meal you will always want to have waiting for you at home.

1 TABLESPOON OLIVE OIL

1 MEDIUM ONION, CHOPPED

2 POBLANO PEPPERS, CHOPPED

1 JALAPEÑO PEPPER, FINELY DICED

3 CLOVES GARLIC

5 CUPS FRESH BABY SPINACH, COARSELY CHOPPED (5 OUNCES)

TWO 15-OUNCE CANS LOW-SODIUM WHITE BEANS, DRAINED AND RINSED

2 TABLESPOONS FRESH LIME JUICE

½ TEASPOON SALT

½ TEASPOON GROUND CUMIN

¼ TEASPOON GROUND CORIANDER

JALAPEÑO PEPPER SAUCE, SUCH AS GREEN TABASCO, OPTIONAL

SIX 8-INCH WHOLE-WHEAT TORTILLAS

1¼ CUPS SHREDDED SHARP WHITE CHEDDAR CHEESE (5 OUNCES)

FOR SERVING:

½ CUP PLAIN LOW-FAT GREEK YOGURT

½ CUP PREPARED TOMATILLO SALSA

1 Heat the oil in a large skillet over medium heat. Add the onion, poblano, and jalapeño and cook, stirring occasionally, until softened, 6 minutes. Add the garlic and cook, stirring, for 30 seconds more. Add the spinach and cook, stirring, until just wilted, 1 minute. Stir in the beans, lime juice, salt, cumin, and coriander. Check for spiciness, depending on the heat of the peppers, and add jalapeño pepper sauce, if desired. If planning to freeze or refrigerate, remove the mixture from the heat at this stage and allow to cool completely, for about 20 minutes, then skip to step 3 and make the burritos with unwarmed tortillas.

2 To continue now, cook until the beans are warmed through, 1 to 2 minutes. Then warm the tortillas on a hot, ungreased griddle or directly over a gas burner, one at a time, for 30 seconds each, turning once. Alternatively, you can wrap the tortillas in a slightly damp paper towel and heat in the microwave for 30 to 40 seconds.

3 Sprinkle each tortilla with about 3 tablespoons of the cheese then, ¾ cup of the mixture and roll up burrito style, with both ends folded under so the burrito is closed.

4 To serve, top each burrito with a dollop of the yogurt and a heaping tablespoon of the salsa.

TO REFRIGERATE AND REHEAT

Wrap the burritos individually in plastic wrap and then in foil and store in the refrigerator where they will keep for up to 3 days. To reheat, unwrap completely, and place on a piece of foil in a 350°F oven until warmed through, 20 to 25 minutes. Alternatively, wrap in a paper towel and microwave for about 1 minute for each burrito.

TO FREEZE AND REHEAT

Wrap the burritos individually in plastic wrap or foil and place in an airtight container or sealable freezer bag and freeze for up to 3 months. There is no need to thaw. To heat, unwrap completely and place on a piece of foil in a cold oven set to 350°F. Once the oven reaches temperature, continue to cook for 30 to 35 minutes, until warmed through. Alternatively, heat in the microwave by unwrapping the frozen burrito completely, then rewrapping it in a paper towel and microwaving on the defrost setting for 6 minutes and then on full power for 90 seconds more for each burrito.

✻ **Serving size:** 1 burrito; **Per serving:** Calories 380; Total Fat 12g (Mono Fat 1.7g, Poly Fat 0.3g, Sat Fat 5g), Protein 20g; Carb 47g; Fiber 10g; Cholesterol 25mg; Sodium 540mg; **Excellent source of:** Calcium, Fiber, Iron, Magnesium, Protein, Thiamin, Vitamin A, Vitamin C, Vitamin K; **Good source of:** Folate, Manganese, Phosphorus, Potassium, Riboflavin, Zinc

Sides

Cauliflower "Rice" Pilaf   • MAKES 6 SERVINGS •

WHEN YOU GRATE RAW CAULIFLOWER florets on a box grater (or in a food processor) you wind up with pieces that look remarkably like grains, such as rice or bulgur. Because cauliflower is so mild tasting, it is like a blank canvas for seasonings, just like grains can be. Here I use it in a classic rice pilaf recipe with sautéed onion, toasted nuts, and fresh herbs for a simple, surprising side. Serve it with anything you might serve with a rice pilaf, like, say, Grandma's Roast Chicken, on page 215. It is also delicious as a bed for the Savory Lamb and Chickpea Stew, page 155.

1 SMALL HEAD OF CAULIFLOWER

3 TABLESPOONS PINE NUTS OR SLICED ALMONDS

1½ TABLESPOONS OLIVE OIL

1 SMALL ONION, DICED

3 TABLESPOONS FINELY CHOPPED FRESH ITALIAN PARSLEY LEAVES

½ TEASPOON SALT

¼ TEASPOON FRESHLY GROUND BLACK PEPPER

1 Cut the head of cauliflower into four or five large pieces, each with some stem attached. Holding each piece by the stem, grate the top part of the cauliflower on the large holes of a box grater to form rice-like pieces, until you have about 6 cups. Alternatively, you can cut the cauliflower into florets, removing as much of the stems as possible, and grate the florets in the food processor using the grater attachment. Save the stems and any remaining cauliflower for another use, such as a soup.

2 In a large, dry skillet, toast the pine nuts or almonds over medium-high heat, stirring frequently, until they are fragrant and golden, 2 to 3 minutes. Transfer them to a plate.

3 Heat the oil in the same skillet over medium heat. Add the onion and cook, stirring occasionally, until softened and beginning to brown, 3 to 5 minutes. Add the cauliflower and cook, stirring frequently, until it is tender, about 5 minutes. Remove from the heat. Stir in the parsley, pine nuts, salt, and pepper.

TO REFRIGERATE AND REHEAT

Place in an airtight container in the refrigerator for up to 4 days.

To reheat, place in a saucepan on the stove over medium-low heat, cover, and cook, stirring occasionally, adding 1 to 2 tablespoons of water if the pan seems dry, for 3 to 12 minutes, depending on the amount. Alternatively, place in a microwave-safe bowl, cover with a splatter guard, and microwave on high for about 30 seconds for one portion.

TO FREEZE AND REHEAT

Place in sealable freezer bags in the portions desired and freeze for up to 3 months.

Thaw in the refrigerator for 18 to 24 hours, then reheat following the "to refrigerate" directions. Or, to thaw quickly, run hot water over the bag for 30 seconds to release the food. Then place in a covered saucepan on the stove with about 1 tablespoon water per portion, and warm over medium-low heat, stirring occasionally and breaking the mixture up with a spoon, for 5 to 20 minutes, depending on the amount. Alternatively, after releasing from the bag, place in a microwave-safe dish, and microwave on the defrost setting for 4 minutes, and then on high for about 1 minute for one portion.

---

* **Serving size:** About ⅔ cup; **Per serving:** Calories 90; Total Fat 7g (Mono Fat 3.3g, Poly Fat 1.8g, Sat Fat 0.75g); Protein 3g; Carb 7g; Fiber 3g; Cholesterol 0mg; Sodium 230mg; **Excellent source of:** Manganese, Vitamin C, Vitamin K; **Good source of:** Folate, Potassium, Vitamin B6

Ginger Soy Roasted Mushrooms

• MAKES 6 SERVINGS •

DELICIOUS DOESN'T GET MUCH EASIER than this. Just toss mushrooms with a soy-ginger dressing, put them on a baking sheet, and let the oven work its magic, caramelizing the dressing and crisping the mushrooms slightly, while tenderizing them and concentrating their deep umami flavor. They are absolutely addictive and will heighten main courses like simply grilled chicken or steak. At room temperature, they would be a delicious addition to the Forbidden Rice Bowl, page 280.

- 4 TABLESPOONS REDUCED-SODIUM SOY SAUCE
- 2 TABLESPOONS HONEY
- 2 TABLESPOONS CANOLA OR PEANUT OIL
- 1 TABLESPOON FINELY GRATED GINGER
- 2 TEASPOONS TOASTED SESAME OIL
- 1½ TEASPOONS CHILI-GARLIC SAUCE, SUCH AS SRIRACHA
- 3 POUNDS ASSORTED MUSHROOMS, SUCH AS CREMINI, OYSTERS, SHIITAKES, AND BUTTON, CUT INTO LARGE (ROUGHLY, 1-INCH) PIECES
- 5 CLOVES GARLIC, SLICED
- ¼ CUP CHOPPED SCALLION GREENS

1 Preheat the oven to 425°F.

2 In a small bowl, whisk together the soy sauce, honey, canola oil, ginger, sesame oil, and chili-garlic sauce. Add the mushrooms and garlic and toss to coat.

3 Divide the mushrooms among two baking sheets and place in the oven. Cook until browned and slightly caramelized, 23 to 25 minutes, stirring once at the halfway point. Sprinkle with the scallions and serve.

✳ **Serving size:** ½ cup; **Per serving:** Calories 140; Total Fat 7g (Mono Fat 3.6g, Poly Fat 2.1g, Sat Fat 0.6g); Protein 7g; Carb 18g; Fiber 2g; Cholesterol 0mg; Sodium 340mg; **Excellent source of:** Copper, Niacin, Pantothenic Acid, Phosphorus, Potassium, Riboflavin, Selenium; **Good source of:** Folate, Manganese, Protein, Thiamin, Vitamin B6, Vitamin K, Zinc

TO REFRIGERATE AND REHEAT
Store the mushrooms in an airtight container in the refrigerator for up to 4 days.

Serve at room temperature or, to warm, place in a saucepan, cover, and heat over medium-low heat, stirring occasionally for 5 to 15 minutes, depending on the amount. Alternatively, warm in the microwave on high for about 40 seconds for one portion.

Freezing the mushrooms is not recommended.

Mediterranean Braised Green and White Beans · MAKES 8 SERVINGS ·

YOU MIGHT NOT ORDINARILY THINK of vegetables as comfort food, but when green beans are simmered in a saucy pot of onions and hand-crushed tomatoes until they are meltingly tender, you are 100 percent in heart-warming, feel-good territory. The addition of white beans gives the dish an extra heartiness, and the flexibility of being a vegetarian entree in larger portions. Fresh parsley, dill, and a dollop of thickened yogurt gives it a rustic, Greek flair. I love it as a main with a hunk of crusty bread, or alongside simply seasoned lamb chops or kabobs.

¼ CUP OLIVE OIL

1 LARGE ONION, THINLY SLICED

4 CLOVES GARLIC, MINCED

2 TABLESPOONS TOMATO PASTE

ONE 28-OUNCE CAN WHOLE, PEELED TOMATOES

2 POUNDS GREEN BEANS, TRIMMED

½ CUP CHOPPED FRESH ITALIAN PARSLEY LEAVES

1 TABLESPOON CHOPPED FRESH DILL OR 2 TEASPOONS DRIED

¾ TEASPOON SALT

½ TEASPOON FRESHLY GROUND BLACK PEPPER

ONE 15-OUNCE CAN NO-SALT-ADDED WHITE BEANS, DRAINED AND RINSED

FOR SERVING:

½ CUP PLAIN LOW-FAT GREEK YOGURT

1 Heat the oil in a large heavy pot, such as a Dutch oven, over medium heat. Add the onion and cook, stirring, until softened, 8 minutes. Add the garlic and cook, stirring, 1 minute more. Stir in the tomato paste and cook until the tomato paste is lightly caramelized, 1 minute more.

2 Add the tomatoes with their juices, crushing each tomato with your hand over the pot before adding it. Add ½ cup of water and bring to a boil. Then, add the green beans, parsley, dill, salt, and pepper. Cover, lower the heat to low, and simmer for 30 minutes. Add the white beans and continue cooking, covered, until the green beans are very tender, 30 minutes more. The dish may be refrigerated or frozen at this stage.

3 Serve with a dollop of the yogurt on top.

Recipe continues

TO REFRIGERATE AND REHEAT

The dish will keep in the refrigerator in an airtight container for up to 4 days. To reheat, place in a pot over medium-low heat, cover, and cook, stirring occasionally, until warmed through, 5 to 20 minutes, depending on the amount. Alternatively, place in a microwave-safe bowl, cover with a splatter guard, and microwave on full power for about 1 minute for a single portion.

TO FREEZE AND REHEAT

Chill in the refrigerator for 30 minutes, then transfer into freezer bags in the portions desired, and freeze for up to 3 months.

Thaw in the refrigerator 24 to 36 hours and then reheat following the "to refrigerate" directions, or, to thaw quickly, run the bag under hot water for 30 seconds to release the frozen food from the bag, then transfer it to a pot along with 1 to 2 tablespoons of water. Cover and cook over medium-low heat, stirring occasionally, until warmed though, 15 to 40 minutes, depending on the number of portions being thawed. Add more water to the pot if the bottom is getting dry. Alternatively, after running the bag under hot water, transfer the stew to a microwave-safe bowl, cover with a splatter guard, and microwave on the defrost setting for about 6 minutes per portion, then heat through on full power for about 1 minute.

＊ **Serving size:** 1 cup beans and 1 tablespoon yogurt; **Per serving:** Calories 190; Total Fat 7g (Mono Fat 4.9g, Poly Fat 0.7g, Sat Fat 1.1g); Protein 6g; Carb 23g; Fiber 6g; Cholesterol 0mg; Sodium 270mg; **Excellent source of:** Fiber, Manganese, Vitamin A, Vitamin C, Vitamin K; **Good source of:** Calcium, Iron, Protein, Thiamin

Ratatouille   • MAKES 6 SERVINGS •

THERE ARE AT LEAST 101 different ways to make this classic, French-country vegetable stew. I keep the dish homey and unfussy, but I do think it is worth the extra step of roasting the eggplant and zucchini separately while the rest of the ingredients are cooked down to a rich sauce. This way, you get that long-cooked, melted base, but rather than everything being reduced to mush, you get distinct chunks of vegetables as well.

The versatility of ratatouille is incredible: serve it over toast with a fried or poached egg on top, as a side for roasted chicken or meat, serve it at a party as a topper for crostini, stuff it into an omelet, or pile it on a whole-grain baguette and top with some mozzarella for a French-bread pizza.

1 MEDIUM EGGPLANT (ABOUT 1 POUND), CUT INTO ¾-INCH PIECES

2 TEASPOONS SALT, DIVIDED

2 MEDIUM ZUCCHINI AND/OR YELLOW SUMMER SQUASH (ABOUT 8 OUNCES EACH), CUT INTO ¾-INCH PIECES

¼ CUP OLIVE OIL, DIVIDED

2 MEDIUM ONIONS, DICED

4 LARGE CLOVES GARLIC, THINLY SLICED

2 MEDIUM RED, ORANGE, AND/OR YELLOW BELL PEPPERS, DICED

3 MEDIUM TOMATOES, DICED

2 TEASPOONS MINCED FRESH THYME LEAVES OR 1 TEASPOON DRIED THYME

¼ TEASPOON FRESHLY GROUND BLACK PEPPER

1 Preheat the oven to 450°F.

2 Place the eggplant in a colander over a bowl and toss with 1 teaspoon of the salt. Allow to sit and drain for 20 minutes, then rinse the eggplant with cold water. Lay the eggplant on paper towels and pat with an additional paper towel to remove as much water as possible.

3 Toss the eggplant and zucchini with 2 tablespoons of the oil and ¼ teaspoon of the remaining salt and arrange on a baking tray. Place in the oven and roast, stirring once or twice, until browned and tender, 35 to 40 minutes.

4 Meanwhile, heat the remaining 2 tablespoons oil in a large, heavy pot, such as a Dutch oven, over medium heat. Add the onions and cook, stirring occasionally, until softened, 6 minutes. Add the garlic and cook, stirring, 1 minute more. Add the bell peppers and cook, stirring occasionally, until softened, 4 minutes. Add the tomatoes, thyme, remaining ¾ teaspoon salt, and the black pepper and cook, stirring, until the tomatoes break down and release their juices, 7 minutes. Lower the heat to low, cover, and cook, stirring, until the vegetables are further softened and melded, 10 to 15 minutes more. Add the roasted eggplant and zucchini and stir to combine.

TO REFRIGERATE AND REHEAT

The ratatouille will keep in the refrigerator in an airtight container for up to 4 days. To reheat, place in a pot over medium-low heat, cover, and cook, stirring occasionally, until warmed through, 4 to 20 minutes, depending on the amount. Alternatively, place in a microwave-safe bowl, cover with a splatter guard, and microwave on full power for about 1 minute for a single portion.

TO FREEZE AND REHEAT

Chill in the refrigerator for 30 minutes, then transfer into freezer bags in the portions desired, and freeze for up to 3 months.

Thaw in the refrigerator for 24 to 36 hours and then reheat following the "to refrigerate" directions, or, to thaw quickly, run the bag under hot water for 30 seconds to release the frozen food from the bag, then transfer it to a pot along with 1 to 2 tablespoons of water. Cover and cook over medium-low heat, stirring occasionally, until warmed though, 6 to 30 minutes, depending on the amount. Add more water to the pot if the bottom is getting dry. Alternatively, after running the bag under hot water, transfer the stew to a microwave-safe bowl, cover with a splatter guard, and microwave on the defrost setting for about 5 minutes per portion, then heat through on full power for about 1 minute for one serving.

∗ **Serving size:** 1 cup; **Per serving:** Calories 130; Total Fat 9g (Mono Fat 6.6g, Poly Fat 1.1g, Sat Fat 1.3g); Protein 2g; Carb 11g; Fiber 4g; Cholesterol 0mg; Sodium 490mg; **Excellent source of:** Vitamin A, Vitamin C; **Good source of:** Fiber, Folate, Manganese, Molybdenum, Potassium, Vitamin B6, Vitamin E, Vitamin K

Roasted Autumn Vegetables

• MAKES 8 SERVINGS •

THE COLORS IN THIS DISH are like those outside your window on an autumn day (in many parts of the country, anyway): red (bell peppers), orange-gold (carrots and butternut squash), and brown (caramelized cauliflower). The sweet and savory balance of the vegetables is enhanced with an earthy, fragrant rub of paprika, cumin, and garlic, for a dish that lifts you easily above those been-there-done-that basic roasted vegetables. They are wonderful served hot or at room temperature, and can be easily eaten with toothpicks at a cocktail party.

3 TABLESPOONS OLIVE OIL

2 TEASPOONS PAPRIKA

1 TEASPOON GROUND CUMIN

¾ TEASPOON GARLIC POWDER

¾ TEASPOON SALT

½ TEASPOON FRESHLY GROUND BLACK PEPPER

1 HEAD (1½ POUNDS) CAULIFLOWER, CUT INTO 1-INCH FLORETS (ABOUT 6 CUPS)

4 CUPS CUBED (1-INCH PIECES) BUTTERNUT SQUASH (1 POUND)

1 POUND (ABOUT 6 LARGE) CARROTS, CUT INTO 1-INCH PIECES

3 MEDIUM RED BELL PEPPERS, CUT INTO 1-INCH PIECES

1 Preheat the oven to 450°F.

2 In a large bowl, whisk together the oil, paprika, cumin, garlic, salt, and pepper. Add the vegetables and toss to coat well.

3 Arrange the vegetables in one layer on 2 baking sheets and roast in upper and lower thirds of oven, switching positions of pans halfway during roasting and stirring occasionally, until golden brown and tender, about 25 to 30 minutes.

Recipe continues

TO REFRIGERATE AND REHEAT

Store the vegetables in an airtight container in the refrigerator where they will keep for up to 4 days.

To reheat, place them on a baking tray in a 400°F oven for about 8 minutes, or in a covered saucepan over medium-low heat, stirring occasionally, for 5 to 20 minutes, depending on the amount. Alternatively, place on a microwave-safe plate, cover with a splatter guard, and microwave on high for 40 seconds for a single portion.

TO FREEZE AND REHEAT

Place in sealable plastic bags in the portions desired and freeze for up to 3 months.

To reheat, run a bag under hot water for 30 seconds to release the vegetables, then place the frozen vegetables onto a baking sheet, uncovered, and put into a cold oven set to 400°F. Once the oven reaches temperature, continue to cook for about 8 minutes, spreading the vegetables out into a single layer once they are thawed, after about 3 minutes.

Alternatively, once released from the bag, place the frozen vegetables on a microwave-safe plate, cover with a splatter guard, and microwave on the defrost setting for 3 minutes, then spread the vegetables out into a single layer and microwave for 40 seconds on high for a single portion.

✻ **Serving size:** 1 cup; **Per serving:** Calories 130; Total Fat 6g (Mono Fat 3.7g, Poly Fat 0.7g, Sat Fat 0.8g); Protein 3g; Carb 20g; Fiber 5g; Cholesterol 0mg; Sodium 280mg; **Excellent source of:** Fiber, Folate, Potassium, Vitamin A, Vitamin B6, Vitamin C, Vitamin K; **Good source of:** Magnesium, Manganese, Molybdenum, Niacin, Pantothenic Acid, Thiamin, Vitamin E

Wild Rice and Barley Pilaf • MAKES 6 SERVINGS •

NUTTY, EBONY WILD RICE AND tender, cream-colored barley are like a grain yin and yang where, when cooked in the same pot, they contrast and balance one another. After cooking they are tossed with a lemon-Dijon dressing, fresh green herbs, a buttery crunch of pistachios, and sweet, chewy dried fruit for an intriguing and flavorful side to accompany, perhaps, some kababs, or the Roasted Salmon and Fennel, page 260.

2 TEASPOONS OLIVE OIL

½ CUP FINELY CHOPPED SHALLOT

¾ CUP UNCOOKED WILD RICE

½ CUP UNCOOKED PEARL BARLEY

1¾ CUPS LOW-SODIUM CHICKEN BROTH

½ CUP SHELLED PISTACHIOS

1 TABLESPOON FRESH LEMON JUICE

2 TEASPOONS DIJON MUSTARD

1 TEASPOON FINELY GRATED FRESH LEMON ZEST

½ TEASPOON SALT

½ TEASPOON FRESHLY GROUND BLACK PEPPER

2 TABLESPOONS WALNUT OIL OR EXTRA-VIRGIN OLIVE OIL

½ CUP DRIED CHERRIES OR APRICOTS, CHOPPED

¼ CUP CHOPPED FRESH ITALIAN PARSLEY LEAVES

1 TEASPOON FINELY CHOPPED FRESH THYME

1 Heat the olive oil over medium heat in a large saucepan. Add the shallot and cook, stirring, until softened, about 2 minutes. Add the rice and barley and cook, stirring, 1 minute. Add the broth and bring to a boil. Lower the heat to low, cover, and simmer until most of the liquid is absorbed and the rice is tender, for 45 to 50 minutes.

2 Meanwhile, toast the pistachios in a dry skillet over medium-high heat, stirring frequently, until fragrant, 3 to 5 minutes. Set aside to cool, then coarsely chop. In a small bowl, whisk together the lemon juice, mustard, zest, salt, and pepper until combined well. Slowly whisk in the walnut or olive oil until well combined.

3 Stir the vinaigrette into the cooked rice until well coated. Then stir in the toasted pistachios, dried cherries or apricots, parsley, and thyme. Serve warm or at room temperature.

Recipe continues

TO REFRIGERATE AND REHEAT

Place in an airtight container in the refrigerator for up to 3 days. Serve at room temperature, or warm in a saucepan, covered, over medium-low heat, with 1 to 2 tablespoons of water, until warmed through, 5 to 15 minutes, depending on the amount. Alternatively, place a single portion in a microwave-safe dish, cover with a splatter guard, and microwave on high for about 1 minute.

TO FREEZE AND REHEAT

Allow to cool slightly so it is no longer steaming, but still quite warm. Place in sealable plastic freezer bags in the portions desired and freeze for up to 3 months.

To reheat, run a plastic bag under hot water for 30 seconds to release the rice, then transfer it to a saucepan with 2 tablespoons of water per portion. Cover and cook over low heat, turning and breaking it up with a fork once or twice, until warmed through, 13 to 30 minutes, depending on the amount.

Alternatively, after running the bag under water to release the food, transfer it to a microwave-safe bowl, cover tightly, and microwave on high for about 2 to 2½ minutes for one portion.

✳ **Serving size:** About ¾ cup; **Per serving:** Calories 290; Total Fat 11g (Mono Fat 6.8g, Poly Fat 2.2g, Sat Fat 1.4g); Protein 8g; Carb 42g; Fiber 8g; Cholesterol 0mg; Sodium 260mg; **Excellent source of:** Fiber, Manganese, Vitamin K; **Good source of:** Iron, Magnesium, Niacin, Phosphorus, Protein, Selenium, Vitamin A, Vitamin C, Zinc

Spaghetti Squash Gratin • MAKES 8 SERVINGS •

THIS GRATIN HAS TWO GLORIOUS layers of swoon-worthy flavor. On the bottom is tender, delicately flavored, orange-gold spaghetti squash, and on top lies a silken blanket of cheese sauce that has the nutty, rich flavor of Swiss Gruyère infused with rosemary and garlic.

It is splendid on a holiday table, but perfect to make on a weekend to enjoy throughout the following week. Serve it with roasted meat or poultry, and/or with a crisp autumnal salad like the Red Cabbage and Kale Salad with Sunflower Seeds and Chickpeas, page 83.

1 LARGE SPAGHETTI SQUASH (ABOUT 3½ POUNDS)

1½ TABLESPOONS OLIVE OIL, DIVIDED

¾ TEASPOON SALT, DIVIDED

½ TEASPOON FRESHLY GROUND BLACK PEPPER, DIVIDED

COOKING SPRAY

2 SLICES WHOLE-GRAIN BREAD (3 OUNCES), PULSED IN THE FOOD PROCESSOR TO MAKE CRUMBS (1½ CUPS)

2 CUPS COLD 1% MILK

¼ CUP WHOLE-WHEAT PASTRY FLOUR OR ALL-PURPOSE FLOUR

1 CLOVE GARLIC, SMASHED

1 SPRIG FRESH ROSEMARY

¾ CUP, LIGHTLY PACKED, GRATED GRUYÈRE CHEESE (3 OUNCES)

⅔ CUP OUNCES GRATED PARMESAN CHEESE (2 OUNCES), DIVIDED

PINCH GROUND NUTMEG

1 Preheat the oven to 400°F.

2 Halve the spaghetti squash lengthwise and scoop out the seeds. Brush the cut sides with ½ tablespoon of the oil total and sprinkle with ¼ teaspoon of the salt and ¼ teaspoon of the pepper.

3 Line a rimmed baking sheet with foil and place the squash on it, cut side down. Bake until the squash can be easily pierced with a fork or metal skewer, 40 minutes. Remove the squash from the oven, and flip it so the cut side faces upward. Allow it to cool until easy to handle, 10 to 15 minutes.

4 Meanwhile, spray one 9 × 13-inch baking dish or two 8-inch square baking dishes with cooking spray. In a small bowl, toss the bread crumbs with the remaining 1 tablespoon oil.

5 Once cooled, scoop the spaghetti squash from its shell back onto the foil-lined baking sheet or into a bowl. Fluff it with a fork to separate the strands of squash, and toss with ¼ teaspoon of the salt. Transfer it to the prepared baking dish(es) and set aside.

Recipe continues

6 Place the cold milk into a medium saucepan and whisk in the flour until it is dissolved. Add the garlic and rosemary, and, stirring all the while, bring to a simmer over medium heat. Continue to cook, stirring, until thickened, 2 minutes. Remove and discard the garlic and rosemary. Add the Gruyère, ⅓ cup of the Parmesan, the nutmeg, and the remaining ¼ teaspoon salt and remaining ¼ teaspoon pepper and cook, stirring, until the cheese is melted. Pour the cheese sauce over the squash. The gratin may be made ahead and refrigerated or frozen at this stage.

7 To continue, sprinkle the top of the gratin with the remaining Parmesan and then the bread crumbs. Bake until bubbly, 20 to 25 minutes.

To make ahead:

TO REFRIGERATE AND SERVE
Wrap the unbaked dish(es) tightly with plastic wrap and refrigerate for up to 3 days. Place the bread crumbs and Parmesan together in an airtight container in the refrigerator.

To serve, allow to sit at room temperature as you preheat the oven to 375°F. Sprinkle with the Parmesan and bread crumbs and bake, uncovered, for about 40 to 50 minutes, until bubbling.

TO FREEZE AND SERVE
Wrap the unbaked dish(es) tightly with plastic wrap and then foil and freeze for up to 3 months. Place the bread crumbs and Parmesan together in a sealable plastic freezer bag and freeze for up to 3 months.

When ready to serve, uncover, sprinkle with Parmesan and bread crumbs, and place in a cold oven set to 375°F. Once the oven reaches temperature, cook until bubbling, about 50 to 60 minutes.

TO REFRIGERATE AND REHEAT ONCE BAKED
Keep leftover gratin in the original baking dish or transfer to a smaller baking dish and cover tightly. Refrigerate for up to 3 days.

To reheat, allow to sit at room temperature as the oven preheats to 375°F. Bake for 25 to 30 minutes, until bubbling. Alternatively, place on a microwave safe plate, cover with a splatter guard, and microwave on high for about 40 seconds for a single portion.

✳ **Serving size:** One 4½ × 3¼-inch square; **Per serving:** Calories 200; Total Fat 10g (Mono Fat 3.8g, Poly Fat 1.1g, Sat Fat 4.2g); Protein 11g; Carb 20g; Fiber 3g; Cholesterol 20mg; Sodium 490mg; **Excellent source of:** Calcium, Manganese, Phosphorus, Protein; **Good source of:** Fiber, Molybdenum, Riboflavin, Selenium, Vitamin B6, Vitamin B12

Mushroom-Herb Stuffing with Pecans • MAKES 10 SERVINGS •

ALTHOUGH THIS FRAGRANT, MOIST-ON-THE-INSIDE, CRISP-ON-THE-OUTSIDE, mushroom-packed, three-herb stuffing is perfect for a holiday dinner with a roasted turkey, you would be remiss to eat it just once a year. Why not make it more often to make everyday special, especially when you can make it once and divide it into two batches, one for tonight, and another to tuck away in the freezer for another day?

9 CUPS ½-INCH CUBES CRUSTY WHOLE-GRAIN BREAD (ABOUT 15½ OUNCES)

1 CUP COARSELY CHOPPED PECANS

2 TABLESPOONS OLIVE OIL

2 TABLESPOONS UNSALTED BUTTER

1¾ POUNDS ASSORTED MUSHROOMS, TRIMMED AND CHOPPED, ABOUT 12½ CUPS

1¼ TEASPOONS SALT, DIVIDED

½ TEASPOON FRESHLY GROUND BLACK PEPPER

4 MEDIUM LEEKS, WHITE AND PALE GREEN PARTS ONLY, SLICED

1 MEDIUM ONION, CHOPPED

2 STALKS CELERY, FINELY CHOPPED

2 CLOVES GARLIC, MINCED

¾ CUP DRY WHITE WINE, SUCH AS CHARDONNAY

2 CUPS LOW-SODIUM CHICKEN BROTH

¼ CUP FINELY CHOPPED FRESH ITALIAN PARSLEY LEAVES

1½ TABLESPOONS FINELY CHOPPED FRESH SAGE

1½ TABLESPOONS CHOPPED FRESH THYME LEAVES

COOKING SPRAY

1 Preheat the oven to 375°F.

2 Arrange the bread on a large baking sheet and bake in the middle of the oven, stirring occasionally, until pale golden and dry, about 12 minutes. Meanwhile, place the pecans on another small baking sheet, place them in the oven, and toast until fragrant, about 10 minutes. Set the toasted bread and pecans aside to cool.

3 Heat the oil and butter in a large pot over medium heat. Add the mushrooms, 1 teaspoon of the salt, and the pepper and cook, stirring occasionally, until they begin to release their liquid, 3 to 4 minutes. Add the leeks, onion, celery, and garlic and cook, covered, stirring occasionally, until softened, about 6 minutes. Add the wine and simmer, uncovered, until reduced by half, about 4 minutes.

4 Remove from the heat, add the bread, broth, pecans, parsley, sage, thyme, and remaining ¼ teaspoon salt and stir until well combined. Spray one 9 × 13-inch or two 8 × 8-inch baking dishes with cooking spray, and fill with the stuffing mixture. The stuffing may be refrigerated or frozen at this stage.

5 To continue, bake, uncovered, in the middle of the oven until golden brown and crisp on top, 30 to 40 minutes.

Recipe continues

To make ahead:

TO REFRIGERATE AND SERVE
Cover the unbaked stuffing tightly and refrigerate for up to 1 day.

To serve, allow to sit at room temperature as you preheat the oven to 375°F. Bake, uncovered, for about 45 to 55 minutes, until warmed through and the top is golden brown.

TO FREEZE AND SERVE
Cover the unbaked stuffing tightly with plastic wrap and then with foil and freeze for up to 3 months.

There is no need to thaw. To serve, remove the plastic wrap and re-cover loosely with the foil. Place in a cold oven set for 375°F. Once the oven reaches temperature, continue to cook for 20 minutes, then uncover and cook until the top is crisp and the stuffing is warmed through, 40 to 50 minutes more.

TO REFRIGERATE AND REHEAT ONCE BAKED
Cover tightly and refrigerate for up to 3 days. Allow to sit at room temperature as the oven preheats to 350°F. Bake, uncovered, for 35 to 45 minutes.

Alternatively, place on a microwave-safe plate, cover with a splatter guard, and microwave on high for about 40 to 60 seconds for a single portion. (Oven reheating is preferred, as stuffing will not re-crisp in the microwave.)

✳ **Serving size:** 1⅓ cups; **Per serving:** Calories 310; Total Fat 15g (Mono Fat 7.4g, Poly Fat 3.7g, Sat Fat 2.9g); Protein 10g; Carb 32g; Fiber 6g; Cholesterol 5mg; Sodium 500mg; **Excellent source of:** Fiber, Folate, Copper, Manganese, Niacin, Phosphorus, Protein, Riboflavin, Selenium, Thiamin, Vitamin K; **Good source of:** Calcium, Iron, Magnesium, Pantothenic Acid, Potassium, Vitamin A, Vitamin B6, Vitamin C, Zinc

Sweet and Sour Red Cabbage with Caraway

• MAKES 6 SERVINGS •

THIS OLD-WORLD, RUBY RED, GERMAN-STYLE favorite gets an exciting update with sweetness from chopped dates and maple syrup balancing the tartness of the cider vinegar. A sprinkling of caraway seeds adds a punch of texture and flavor. Enjoy it alongside the Stout-Marinated Pork Chops, page 170.

- 2 TABLESPOONS OLIVE OIL
- 8 CUPS SHREDDED RED CABBAGE (FROM 1 MEDIUM HEAD)
- 1 MEDIUM RED ONION, SLICED INTO HALF-MOONS
- ¼ CUP CHOPPED PITTED DATES
- 5 TABLESPOONS CIDER VINEGAR, PLUS MORE TO TASTE
- 2 TABLESPOONS PURE MAPLE SYRUP
- 1 TEASPOON CARAWAY SEEDS
- 1 TEASPOON SALT, PLUS MORE TO TASTE
- ½ TEASPOON FRESHLY GROUND BLACK PEPPER

1 Heat the oil in a medium pot over medium heat. Add the cabbage, onion, ½ cup of water, the dates, vinegar, maple syrup, caraway seeds, salt, and pepper and bring to a boil. Lower the heat to medium-low, cover, and simmer, stirring occasionally, until the cabbage is tender, 12 to 15 minutes. Season with additional vinegar and salt to taste.

TO REFRIGERATE AND REHEAT
The cabbage will keep in the refrigerator in an airtight container for up to 4 days. To reheat, place in a pot over medium-low heat, cover, and cook, stirring occasionally, until warmed through, 5 to 20 minutes, depending on the amount. Add 1 to 2 tablespoons of water to the pan if it seems to be getting dry. Alternatively, place in a microwave-safe bowl, cover with a splatter guard, and microwave on full power for about 1 minute for a single portion.

TO FREEZE AND REHEAT
Chill in the refrigerator for 30 minutes, then transfer into freezer bags in the portions desired, and freeze for up to 3 months.

To reheat, run the bag under hot water for 30 seconds to release the frozen food from the bag, then transfer it to a pot along with 1 to 2 tablespoons of water. Cover and cook over medium-low heat, stirring occasionally, until warmed through, 8 to 30 minutes, depending on the amount. Add more water to the pot if it is getting dry. Alternatively, after running the bag under hot water, transfer to a microwave-safe bowl, cover with a splatter guard, and microwave on full power for 2 minutes for a single serving.

＊ **Serving size:** 1 cup; **Per serving:** Calories 120; Total Fat 5g (Mono Fat 3.3g, Poly Fat 0.6g, Sat Fat 0.7g); Protein 2g; Carb 20g; Fiber 3g; Cholesterol 0mg; Sodium 420mg; **Excellent source of:** Manganese, Vitamin A, Vitamin C, Vitamin K; **Good source of:** Fiber, Potassium, Riboflavin, Vitamin B6

Wild Mushroom Shepherd's Pie • MAKES 6 SERVINGS •

IMAGINE HAVING ALL THE COMFORTING pleasure of a classic Shepherd's pie—a creamy layer of mashed potatoes blanketing a savory, meaty base—but in a much healthier way. Well, here you have it! In this double-decker pie, cauliflower is mashed with the potatoes on top; they blend seamlessly and are steamed together so there's no extra effort involved. The lower layer gets its meaty depth of flavor from a mix of mushrooms sautéed with onions and thyme in a thick mushroom gravy. Enjoy it as a side with some lamb chops or roast chicken, or as a vegetarian main with a Red Cabbage and Kale Salad with Sunflower Seeds and Chickpeas, page 83, alongside.

1½ POUNDS OF YUKON GOLD OR CREAMERY POTATOES, UNPEELED, CUT INTO 2-INCH PIECES

1 SMALL HEAD CAULIFLOWER (ABOUT 2 POUNDS), CUT INTO FLORETS

⅔ CUP 1% MILK

2 TABLESPOONS BUTTER

1 TEASPOON SALT, DIVIDED

1 TABLESPOON OLIVE OIL

1 LARGE ONION, CHOPPED

2½ POUNDS MIXED WILD MUSHROOMS, CHOPPED

2 TEASPOONS CHOPPED FRESH THYME OR 1 TEASPOON DRIED

1 TABLESPOON ALL-PURPOSE FLOUR

½ CUP VEGETABLE BROTH OR WATER

2 TEASPOONS WORCESTERSHIRE SAUCE

1 TEASPOON SHERRY VINEGAR

¼ TEASPOON FRESHLY GROUND BLACK PEPPER

1 Place the potatoes in a large steamer basket set over boiling water, cover, and steam for 10 minutes. Add the cauliflower to the basket and cook until the potatoes and cauliflower are tender when pierced with the tip of a knife, about 15 minutes longer. Mash the vegetables with a potato masher until smooth. Heat the milk and butter and stir into the potato mixture along with ¾ teaspoon of the salt.

2 Meanwhile, heat the oil in the skillet over medium heat. Add the onion and cook, until softened and beginning to brown, about 6 minutes. Add the mushrooms and thyme and cook, uncovered and stirring occasionally, until the mushrooms are soft, their liquid has evaporated, and they are browned, about 18 minutes longer. In a small bowl or spouted measuring cup, whisk together the flour and broth or water. Add the flour-broth mixture gradually to the pan with the mushrooms, stirring all the while. Stir in the Worcestershire sauce, sherry vinegar, the remaining ¼ teaspoon of salt, and the pepper and bring to a simmer, scraping up any brown bits from the bottom of the pan. Cook until the broth has thickened, 1 to 2 minutes more. Pour the mixture into one 9 × 13-inch baking dish, two 8-inch square dishes, or six 2-cup capacity individual ovenproof crocks. Spread the potato mixture on top of the mushroom mixture. Refrigerate or freeze at this stage.

Recipe continues

3 To continue, preheat the oven to 375°F. Bake until heated through, bubbling at the edges, and the top is lightly browned, 20 to 25 minutes.

To make ahead:

TO REFRIGERATE AND SERVE

Cover unbaked pie(s) tightly and refrigerate for up to 5 days. When ready to serve, allow to sit at room temperature as the oven preheats to 375°F. Cook, uncovered, until bubbling at the edges and top is lightly browned, about 40 minutes.

TO FREEZE AND SERVE

Cover unbaked pie(s) tightly and refrigerate for 30 minutes, then freeze for up to 3 months. There is no need to thaw. When ready to serve, uncover and place in a cold oven set to 375°F. Once the oven reaches temperature, cook until bubbling and lightly browned on top, about 50 to 60 minutes.

TO REHEAT ONCE BAKED

Scoop an already baked pie onto a microwave-safe plate, cover with a splatter guard, and microwave for 60 to 90 seconds for one portion.

✱ **Serving size:** About 1⅔ cup; **Per serving:** Calories 250; Total Fat 6.5g (Mono Fat 2.8g, Poly Fat 0.6g, Sat Fat 3.1g); Protein 11g; Carb 40g; Fiber 7g; Cholesterol 10mg; Sodium 490mg; **Excellent source of:** Copper, Fiber, Folate, Manganese, Niacin, Pantothenic Acid, Phosphorus, Potassium, Protein, Riboflavin, Selenium, Thiamin, Vitamin C, Vitamin B6, Vitamin K; **Good source of:** Calcium, Iron, Magnesium, Molybdenum, Zinc

Savory Tomato Tart • MAKES 6 SERVINGS •

THIS SPECTACULAR SUMMER TART WILL be the crowning glory of your table, sure to elicit oohs and ahhhs even before anyone digs in. It's not only gorgeous, it is scrumptious, with an olive oil crust that has just the right amount of crumble, a fragrant basil pesto, and a mound of colorful grape tomatoes. It is baked just long enough to soften the tomatoes slightly and allow the ingredients to meld, so while savory and cooked, it still has a real freshness to it.

You can fully make the crust as well as the pesto ahead of time, so all you need to do to pull it together is cut the tomatoes, toss the elements together, and bake.

1 RECIPE MELT-IN-YOUR-MOUTH NO ROLL OLIVE OIL CRUST, PAGE 35, PRE-BAKED IN A TART PAN AS PER THE RECIPE INSTRUCTIONS, THAWED IF FROZEN

½ CUP BASIL PESTO, PAGE 107, OR STORE-BOUGHT PESTO

2½ CUPS GRAPE TOMATOES, HALVED

2 TABLESPOONS FINELY GRATED PARMESAN CHEESE

½ TEASPOON FRESHLY GROUND BLACK PEPPER

1 Preheat the oven to 375°F. Spread the pesto on the bottom of the crust and top evenly with the tomatoes. Sprinkle with the Parmesan and pepper. Bake in the middle of the oven until the cheese is melted and the tomatoes are slightly wilted, about 20 minutes.

2 Transfer the tart in the pan to a rack to cool completely. Carefully remove the rim of the pan and place on a serving plate still on the bottom of the pan. Cut into wedges and serve within 2 hours.

Recipe continues

✱ Serving size: 1 wedge; **Per serving:** Calories 280; Total Fat 20g (Mono Fat 13g, Poly Fat 2.4g, Sat Fat 3g); Protein 5g; Carb 22g; Fiber 3g; Cholesterol 5mg; Sodium 170mg; **Excellent source of:** Vitamin K; **Good source of:** Fiber, Manganese, Protein, Thiamin, Vitamin A, Vitamin C, Vitamin E

Make ahead:

The crust may be made ahead and refrigerated or frozen and thawed as per the recipe instructions on page 35.

The pesto may be made ahead and refrigerated or frozen as per the recipe instructions on page 107.

Once the tart is cooked, refrigerating or freezing is not recommended.

Sweet Potato Vegetable Bake

• MAKES 8 SERVINGS •

THIS DISH IS WHAT MY Grandma would have called a vegetable kugel, a pile of grated vegetables bound with egg, simply seasoned with onion, salt, and pepper and baked until tender inside and crisp outside. This one has a colorfully healthy array of shredded sweet potato, broccoli stalks (why toss them?!), zucchini, and carrots, and comes out almost like a vegetable pancake. It is simple, wonderful comfort food, which can be a vegetarian main course, along with a soup or salad, or pair, naturally, with Grandma's Roast Chicken, page 215.

1 LARGE HEAD OF BROCCOLI (ABOUT 1¾ POUNDS)

1 LARGE OR TWO MEDIUM ZUCCHINI (ABOUT 1 POUND TOTAL)

1 MEDIUM SWEET POTATO (ABOUT 12 OUNCES), SKIN ON

½ POUND CARROTS

1 LARGE ONION

5 LARGE EGGS, BEATEN

¼ CUP OLIVE OIL

¼ CUP WHOLE-WHEAT PASTRY FLOUR

1 TEASPOON SALT

¼ TEASPOON FRESHLY GROUND BLACK PEPPER

COOKING SPRAY

1 Preheat the oven to 400°F.

2 Remove the florets from the head of broccoli and set aside for another use. Using the wide holes of a box grater or the grater attachment of a food processor, grate the broccoli stalks so they are shredded. Shred the zucchini, sweet potato, carrots, and onion.

3 In a large bowl, combine all the shredded vegetables, eggs, oil, flour, salt, and pepper. Spray a 9 × 13-inch baking dish with cooking spray and pour the vegetable mixture into the baking dish. Bake until the top is golden and the underside and edges are browned, about 1 hour and 15 minutes.

4 Allow to cool on the countertop to set, for about 20 minutes, then cut into 8 equal-sized pieces.

TO REFRIGERATE AND REHEAT

Once cooked, cover tightly in the baking dish or transfer to an airtight container. Refrigerate for up to 4 days. To reheat, allow to sit at room temperature as the oven preheats to 350°F. Bake, uncovered, in the baking dish or on a baking sheet, for 20 minutes, until warmed through and somewhat crisped on the outside.

Microwave reheating is not recommended.

TO FREEZE AND REHEAT

Once cooked, allow to chill in the refrigerator for 30 minutes, then wrap individual squares in plastic wrap or foil, and place in sealable plastic freezer bags in the freezer for up to 3 months.

To reheat, there is no need to thaw. Place uncovered on a piece of foil or baking sheet in a cold oven set for 350°F. Once the oven reaches temperature, continue to cook until warmed through and slightly crisped, 30 to 40 minutes.

Microwave reheating is not recommended.

---

* **Serving size:** 1 piece; **Per serving:** Calories 200; Total Fat 10g (Mono Fat 6.1g, Poly Fat 1.4g, Sat Fat 1.9g); Protein 8g; Carb 22g; Fiber 5g; Cholesterol 115mg; Sodium 410mg; **Excellent source of:** Fiber, Folate, Manganese, Vitamin A, Vitamin C, Vitamin K; **Good source of:** Iodine, Iron, Magnesium, Molybdenum, Pantothenic Acid, Phosphorus, Potassium, Protein, Riboflavin, Selenium, Vitamin B6, Vitamin E

Indian Rice and Vegetable Pilaf (Biryani) • MAKES 6 SERVINGS •

THE AROMA THAT FILLS YOUR kitchen when you make this dish is like a siren's call. The combined floral fragrance of the basmati rice, the rich scent of coconut oil, and the warm toasted spices is absolutely intoxicating. And that is just a hint of the wonderful flavors to follow when you taste it. It is chock-full of flavorful, colorful goodies too: carrots, peas, fresh cilantro, and crunchy nuts.

Try it with the Green "Tandoori" Grilled Chicken, page 209.

2 CARDAMOM PODS

½ TEASPOON WHOLE CUMIN SEEDS

½ TEASPOON MUSTARD SEEDS

½ TEASPOON CORIANDER SEEDS

1 CINNAMON STICK

1 TABLESPOON VIRGIN COCONUT OIL OR CANOLA OIL

1 LARGE ONION, CHOPPED

1 CUP BASMATI BROWN RICE

¾ TEASPOON SALT

1 LARGE CARROT, SHREDDED (1½ CUPS)

1 CUP PEAS, NO NEED TO THAW IF FROZEN

FOR SERVING:

¼ CUP CHOPPED FRESH CILANTRO LEAVES

⅓ CUP COARSELY CHOPPED, TOASTED CASHEWS OR ALMONDS

1 Bring 1¾ cups of water to a boil in a kettle or covered pot.

2 Meanwhile, heat a 4-quart saucepan over medium heat. Add the cardamom, cumin, mustard, coriander, and cinnamon and toast until fragrant, 1 minute. Transfer the spices to a plate.

3 Heat the oil in the same saucepan over medium heat. Add the onion and cook until soft and golden, stirring occasionally, 9 to 10 minutes. Stir in the rice and cook until glossy, 1 minute. Return the spices to the pan, add the boiling water and salt, and return to a boil. Lower the heat to low, cover, and cook until the rice is tender and most of the liquid is absorbed, 50 to 55 minutes. Add the carrot and peas and cook, covered, until everything is warmed through and the liquid is absorbed, 7 to 10 minutes. Remove from the heat and let rest, covered, for 10 minutes. Uncover, remove the cinnamon stick, and fluff with a fork. To make ahead, freeze at this stage. Serve garnished with the cilantro and nuts.

* **Serving size:** About ⅔ cup; **Per serving:** Calories 180; Total Fat 6g (Mono Fat 2.1g, Poly Fat 1.1g, Sat Fat 2.4g); Protein 5g; Carb 30g; Fiber 4g; Cholesterol 0mg; Sodium 325mg; **Excellent source of:** Vitamin A; **Good source of:** Fiber, Protein, Vitamin K

Refrigeration is not recommended. For best results, freeze while still hot.

TO FREEZE AND REHEAT

Allow the rice to cool slightly so it is no longer steaming, but still quite warm. Place in sealable plastic freezer bags in the portions desired and freeze for up to 3 months.

To reheat, run the plastic bag under hot water for 30 seconds to release the rice, then transfer it to a saucepan with 2 tablespoons of water per portion. Cover and cook over low heat, turning and breaking it up with a fork once or twice, until warmed through, 13 to 30 minutes, depending on the amount.

Alternatively, after running the bag under water to release the rice, transfer it to a microwave-safe bowl, cover tightly, and microwave on high for about 2 to 2½ minutes for one portion.

Roasted Shredded Brussels Sprouts with Apricots and Sunflower Seeds

• MAKES 6 SERVINGS •

BY NOW JUST ABOUT EVERYONE I know is a fan of roasted Brussels sprouts. And who wouldn't be? Roasting the vegetable mellows it, brings out its nutty sweetness, and crisps its edges enticingly. This recipe takes that old favorite for a new spin by shredding the sprouts first, turning them into a kind of tender-crisp, savory slaw. With the addition of sweet apricots, nutty sunflower seeds, and a quick cider-maple vinaigrette, you get roasted Brussels sprouts in a new, exciting, and exceptionally tasty way.

1½ POUNDS BRUSSELS SPROUTS, TRIMMED, HALVED, AND CUT CROSSWISE INTO SHREDS (ABOUT 8 CUPS)

3 TABLESPOONS OLIVE OIL, DIVIDED

½ TEASPOON SALT

½ TEASPOON FRESHLY GROUND BLACK PEPPER

¼ CUP UNSALTED HULLED SUNFLOWER SEEDS

1½ TABLESPOONS CIDER VINEGAR

½ TABLESPOON PURE MAPLE SYRUP

1 TEASPOON DIJON MUSTARD

¼ CUP DRIED APRICOTS, SLICED

1 Preheat the oven to 400F.

2 In a large bowl, toss the Brussels sprouts with 2 tablespoons of the oil and the salt and pepper. Spread out on a large sheet pan in one layer and roast in the middle of the oven, stirring occasionally, until golden brown, 22 to 25 minutes.

3 Meanwhile, place the sunflower seeds on a small baking sheet and place in the oven until toasted and fragrant, about 10 minutes.

4 In a large serving bowl, whisk together the vinegar, maple syrup, and mustard until well combined. Slowly whisk in the remaining tablespoon of oil until emulsified.

5 When the Brussels sprouts are done, immediately transfer them to a serving bowl and toss with the dressing to coat. Stir in the apricots and sunflower seeds.

Recipe continues

* **Serving size:** A heaping ½ cup; **Per serving:** Calories 180; Total Fat 10g (Mono Fat 5.5g, Poly Fat 2.6g, Sat Fat 1.3g); Protein 5g; Carb 21g; Fiber 6g; Cholesterol 0mg; Sodium 250mg; **Excellent source of:** Fiber, Folate, Manganese, Vitamin A, Vitamin C, Vitamin K; **Good source of:** Iron, Phosphorus, Potassium, Protein, Thiamin, Vitamin B6, Vitamin E

TO REFRIGERATE AND REHEAT

Allow to cool at room temperature for 30 minutes, then place in an airtight container in the refrigerator for up to 4 days. To reheat, spread out on a baking sheet in one layer and place in a preheated 400°F oven for 10 minutes, until warmed and crisped.

Microwave reheating is not recommended.

Freezing is not recommended.

Chili-Spiced Sweet Potato Wedges with Maple Pecans

• MAKES 6 SERVINGS •

THE ONLY PROBLEM WITH THESE sweet potato wedges is that they are so good it is almost impossible to stop eating them. The potatoes are tossed with a sweet, spiced (but not too hot) mix of maple syrup and chili powder, then baked until soft inside and caramelized outside. A finishing sprinkle of crunchy "candied" pecans sweetens the deal. Try them with the Almond-Crusted Chicken Tenders, page 176, the Mini Turkey Meatloaves, page 217, or the Grilled Chicken with Cherry Bourbon BBQ Sauce, page 185.

- 3 LARGE SWEET POTATOES (2 POUNDS), UNPEELED
- 3½ TABLESPOONS PURE MAPLE SYRUP, DIVIDED
- 2 TABLESPOONS OLIVE OIL
- 2 TABLESPOONS CHILI POWDER
- 1¼ TEASPOONS SALT, DIVIDED
- ⅛ TEASPOON CAYENNE PEPPER, OPTIONAL
- ½ CUP PECANS

1 Preheat the oven to 450°F. Cut the potatoes in half lengthwise and cut each half lengthwise into 4 wedges. Cut each wedge in half crosswise, on the diagonal, so you wind up with 48 pieces.

2 In a large bowl, whisk together 2 tablespoons of the maple syrup, the oil, chili powder, 1 teaspoon of the salt, and the cayenne, if using. Add the potatoes and toss until coated well. Arrange in one layer on 2 parchment-lined large baking sheets and roast for 12 minutes. Turn the potatoes over with a spatula and continue to roast until tender and caramelized, 8 to 10 minutes more.

3 Meanwhile, add the pecans, the remaining 1½ tablespoons of maple syrup, and ¼ teaspoon salt to a small saucepan. Cook over medium heat, stirring frequently, until the maple syrup is reduced to a glaze, 3 to 4 minutes. Transfer the nuts to a cutting board and allow to cool, then coarsely chop them.

4 Serve the potato wedges with the pecans sprinkled on top.

Recipe continues

TO REFRIGERATE AND REHEAT

Store the potatoes and pecans in separate airtight containers in the refrigerator. The potatoes will keep for up to 4 days and the pecans will keep for 2 weeks.

To reheat the potatoes, place them on a parchment- or foil-lined baking tray and heat in a 400°F oven for about 8 minutes. Alternatively, place on a microwave-safe plate and microwave on high for 1 minute for a single portion. Serve topped with the pecans.

TO FREEZE AND REHEAT

Wrap the potatoes in individual portions in foil, then place in a sealable plastic bag. Place the pecans in a separate sealable plastic bag. Freeze for up to 3 months.

To reheat, place the frozen potatoes on a baking sheet, uncovered, and put in a cold oven set to 400°F. Once the oven reaches temperature, continue to cook for 12 minutes, spreading the potatoes out into a single layer once they are thawed, at about the midway point.

Alternatively, place the potatoes on a microwave-safe plate, cover with a splatter guard, and microwave on the defrost setting for 4 minutes, then spread the potatoes out into a single layer and microwave for 30 seconds on high for a single portion.

To thaw the pecans, leave out at room temperature for 2 hours.

---

* **Serving size:** 8 wedges and 1 heaping tablespoon of pecans; **Per serving:** Calories 260; Total Fat 11g (Mono Fat 6.7g, Poly Fat 2.5g, Sat Fat 1.2g); Protein 3g; Carb 41g; Fiber 6g; Cholesterol 0mg; Sodium 600mg; **Excellent source of:** Fiber, Manganese, Vitamin A; **Good source of:** Copper, Magnesium, Molybdenum, Pantothenic Acid, Phosphorus, Potassium, Riboflavin, Thiamin, Vitamin B6, Vitamin E, Vitamin K

Herb-Marinated Grilled Vegetables · MAKES 10 SERVINGS ·

ONE OF THE BEST THINGS you can do in the summer to make eating deliciously and healthfully easy is to grill up a big batch of vegetables. You can grill whatever is available at the market, but I have included some all-time favorites here—eggplant, zucchini, peppers, mushrooms, and onions—and marinated them first with an herbed vinaigrette for an extra punch of flavor. The list of what you can do with them is so long I barely know where to start: layer them on sandwiches, cut them up into salads, use them to top homemade pizzas, put them on an antipasto plate, or simply serve as a side dish, just to name a few.

½ CUP PLUS 2 TABLESPOONS RED WINE VINEGAR

½ CUP OLIVE OIL

⅓ CUP CHOPPED FRESH BASIL

⅓ CUP CHOPPED FRESH ITALIAN PARSLEY LEAVES

1 TEASPOON SALT

½ TEASPOON FRESHLY GROUND BLACK PEPPER

2 MEDIUM EGGPLANTS, TRIMMED AND CUT LENGTHWISE INTO ¼-INCH-THICK SLICES

3 MEDIUM ZUCCHINI, TRIMMED AND CUT LENGTHWISE INTO ¼-INCH-THICK SLICES

3 MEDIUM ASSORTED BELL PEPPERS, STEMMED, SEEDED, AND CUT INTO 3-INCH-WIDE PIECES

6 PORTOBELLO MUSHROOM CAPS, STEMS REMOVED

2 MEDIUM RED ONIONS CUT INTO ¼-INCH-THICK ROUNDS

4 CLOVES GARLIC, SMASHED

1 In a large spouted measuring cup or bowl, whisk together the vinegar, oil, basil, parsley, salt, and pepper. Divide the marinade between 2 (gallon-sized) resealable plastic bags. Add half of the vegetables along with 2 of the garlic cloves to each bag. Seal the bags, tossing to coat the vegetables, and marinate at room temperature for 30 minutes.

2 Preheat a lightly oiled grill or grill pan to medium-high. Remove the vegetables from the marinade and grill, in batches if necessary, turning once, until tender and grill marks have formed, 4 to 5 minutes for the zucchini and eggplant, 6 to 8 minutes for the onion and mushroom, and about 10 minutes for the peppers. Transfer to a platter as grilled.

* **Serving size:** 1 cup; **Per serving:** Calories 130; Total Fat 8g (Mono Fat 5.9g, Poly Fat 0.9g, Sat Fat 1.2g); Protein 3g; Carb 12g; Fiber 4g; Cholesterol 0mg; Sodium 180mg; **Excellent source of:** Vitamin C, Vitamin K; **Good source of:** Copper, Fiber, Manganese, Niacin, Pantothenic Acid, Potassium, Riboflavin, Selenium

TO REFRIGERATE AND SERVE

Allow to cool at room temperature for 30 minutes, then place in an airtight container and refrigerate for up to 4 days. Serve at room temperature, or reheat on a baking tray in a 375°F oven for 10 minutes. Alternatively, you can place on a microwave-safe plate, cover with a splatter guard, and microwave for about 40 to 60 seconds for one portion.

Freezing is not recommended.

INDEX

Page numbers in **boldface** indicate illustrations